Inescapable Romance
Studies in the Poetics of a Mode

Inescapable Romance

Studies in the Poetics of a Mode

Patricia A. Parker

Princeton University Press

All Rights Reserved
Library of Congress Cataloging in Publication Data will be
found on the last printed page of this book

This book has been composed in VIP Bembo

Clothbound editions of Princeton University Press books
are printed on acid-free paper, and binding materials are
chosen for strength and durability.

Printed in the United States of America by Princeton
University Press, Princeton, New Jersey

Material from Chapter III is included in an article entitled "Eve, Evening,
and the Labor of Reading in *Paradise Lost*," copyright © *English Literary
Renaissance*, Vol. 9, No. 2 (Spring 1979).

The text used in all citations from Valéry is the Pléiade edition of his
Oeuvres, 2 vols., ed. Jean Hytier, copyright © Gallimard 1957. "Les Pas" is
quoted in full.

Grateful acknowledgment is made to Alfred A. Knopf, Inc. for permission
to quote from the copyrighted works of Wallace Stevens.

To My Family

Contents

Acknowledgments

In the preparation of this book I have received help of many kinds. The debts recorded in the footnotes speak for themselves. I would like, however, to express my particular gratitude to scholars, colleagues, and friends who have helped make its completion possible: to the teaching, at Yale, of Harold Bloom, John Freccero, Paul de Man, and Leslie Brisman, which has left its imprint on this work even where it departs from them; to Geoffrey Hartman, who was director of this study when it began as a dissertation in 1976 and has been ever since an encouraging and patient presence; to A. Bartlett Giamatti and Thomas M. Greene, who gave careful attention to particular chapters at times of heavy administrative responsibility; and to Jaroslav Pelikan, who cheerfully offered clarification of some central theological terms.

I would also like to express my thanks, here, to my early teachers Raymond Longfield, Alice Hamilton, and Walter Swayze; to James Nohrnberg, for his friendship and unstinting scholarly generosity; to colleagues and friends at Toronto who generously took time from their own work to give careful scrutiny to sections of the argument in unchastened form—in particular, to James Carscallen, Eleanor Cook, Graham Falconer, Nancy Lindheim, Hugh MacCallum, Peter Marinelli, Peter Nesselroth, and Lee Patterson, who are responsible for much of what finally came out right and, with the other readers of the manuscript in its various forms, are to be dissociated from the errors, which are my own. I also must acknowledge my debt to Timothy Reiss of the University of Montreal, whose perceptive comments helped me to rethink the argument at a crucial stage, and to the continuing presence in my thinking of the work and teaching of Northrop Frye.

For assistance with the inevitable practicalities of research, I would like to thank the librarians of Yale, Harvard, and the

University of Toronto, and in particular the staff of Pratt Library of Victoria College, who patiently overlooked my constant impositions on their good graces. I also owe particular thanks to the readers and editors of Princeton University Press: to the readers for their detailed suggestions on the most problematic issues; to Polly Hanford, for her scrupulous work on the typescript; and to Joanna Hitchcock, for her helpfulness and encouragement from a very early stage.

Some of my debts are less specific: to my students, whose freshness to the subject perpetually renewed my own; to David Quint, whose gracious sharing of his own discoveries constitutes a debt no footnote can adequately record; to conversations with Dennis John Costa and L. Brown Kennedy which made their way indirectly into this study; to Christine Schulze, who helped keep me sane and laughing through periods of intellectual intensity; and to Connie and Kelly Holliston, who were part of my daughter's extended family during her infancy and the infancy of this book.

The last debts are the most difficult to express. To my mother and father, who provided me very early with the time and space for study and who have since, as parents and grandparents, cheerfully provided the support which has made it possible to indulge in the solitary activity of writing. To my husband Ian, whose intellectual range, incisive suggestions, and outrageous sense of humor have been part of the delight of the labor of revision. And finally to our children: to Jacqueline, whose only objections to the book were that it had no pictures and couldn't be eaten; and to Joshua, who slept.

Dedications are meant, perhaps, to be singular, but this dedication must be made to my family, in every sense.

Inescapable Romance
Studies in the Poetics of a Mode

ABBREVIATIONS

Od.	*Odyssey*
Aen.	*Aeneid*
Met.	*Metamorphoses*
ST	*Summa Theologiae*
Inf.	*Inferno*
Purg.	*Purgatorio*
Par.	*Paradiso*
OF	*Orlando furioso*
FQ	*The Faerie Queene*
PL	*Paradise Lost*
PR	*Paradise Regained*

Introduction

Thus at length the magic of the old romances was perfectly dissolved. They began with reflecting an image indeed of the feudal manners, but an image magnified and distorted by unskilful designers. Common sense being offended with these perversions of truth and nature . . . the next step was to have recourse to *allegories*. . . . Under this form the tales of faery kept their ground, and even made their fortune at court. . . . But reason, in the end . . . drove them off the scene, and would endure these *lying wonders*, neither in their own proper shape, nor as masked in figures.

Henceforth, the taste of wit and poetry took a new turn: And *fancy*, that had wantoned it so long in the world of fiction, was now constrained, against her will, to ally herself with strict truth, if she would gain admittance into reasonable company.

What we have gotten by this revolution, you will say, is a great deal of good sense. What we have lost, is a world of fine fabling. . . .

Bishop Hurd, *Letters on Chivalry and Romance*

Inescapable romance, inescapable choice
Of dreams . . .

Wallace Stevens, "An Ordinary Evening
in New Haven"

THE study contained in the chapters which follow has a number of related purposes. The first is to continue, and to extend, the work on romance done by such scholars as Ker, Vinaver, Auerbach, and Frye,[1] and to follow its implications into the field of recent speculation on the problem of poetic closure or of narrative "ending."[2] The second is to develop a synthesis of critical insights into particular poems as a way of perceiving both the fertility of the romance imagination and the variations which have marked its appearance in different poets and historical periods. The third is to suggest some of the affinities between the romance and lyric poetry, affinities frequently acknowledged but less frequently analyzed. The last is to provide a context for modern theories of narrative and linguistic "error" by suggesting that "error's" romance, and Romantic, history.

The approach to romance adopted here follows one of its earliest theorists, Bishop Richard Hurd, in focusing less on its content or *materia* than on its form or "design," an approach which allows us to explore not only the structure of narrative romance but also the "brief romance" of the epiphanic or object-centered lyric. One of the problems in discussing the form of romance has always been the need to limit the way in which the term is applied. I have chosen to approach the subject in a way which does not cover all the forms we call "romance" but may provide what a romance poet might call a "prospect" on them.

The studies, therefore, constitute not so much an exhaustive survey of romance itself as a prospect which uses "romance" as an organizing principle for the interpretation of works of four major poets—Ariosto, Spenser, Milton, and Keats—and of the restatement of romance in modern poetry and poetic theory. "Romance" is characterized primarily as a form which simultaneously quests for and postpones a particular end, objective, or object, a description which Fredric Jameson approaches from a somewhat different direction when he notes that romance, from the twelfth century, necessitates the projection of an Other, a *projet* which comes to an end when that Other reveals his identity or "name."[3] This description has the advantage of comprehending historical difference even as it reveals certain structural affinities. When the "end" is defined typologically, as a Promised Land or Apocalypse, "romance" is that mode or tendency which remains on the threshold before the promised end, still in the wilderness of wandering, "error," or "trial." When the posited Other, or objective, is the terminus of a fixed object, as in a poem of Keats or Valéry, "romance" is the liminal space before that object is fully named or revealed. Finally, when the end is not, typologically, an apocalyptic fulfillment but rather abyss or catastrophe, as in Mallarmé's *Un Coup de dés*, "romance" involves the dilation of a threshold rendered now both more precarious and more essential. This connection between naming, identity, and closure or ending remains a persistent romance phenomenon, from the delaying of names in the narratives of Chrétien de Troyes to Keats's preference for the noumenal over the nominal, for "half-knowledge" over "certainty" or "fact." For poets for whom the recovery of identity or the attainment of an end is problematic, or impossible, the focus may be less on arrival or completion than on the strategy of delay. In this respect, though their tendencies are different, Mallarmé's deferral of revelation in the prose poem "Le Nénuphar blanc" falls as much within the sphere of romance as the period before the unmasking of the "Other" in the *Erec et Enide*.

The term "romance" is intended here neither as fixed generic prescription nor as abstract transhistorical category. The former is rendered impossible by the poets' own extension of the term beyond its strictly generic meaning, and therefore is invoked only where appropriate, in relation to Ariosto's deliberate playing of epic conventions off against the "errors" of the *romanzo* or to Milton's decision to write in the style of Homer and Virgil rather than of Spenser. The latter is invalidated by the changing connotations of the word "romance" in the centuries after Chrétien and his Renaissance successors, and by the discontinuities as well as continuities between the manifestations of a form which historically has had an extraordinary resilience, a tendency to turn up, Proteus-like, in a multiplicity of different guises. By the time Keats was writing his "Poetic Romance" *Endymion*, "romance" had acquired connotations well beyond the strictly generic, associations which made it frequently a synonym for the escapism of "pure fiction" or allied it with the passive states of trance and dream. Keats's later willed farewell to the genre of romance as a "Syren" form is therefore less telling than his more subterranean encounters with the romance of "entrancement" or passivity, a struggle which continues in the contest of poetic voice and the "sable charm" of silence in *The Fall of Hyperion*.

Milton's relation to romance is instructive in this regard. His rejection of the genre is explicit and well documented. But the engaging of romance nevertheless may be seen to take, in *Paradise Lost*, more subtle and less readily identifiable forms. The period of "respite" or "dilation" between First and Second Coming—a period which in Spenser resembles the space between the initial vision and hoped-for return of the Faerie Queene—also assumes in Milton a crucial ambiguity, as a time when the end is both "at hand" and yet to come; and its dark doubles are the Satanic maze of endless wandering and the "staying" or dangerous suspension of the "shadowy Type." Milton rejects the genre and *materia* of romance for "the better fortitude / Of Patience and Heroic Martyrdom / Unsung" (*PL* IX. 31-33). But "patience," even as it turns from the externals of romance to a different, and more inward, subject, continues to inhabit that liminal or preliminary space of "trial" which is the romance's traditional place of testing. The interval which in Milton is both the locus of trial and the threshold of choice shares in the same ambivalence as the dilated or suspended threshold of romance, but this ambivalence enters *Paradise Lost* not directly, or generically, but rather through the poem's constant variations on the problem of "error," and on the "suspensions" or "pendency" of a potential endlessness. The chapter on Milton, therefore, begins not with the epic's explicit references to romance, or with Milton's own reasons for rejecting romance as genre, but rather with the problem of the pendant or pivotal in one of its most crucial Miltonic moments—the interval in which Eve reflects upon her own image in the pool, and the extension of the implications of that interval to Book IV's temporal image of suspension, the realm of evening or twilight, poised between the Either-Or of darkness and light.

One of the problems the writing of literary history inevitably encounters is the problem of continuity and historical change, of suggesting the continuation of a particular line

without sacrificing specificity to the Moloch of a particular
thesis. The organization of the present work into discrete
studies of individual poets is intended to enable the situating
of particular works within the concrete associations and implications of "romance" in their time, to attempt what Jameson calls a "genuinely *historical* account"[4] of the form. Each of
the chapters is therefore conceived, in the first instance, as an
exploration of individual texts, which opens then secondarily
upon questions of historical context or relation—the debate
over epic and romance in the century after Ariosto, the attack
on the "error" of figurative language in the period between
Spenser and Milton, the revival and ambivalence of romance
in the decades before Wordsworth and Keats. This procedure
in part involves turning thematic criticism inside out, starting
from the study of texts and working from there to questions
of poetic interrelation.

In a tradition in which Spenser inherits the genre of
Ariosto, Milton knows intimately the poems of both, and
Keats openly records his debts to "old Romance," the bor-
rowings of the poets themselves provide a way of identifying
explicit transformations and continuities. But the resilience of
romance as a form is also matched by the persistence of certain romance terms and images which provide among these
poets a network of more implicit relations. Oliver Goldsmith, in his essay *Poetry Distinguished from other Writing*,
pointed to the recurrence of the term "hanging" or "pendant"
from Virgil to Milton as an index of the figurative or picture-making power of poetry, and his comments on these related terms provide for those poets a suggestive "concord-
ance." In the texts studied here, a series of images and
etymological complexes also emerges and reveals the capacity
of romance to generate metaphors for its own description.
The fertile multiplicity of the meanings of "error," and its
associations—mental, geographical, and narrative—with
varieties of "de-viation," inform not only the wandering
structure of the poems of Ariosto and Spenser but also the devious romance of figure and trope which Mallarmé identifies
with the "erreur" of poetry itself. Ariosto's reliance on con-

tinual narrative deferral and on the romance proliferation of different story lines is both continued and transformed in Spenser's version of *dilatio* or "dilation" and in the dilated or embowered moments of Keats's *Endymion*. The series of adventures which, as Auerbach remarks, is raised in earlier, courtly romance to the status of a fated and graduated test of election,[5] is recalled and simultaneously transformed in later versions of the "gradual," in Milton's conception of education by degrees and in the trial of the poet in Keats's *Fall of Hyperion* before steps he must ascend in order to exist at all. Finally, the complex of "suspended," "pendant," and, in Milton, "pensive" and even "penseroso" provides a subtle but persistent link between the suspended threshold of romance and the suspensions of Dante's Limbo, a link only too ominous when the contemplative Miltonic "penseroso" becomes, in Keats, that potentially immobilizing interval of seeing when giant forms weigh "ponderous" upon his senses. The reappearance of this etymological play—in Barthes' concept of the "texte pensif" or Vendler's description of Stevens' "pensive" style[6]—serves to recall the links within this recurrent romance metaphor, from the "sospeso" which in Ariosto is so frequent a term for spiritual, and narrative, irresolution to the "suspens vibratoire" which is Mallarmé's central figure for the liminal and momentary status of poetic language before its "end."

These concepts are not conceived as structuring the recurrence of a fixed form, but their reappearance—and cumulative associations—do provide a way of identifying both continuities and differences. The implied echo of Spenser's indolent Phaedria in Keats's "Indolence Ode" and its counsel to take no thought for the morrow suggests its own history of romance as that form became increasingly synonymous with one of its own archetypes—the protective but potentially indolent bower—and provides an insight into the fortunes of romance in the increasingly commercial world of the English "Mammon," from Book VI of *The Faerie Queene* to the anxieties of Keats and Coleridge. Similarly, the notion of trespass links aspects of both "old" romance and "new": Spenser's "faerie" has much less clear a geography than the cosmos of Dante or of Milton and "trespass" in it is therefore not only a theological and moral concept, but also something much less easy to define; Keats's conception of the poet's "negative capability" blurs the boundaries of individual identity and thus makes even more threatening the possibility of a trespass, or violation, of the self. But the relation cannot be understood simply as quest romance internalized, since it is finally impossible to say what if anything in old romance remains "external." Finally, romance traditionally invokes the past or the socially remote; and Auerbach's perception that chivalric romance both embodied the ideals of a ruling class and, in its retreat from specific space and time, concealed that class's social basis, may equally illuminate more modern romance evasions of the ends of a bourgeois world, a withdrawal which may appear not to be in that world, but may still be of it.

In each of the chapters included here, the intention has been both to offer a reading of the poems themselves and to suggest what, poetically, became of them, their influence, and significance, within the transformations of a recurrent mode. Ariosto's use of romance and its much-maligned "error" as a tool for dismantling hierarchies both generic and social is a revelation of romance as what Frye calls "the structural core of all fiction."[7] To suggest that the *Furioso*'s revelation of the ubiquity of fictions and its subversion of hierarchies founded on stable centers of "truth" is a signal event of the Renaissance is not to set up yet another, historical, hierarchy or naive progressive contrast with what had gone before: what is said of Ariosto here might be said, in part, of any poet of the Lucianic, or deconstructive, mode. But Ariosto's poem, as evidence of a fictive self-consciousness that twentieth-century literary theory has begun to rediscover, does provide a critique, long before the modern texts which this theory so often privileges, of the teleological model of narrative and the "end" or "center" of revelation it presupposes. Etymology and its inevitable offspring, the serious pun, have recently become tools of much critical investigation: Jacques Derrida

uses the common etymology of "to differ" and "to defer" in
his punning "différance," a neologism for the simultaneous
proliferation of difference and deferral of presence, a complex
which, as we shall see with Spenser, also includes "dilation."[8]
But Ariosto's continual "differire" already suggests the relation between the romance narrative's extension in space and
its endless deferral of endings. To point to the reappearance,
in Derrida's concept, of a venerable romance pun is not to ad-
vocate any literary-historical return of the same or to ignore
the Cartesian gulf between the two periods, but rather simply
to suggest that Ariosto's critique of presence and his subversion of the teleological model of meaning was, in relation to
his predecessors, at least as thoroughgoing and radical.

Similarly, reading *The Faerie Queene* within the context of
"romance" involves a consideration of the poem both in its
own terms, and time, and in contrast with the later transformations of its central images. Multivalence, or "wandering,"
is, through most of Spenser's poem, sustained by, and
grounded in, the permanent and the eternal, that ordering
frame which enables divagation to be a species of delight. But
The Faerie Queene is also filled with images of a darker strain,
which later romance poets were to enlarge upon and develop.
To perceive this development is not to substitute a Romantic
reading of the poem for a more strictly historical one but
rather to explore why Spenser's poem should have been for
subsequent romance poets so powerful a precursor, and to
suggest a more open conception of poetic history, which
would include both the influence of a text on later texts and
the changing social circumstances which were to make the
opposition between "bower" and Mammon world increasingly more anxious. If we may adopt a concept from a
slightly different context in Dante, we may perhaps speak of
the way in which a text, like Spenser's (or Virgil's), may be
seen retrospectively to have contained, or "prophesied," a
strain of which it was itself, so to speak, unaware. Yeats's remark that Spenser let romance suffer at the hands of the
Mammon of allegory is thus, however much a misreading of
The Faerie Queene itself, a perceptive reading of this tension's

subsequent history, the cloven fiction of an increasingly remote, or evasive, "faery land" and an increasingly pressing
"reality."

Romantic readings tended to attach themselves to different
parts of Spenser's mammoth poem and to shift the significance of episodes or images in the very act of making them
pasturing places of the imagination. Phaedria and Mammon
divide Book II of *The Faerie Queene* between them, splitting
and therefore collapsing the dialectical tension of *festina lente*,
or between the Gospel injunctions both to "Take no thought
for the morrow" and to "Seek and ye shall find." Spenser's
distance from both temptations in this Book makes it possible
to present clearly their parodic forms—the degeneration of
patience into sloth and the perversion of active seeking into
the doctrine of acquisition. But the appeal of Phaedria's
bower would seem for Keats to be both more complex and
more direct; and Spenser's division of his Legend of Temperance between the invitation to careless ease and the figure
who urges "care" for this world provides a compelling model
for the later poet's struggle to temper the indolence of creative
repose and the pressures of relevance.

A similar duality of perspective, from our post-Romantic
vantage point, is necessarily involved in the reading of
Paradise Lost. Milton is, in the history of romance as in so
much else, a pivotal figure. The argument over *Paradise Lost*
has most frequently been a conflict of historical views, between adherents of Blake's "Of the Devil's Party without
knowing it" and the attempt to reconstruct a more
theological—or seventeenth-century—reading, behind, or
beyond, the Romantic distortions. I have tried, in this study,
to point to the tensions within Milton's poem in its own
terms—the relation between gradual and "Immediate," between dilation of the threshold state and precipitation of its
ending—and then to suggest how certain of the images for
this tension come in their historical afterlife to have a significance traceable perhaps only in retrospect to the poem itself.
Dwelling on the twilight space of creation or trial is clearly in
Milton part of the lesson of patience, of submission to the dis-

cipline of time or temperance in contrast to the apocalyptic impulse in its Satanic form. But there is also latent even within this Miltonic twilight a duality which informs both the delight and the despair of subsequent "evening" visions, both a preference for its soothing *chiaro-oscuro* and a species of *melancholia* which might be called a "melancholy of the sign." Gray and Collins celebrate the graduated, gentler light of evening as one of the delights of an *Abendland* or English climate, of a place which, if farther from the sun or "source," yet literally has more latitude. And the countless Odes to Evening which, after Milton, take their inspiration from "Il Penseroso" and Book IV of *Paradise Lost*, move, like the "dewy Eve" of the Mulciber simile, away from polar opposites and the immediate pressures of a decision Either-Or. There is also, however, in this post-Miltonic strain a sense of "evening" as decline or distance, of exile both from Light and from final or definitive meaning, an exile which frequently recalls more the notes of elegy than those of prophecy in the epic's closing lines.

The suspended realm of evening or twilight, therefore, is not only the archetypal space of romance but, for English poets after Milton, an inevitable recall of the lingering "Twilight gray" of *Paradise Lost*, and its power, at the more subtle level of the image, is that it carries with it the stored ambivalence of Milton's more learned use, even after its exegetical content has been forgotten or misunderstood. The romance implications of "pendency" and suspension are conveyed in an image which continues the Miltonic preoccupation with the balance or pivot, even among poets whose chief, if submerged, anxiety is only the precarious or suspended middle of their own social class. Far from shading—as has frequently been suggested—into natural description for its own sake, Evening after Milton seems to become even more intensely a figure for the figural, part of the larger question of the relation of poetic fable to "Truth." Milton's translation of the "error" of romance into the errancy of figures, however impressively that error in his epic might be controlled, provides perhaps part of the clue to the poem's subsequent history. What Marvell glimpsed as a bringing down of Truth to fable—rather than fable in its ruin leading up to Truth—was at least prophetic of the future of Milton's great poem, and of that Romantic descendental movement which was both to undermine more canonical readings of the epic and to heighten the sense of figuration as a threshold which might not lead up at all.

Romantic poetry frequently collapses the distinction between the eternal and the apocalyptic, shifting the permanence which, for Spenser and other Renaissance poets, sustained the temporal, to a fulfillment identified only with time's "end." In the approach to romance adopted in what follows, its characterization as a form which both projects and postpones or wanders from a projected ending may seem, as well, to be tending towards that conflation, an identification appropriate for Romantic poets but not for such figures as Spenser or Milton. The poetry we treat of includes both extremes, the faith in so much of Spenser in a permanence which subtends the natural cycle and the sentence which hangs suspended in *Un Coup de dés* before a catastrophic "period." But even this difference cannot be stated absolutely; and it is romance itself as a form which enables us most clearly to perceive the terms of the problem. Northrop Frye has described romance as "a sequential and processional form."[9] This feature derives from its dependence on the quest, or adventure. One of the implications of the sequential, however, is that it remains, like time itself, within a frame in which presence, or fulfillment, is always in some sense placed at a distance. For Keats, the consequence of this prospective mode is frequently a future- or end-hauntedness, its darkest version a despair of any final fulfillment. But even for the earlier poets, the temporal paradox of the *nunc et nondum*, of an end available "now" and yet still "to come," implies a perspectivism which allies the form of romance to the sequence of history. The threshold or "twilight" space before final revelation or ending is thus not only the veil of an unfolding narrative but part of the nature of all mediation, including the medium of time. In Milton, this paradox takes the form of a tension between the Reformer's sense that every time, or place, is equal before its Maker and the conception of human history as a gradual stepping to Truth. But even in Spenser, the tension emerges, in those *Cantos of Mutabilitie* which contain both an affirmation of the sustaining or permanent and a prayer for its final victory.

The study of romance which follows necessarily focuses on only certain of this form's Protean varieties: it is intended to be suggestive rather than inclusive. It does not pursue the extension of romance into such forms as the Gothic, though the gothic terrors of speechlessness and suffocation reappear to haunt the poet of "Negative Capability" in Keats's *Fall of Hyperion*. Neither does it attempt to include all of romance history. The play on deviation and deferral in the already "late" romances of Ariosto and Spenser is simply not to be found, for example, in the work of Chrétien de Troyes, though the future or prospective mode of *avanture* links this kind of medieval romance with its Renaissance descendants and with the sense of "prospect," virtuality, or perpetual "à venir" in Keats and Valéry. The displacement, and transformation, of romance in the novel is also not expressly treated, though the remarks in the Epilogue on contemporary narrative theory, on Derrida's "différance" and Barthes' "espace dilatoire," are intended to suggest echoes of the novel's romance inheritance, the dilated, or dilatory, space of a form which simultaneously moves towards and delays a definitive resolution or presence.

The chapters proceed chronologically, beginning with Ariosto, a poet for whom romance is already both established and open to an anatomy of its deviance, an anatomy which makes the *Orlando furioso* a sequel not just to Boiardo but to the whole tradition it recapitulates and transforms. The *Furioso* is considered initially as a culmination, and rewriting, of this previous tradition rather than as a quarry for future poets, the subtext it was to become for Spenser. But the intricacies of its influence on later poets emerge, retrospectively, in the chapters that follow, in Spenser's extension of Ariostan deviation, in the echoes of the *romanzo* in Milton's epic, and in Keats's professed preference for the human tales of Chaucer over the marvels of the horn and hippogriff. The exploration of Ariosto's exposure of romance "error" is followed by the study of *dilatio* in Spenser, and its relation to the polarities of romance in the several Legends of *The Faerie Queene*. The chapter on Milton begins with the pendency, or suspension, of Eve and evening, and moves to the implications in *Paradise Lost* of the "shadowy Type." The transition from Milton to Keats is approached through the tension between romance and "enlightenment" in the century after *Paradise Lost*, a tension which provides a context for Keats's own attempts to bid farewell to a siren form. The Epilogue, finally, begins with modern discussions of the aberrance of figurative language and concludes with the restatements of romance in the work of Mallarmé, Valéry, and Stevens.

Bishop Hurd, with others of his century, saw romance as a receding form, a world of fine fabling being crowded out by the advance of mind. Walter Pater described it as an ever-present and enduring principle of the artistic spirit. The hope in this present study of romance—of its transformations and its continuities—is that it might somehow comprehend the insights of both.

I. Ariosto

"Ne point errer est chose au-dessus de mes forces."
                                        La Fontaine

Ariosto and the "Errors" of Romance

AT the beginning of the final canto of the *Orlando furioso*, before the long review of friends waiting to congratulate him on the completion of his labors, Ariosto employs one of the oldest of literary *topoi*—the poetic voyage—to identify his entire poem as a kind of "erring":

> Or, se mi mostra la mia carta il vero,
> non è lontano a discoprirsi il porto;
> sì che nel lito i voti sciolier spero
> a chi nel mar per tanta via m'ha scorto;
> ove, o di non tornar col legno intero,
> o d'errar sempre, ebbi già il viso smorto.
> Ma mi par di veder, ma veggo certo,
> veggo la terra, e veggo il lito aperto.[a]
>
> (XLVI. 1. 1-8)[1]

The stanza provides, in miniature, a perfect example of the difficulty of knowing just how to take this omnipresent narrator and his frequent comments on the conduct of his narrative. Its "errar sempre" could be the real anxiety the repetition of "veggo" suggests, or it could be just another instance of the famous *sorriso dell'Ariosto*, a sly pretense of anxiety in a writer whose ability to bring together his many separate

---

[a] "Now if my map shows me the truth, the harbor is not far out of sight, so I hope to fulfil on the shore my vows to Him who has protected me during such a long journey on the sea, where earlier my face was pale with the fear I would not return with my ship uninjured or would wander forever. But I seem to see, but I certainly see, I see land, and I see the open shore."

stories is as little in doubt as the fact that each page turned ("carta" conveniently meaning both "page" and "chart") brings reader and author steadily closer to the book's inevitable end. The possibility of both these readings, or the tension between them, is probably more revealing than either reading by itself. But the image of "error" for a poem which adopts the "materia" of the "cavallieri erranti" and presents itself as a long poetic wandering is in itself a central revelation and suggests a way of looking at the *Furioso* and its interpretation.

The importance of "error" in Ariosto has been remarked by virtually all of his readers, from Renaissance Aristotelians, for whom his choice of the digressive romance form was an aberration from the higher path of epic, to a modern critic who finds in the different senses of "errare" and "errore" a suggestion of Ariosto's relation to the theme of "the One and the Many."[2] To understand how this play upon the notion of error might suggest an interpretation of this long and complex poem, we must first turn to the criticism of the *Orlando furioso* which most clearly judged its "errors" in both senses—as Ariosto's deviation from the epic norm, and as the sin of its weak-willed, errant knights. Raffaello Ramat and others have indicated the catalogue of complaints against Ariosto's poem which grew, both in Italy and in France, as Aristotle's *Poetics* became increasingly the bible of narrative form: its title was misleading in a poem that dealt at least as much with Ruggiero as with Orlando; its language did not meet the standards set by Bembo; its narration, far from being Aristotle's "single action," was frequently interrupted by digressive episodes; its indulgence, finally, in the fabulous material of the *romanzi* disqualified it from the true epic dignity of the *Iliad* and the *Aeneid*, both founded upon serious historical events.[3]

Its irregular mixing of different genres was, it seems, its most obvious departure from the Aristotelian norm, but this structural criticism—of a poem in its form as "errant" as its characters—was inextricably tied to "error" in the moral sense as well. The concept of a hierarchy of genres in *Cin-*

quecento Italy was very much related to other hierarchies, social and moral. For Antonio Minturno in the *Arte poetica* of 1564, not the least of the "Errori degli scrittori de' Romanzi" was the writer's erring in imitation of his own subject, a weakness of poetic will which might gain popularity with the "vulgo" but which inevitably led the poet away from the nobler path of epic:

> *Vesp.* Che monta, che non vi sia quella, ma un' altra dagli Oltramontani trovata, e dagl'Italiani illustrata, e fatta più bella, purché al mondo piaccia, e da lui si vegga meravigliosamente accettata e ricevuta?
> *Min.* Del vulgo io non mi meraviglio, il quale spesse volte accetta quelle cose, che non conosce; e, poiché una volta l'ha con molto suo piacere accettate, sempre le ritiene, e favorisce; né se migliori di quelle poi le si presentino, volentieri le riceve: sì può l'opinione saldamente nella mente umana impressa. Ma non posso non prender meraviglia grandissima, che si trovino alcuni scienziati . . . i quali (per quel, che se n'intende) confessino già ne'Romanzi non esser la forma e la regola, che tennero Omero e Virgilio, e doversi tenere Aristotele ed Orazio comandarono, e nondimeno s'ingegnino di questo errore difendere: anzi, perciocché tal composizione comprende i fatti de' Cavalieri erranti, affermino ostinatamente, non pur la Virgiliana ed Omerica maniera di poetare non convenirle; ma esserle richiesto, ch'ella anco errante sia, passando di una in altra materia, e varie cose in un fascio stringendo.[b4]

[b] "*Vesp.* What does it matter that it is not that one, but another one found over the mountains, and made famous by the Italians, and more beautiful, as long as the world likes it and it is marvellously accepted and received? *Min*: I do not wonder at the common people who often accept those things that they do not know, and because they have accepted them with great pleasure once, always keep and favor them; and if better things than those present themselves later, they are not willingly received; this is what an opinion solidly impressed upon the human mind can do. But I cannot help but marvel greatly that there are some learned people . . . who (as far as I understand) confess that in the Romances the form and the rules are no longer as Homer

"Error" is the operative word in this criticism, both as a structural fault and as the danger of a genre whose "endroits fâcheux," according to Madame de Sévigné, might well lead its younger readers astray.[5] If the errant knights of romance were assimilated to the erring will as opposed to the reason, one of the "errori" of the romance form was its appeal to the senses, the counterpart in the hierarchy of the faculties to the "volgari" in the body politic. When Horace was added to Aristotle, Ariosto's error was to come too close to the *dulce* side of the famous Horatian dictum, to succumb to the attractions of diverting fable over the essential, if perhaps less interesting, moral kernel. The *Orlando furioso* was read more widely in France than its condemnation by the rules of *Classicisme* might suggest, but when the poem was condescended to, it was frequently as a mere "divertissement" from more serious concerns, a kind of "jolie péché."[6]

One of the issues raised in the earliest Italian criticism of the poem was the question of whether Ariosto deviated from the Aristotelian epic norms through ignorance or was deliberately writing a different kind of poetry. The problem was, of course, where to fit a poem which was highly popular with a more than merely "vulgar" audience and filled with more epic conventions than the other *romanzi*.[7] He clearly was writing a different kind of poem from that described by Aristotle, however hard his more enthusiastic readers might try to prove that the *Furioso* was as regular as the *Iliad* or the *Aeneid*.[8] As early as 1554, Giambattista Pigna had argued that if Ariosto had deviated from the model set down by Virgil, it was because he was choosing another path to Helicon, a genre which was not inferior to epic on its own ground, but simply different.[9] And through the century this voice was heard along with the more rigid Aristotelian condemnations.[10]

---

and Virgil followed them, and as Aristotle and Horace ordered that they should be followed, and yet strive to defend this error; in fact, because such a composition includes the deeds of errant knights, they obstinately affirm not only that the Virgilian and Homeric manner of writing is not applicable, but that it is necessary for the poetry to be errant as well, passing from one subject to another, and tying various things together in a single bundle." (trans. mine)

Because the *Orlando furioso* appeared before the controversy over epic had begun in earnest, all of this criticism has necessarily something anachronistic about it. Precisely because it extends so variously the connotations of Ariosto's "errori," however, it provides a highly suggestive starting point for a reading both of Ariosto's poem in itself and of its place within poetic history. "Error" in the *Furioso* ranges from the diversions of chivalric adventure to the terrifying spectacle of Orlando's madness, from a pleasing "divertimento" to a willful deviation from epic and its single path. So insistent are Ariosto's own variations on "errare" and "errore" that they suggest not ignorance but rather a highly deliberate choice of romance and its aberrance, a choice whose implications turn a possible criticism of the poem into a perspective on the nature of all fictions. "Error" is not only a romance pun, sign of the interplay between mental and geographical "wandering"; it is also the concept which connects the diverse aspects of a long and complex poem. We shall proceed, therefore, by exploring what might be called the gradations of error in the *Furioso*, from the author's exploitation, and imitation, of the divagations of his errant knights; through the tension between a deviant narrative and the demands of closure; to the *selva* of allusions which reveal a pattern of "error" or deviation within literary history; and to the revelation, on the Moon, of the error of all poetic constructs or "authorized versions," including even those of Dante and of Virgil.

More than one modern reader has remarked the frequency with which the verb "errare" and its many variants occur throughout the *Furioso*. In the very first canto of the poem, when Orlando's expected possession of Angelica is interrupted by an unforeseen Saracen victory, the narrator comments, "Ecco il giudicio uman come spesso erra!"[c] (i. 7. 2), and one of the most important of the myriad senses of "error" through the rest of the poem is just such a failure of expectation, a misconception about future events. This kind of error seems to be the inevitable result of not knowing the plot in advance, somewhat like Malagigi in the so-called *Cinque canti*,

[c] "Lo, how often human judgment errs!"

or "five cantos," who does not share the author's or the reader's knowledge of the "Gran Consiglio delle fate" and therefore cannot know that he is calling on the infernal spirits in vain.[11] The possibility of such a dual perspective reminds us at once of the archetypal locus of romance, the "selve e boscherecci labirinti"[d] (XIII. 42. 4) in which the direct route is obscured. Daedalus, creator of the Cretan labyrinth in which even he might get lost, was not accidentally the mythical inventor of human flight, and this polarity in Ariosto's poem becomes the contrast between the earth-bound wandering of errant knights and the authorial hippogriff's-eye view.

This, however, is only one of the verb's fertile senses in a linguistic universe where "errare" can mean both "to wander" and "to err." Grifone's unreasonable attachment to the wicked Orrigille—"Grifone, / che non si può emendare, e il suo error vede"[e] (XVI. 4. 1-2)—provides an indication that error, in the moral sense, is a symptom of the Pauline wayward will (Rom. 7: 19), Petrarch's "io fallo e vedo il mio fallir."[f] That Grifone's error is specifically that of love makes him one example among many of the *furor* which gives Ariosto's poem its title. More than one Renaissance commentator allegorized the *Furioso*'s principal enchanter, Atlante, as "Amore," and its English translator, Sir John Harington, described Atlante's "palazzo incantato" (XXII. 17. 1) as an "infinite laberinth" where "so many brave young men of great vallor, loose themselves in seeking their loves."[12] Harington goes on to characterize such seeking as idolatry, and indeed there is perhaps no more terrifying Renaissance version of the *idolon* and its emptiness than the palace where each man pursues the phantom of his own desire, alone. The incarnation of this phantom in the first part of the poem is, of course, Angelica, the universal object of pursuit that Ariosto takes over from Boiardo's *Orlando innamorato* and makes into a symbol of the erotics of scarcity. When so elusive a "commodità" (XXIII. 108. 6) virtually squanders herself on the

---

[d] "woods and shady mazes"

[e] "Grifon, who cannot correct himself and sees his error"

[f] "I fail and see my failing" (trans. mine)

newcomer, Medoro, there remains from this anticlimax the overwhelming sense of an excess of desire with nowhere to go. Ariosto's version firmly takes over from Boiardo's at this point, and Orlando's love deepens into madness.

That Orlando's madness is also the result of a mistake in perception suggests yet another of the senses of "error" in the *Furioso*. Ariosto, like Spenser after him, often introduces the characters of his poem by the way in which they first appear to other characters, and the deceptive nature of appearance, and the errors it leads to, become part of the labyrinthine "selva oscura." Ruggiero is a pupil with almost no retention, and falls prey to the attractive seeming of Alcina's court despite the instructions given him by Astolfo. Bradamante, similarly instructed by Melissa, still believes the *imago* of Ruggiero to be the real one (XIII. 76). Even the angel Michele has to trust to appearances (XIV. 91), and if the "errore" of Norandino in judging too quickly by appearance is finally righted in the case of Grifone in canto XVIII, the more sinister "apparenza" of Pinabello (II. 30-76) prepares us for the darker world of the *Cinque canti* where the true story is almost impossible to perceive. The terrifying image of Orlando roaming the countryside in his madness unearths the despair just beneath the surface of the poem's delights, a wandering which is no longer an engaging diversion but the *contrapasso* of a crippling blindness:

> Varii gli effetti son, ma la pazzia
> è tutt'una però, che li fa uscire.
> Gli è come una gran selva, ove la via
> conviene a forza, a chi vi va, fallire:
> chi su, chi giù, chi qua, chi là travia.[g]
>
> (XXIV. 2. 1-5)

An "erring" which had seemed to be a form of looseness, even of flexibility, becomes instead the rigidity of an individual obsession, the final form of the labyrinth of desire.

---

[g] "Varied are the effects, but the madness that brings them out is nevertheless all one. It is like a great forest, where of necessity the way must deceive him who goes there; one up, one down, one here, one there goes astray."

The "nuovo error" of Atlante's palace (xxii. 17-20) seems to exempt at least the reader, who can look down as if upon a maze or hall of mirrors and see each character imprisoned within his own fixation. But not even the reader is always admitted to this privileged perception, and the suggestion in one canto opening that he has his Ganelon in the enchanters who work not with spirits but with simulation and fraud (viii. 1) extends the problem of ineluctable error to the larger problem of "reading" outside the boundaries of the text. The *exordia* of Ariosto's poem open out the seemingly closed, and distanced, form of the romance onto a world which, by implication, is part of its "gran selva." However insistently literary, the *Furioso* retains at least this element of the oral fiction of Boiardo's poem, where the poet frequently addresses an audience pictured as present and participating in the performance by its response. Ariosto's sequel alternates slyly between the oral and the literary, and the reader who enjoys, as "lettor," a distanced view of the wandering of characters within a circumscribed text, may suddenly find himself addressed within that maze, and his own flexibility of movement denied.

Orlando's error, according to St. John in canto xxxiv, was to turn away "dal camin dritto le commesse insegne"[h] (62. 6). And this metaphor of deviation gathers up another of the poem's "errors," the straying of the knights from duty into love, from loyalty to the epic *agon* of the Holy War into the "selva amorosa" of romance. So constant is the alternation between the two worlds—as, for example, in canto xvii, where the poet signals his departure from the epic siege at Paris to follow the more Odyssean exploits of Astolfo (xvii. 17. 1-2)—that we begin to suspect that one of the *Furioso*'s subjects is the difference between epic and romance, that the "straying" noted by his Aristotelian critics was, generically, a deliberate one. Melissa, the spirit behind the single epic intent of bringing Ruggiero, like Aeneas, to a destined marriage, shows his future wife Bradamante the most direct route to this goal:

[h] "from the straight road the ensigns entrusted"

Tosto che spunti in ciel la prima luce,
piglierai meco la più dritta via
ch'al lucente castel d'acciai' conduce,

. . . .

t'insegnerò, poi che saren sul mare,
sì ben la via, che non potresti errare.—[i]

(III. 63. 1-3, 7-8)

But when this direct path has been obstructed by the machi-
nations of the old enchanter, Atlante, Bradamante's aimless
wandering is deliberately contrasted with Melissa's superior
knowledge and more steadfast purpose:

Or tornando a colei, ch'era presaga
di quanto de' avvenir, dico che tenne
la dritta via dove l'errante e vaga
figlia d'Amon seco a incontrar si venne.[j]

(VII. 45. 1-4)

The powerful centrifugal force of such "error" makes the
"dritta via" of epic virtually impossible, just as the multiplicity of claims on the knights' time makes it difficult to will one
thing. The review of the Saracen army in canto XIII, though
an obvious parallel to the review of Turnus' troops in the
Aeneid, reveals instead the supreme difficulty of ordering "le
diverse squadre e le nazioni / . . . errando senza guida propia"[k]
(XIII. 82. 5-6) and suggests why Tasso's return to Virgilian
epic takes the form of a pointed correction of Ariosto's deviation.[13]

This wandering from epic appears unquestionably deliberate in a poem whose constant digressions—one of the "Errori
degli scrittori de' Romanzi"—are presented as the unavoidable result of the erring loves of its characters. The various

---

[i] "As soon as the first light dawns in the sky, with me you will take the
shortest way that leads to the shining steel castle. . . . when we are on the
seashore, I shall show you the way so well that you cannot err."

[j] "Now returning to that one who divined all that was to come, I say she
kept the very road where the wandering and uncertain daughter of Amon
came to meet her."

[k] "the different squadrons and the nations . . . wandering about without
suitable leaders"

ways in which the knights deviate from a single, straightforward intent have their counterpart in the narrator's comments on his own poem, on the impossibility of keeping to a single narrative line and on such straying as the authorial version of the chivalric desire to "please." The punning connection between a romance presented as "divertimento" (I. 4. 6-8) and the distractions which lure his characters from the path of duty is simply another reminder that all such spatial metaphors for error have their narrative counterparts—deviation, diversion, and digression. Dalinda tells Rinaldo how, blinded by love to the false seeming of Polinesso, she was an unwitting accomplice in his evil design against Ginevra (v. 11), and thus leads the knight, and the poem, into another episodic adventure. Orlando is deterred from pursuing the straightest path to Angelica by the plight of Olimpia (IX. 18), a distraction for him which is at the same time yet another digression for the poem. Ruggiero's explanation to the beautiful ladies of Alcina's court of the service demanded of "un cavalliero errante" (VI. 80. 3-8) reminds us of the narrator's defense of his digressions as a sense of being diverted by one obligation after another.

So ubiquitous is this problem of "errore" that it comes as no surprise when the narrator confesses his share in its moral consequences as well and speaks of his momentary freedom from it as a "lucido intervallo" (XXIV. 3. 4). Robert Durling and others have observed how closely the moral erring of the poem's characters is paralleled by the poet's confession of his own weakness.[14] The very first mention of the madness of Orlando is accompanied by a reference to the poet's own madness, to a love which threatens the very completion of his promised poem:

> se da colei che tal quasi m'ha fatto,
> che 'l poco ingegno ad or ad or mi lima,
> me ne sarà però tanto concesso,
> che mi basti a finir quanto ho promesso.[1]

(I. 2. 5-8)

[1] "if by her who has almost made me the same, who all the time files away my small ability, so much of it is still granted me as may suffice to finish what I have promised."

This confession of like weakness is repeated in the poet's comment on Orlando after the hero has deviated from his duty to Charlemagne in order to pursue "un vano amor" (IX. 1. 7), a comment which once again suggests the origin of error in the Pauline wayward will:

> Ma l'escuso io pur troppo, e mi rallegro
> nel mio difetto aver compagno tale;
> ch'anch'io sono al mio ben languido et egro,
> sano e gagliardo a seguitare il male.[m]
>
> (IX. 2. 1-4)

And, at the center of the poem, when Orlando's brain finally turns at the confirmation of Angelica's betrayal, the parallel reappears:

> Ben mi si potria dir: — Frate, tu vai
> l'altrui mostrando, e non vedi il tuo fallo. —
> Io vi rispondo che comprendo assai,
> or che di mente ho lucido intervallo;
> et ho gran cura (e spero farlo ormai)
> di riposarmi e d'uscir fuor di ballo:
> ma tosto far, come vorrei, nol posso;
> che 'l male è penetrato infin all'osso.[n]
>
> (XXIV. 3)

This admission of a share in the madness of error and the suggestion that it is only a "lucido intervallo" that enables him to write the poem at all is the counterpart, on the moral level, to the structural play of distance and involvement in the narrator's perspective on his own work. The confession of a brotherhood in weakness softens the inevitable sense of a judging distance between narrator and poem, but when the

---

[m] "But I excuse him only too much and congratulate myself at having such a companion in my failure; for I too am weak and sick as to my own good, healthy and strong in following evil."

[n] "It may well be said to me: 'Brother, you go on showing another man his error and do not see your own.' I answer you that I understand well, now that my mind has a lucid interval, and I am taking great care (and I hope always to do so) to rest and get out of the dance, but I cannot do it as quickly as I should like, for the malady has penetrated to my bones."

parallel returns, once again, after Astolfo's journey to the
moon, we begin to suspect that something more than sincere
fellow feeling is involved:

> Chi salirà per me, madonna, in cielo
> a riportarne il mio perduto ingegno?
> che, poi ch'uscì da' bei vostri occhi il telo
> che 'l cor mi fisse, ognior perdendo vegno.
> Né di tanta iattura mi querelo,
> pur che non cresca, ma stia a questo segno;
> ch'io dubito, se più si va sciemando,
> di venir tal, qual ho descritto Orlando.
>
> Per rïaver l'ingegno mio m'è aviso
> che non bisogna che per l'aria io poggi
> nel cerchio de la luna o in paradiso;
> che 'l mio non credo che tanto alto alloggi.
> Ne' bei vostri occhi e nel sereno viso,
> nel sen d'avorio e alabastrini poggi
> se ne va errando; et io con queste labbia
> lo corrò, se vi par ch'io lo rïabbia.º

(xxxv. 1-2)

Apart from the obvious fact that this "Cure of Folly" is quite
the opposite of that provided for Orlando's error, under the
pretense that his less extreme case calls for a less drastic solution, this confession of weakness pushes the poet's supposed
sincerity just far enough to make the opening question, literally, rhetorical, and to extend its suggestion of hyperbole
back over all such confessions in the poem.

If this irony applies on the moral level to all such admis-

º "Who will mount up to the sky for me, my Lady, to bring back my lost
wits? which, since the weapon that pierced my heart came from your beautiful eyes, I keep on losing every hour. Yet I do not complain of so great a loss,
if only it does not increase but remains at this point, for I fear, if they go on
getting less, I shall come to be such as I have described Orlando. // To get my
wits again I think I do not need to mount in the air to the circle of the moon
or to paradise, for I do not think mine dwell so high. In your beautiful eyes
and in your calm face, in your ivory bosom and alabaster hills they are wandering, and I will gather them in with these lips, if it seems to you I may have
them again."

sions of a share in his characters' errors, it also applies to the play in the narrative itself between detachment and involvement. In canto VIII, the narrator pretends to be so overcome with emotion at the spectacle of the fair Angelica chained naked to the rock that he cannot go on with her story (66–67), a sympathy as frustrating to the reader's expectations as the pretense that the story is becoming tedious just as Ruggiero is about to succeed in untying his troublesome knots (x. 115). It is on the same level as Ariosto's claim that even he is taken in by the golden appearance of Alcina's city (VI. 59) and the pushing of his supposed identification with the oral delivery of the *cantastorie* to its logical conclusion: "Non più, Signor, non più di questo canto; / ch'io son già rauco, e vo' posarmi alquanto"[p] (XIV. 134. 7–8). If the digressive, errant nature of the poem appears as the unavoidable result of the errors of its characters, this too may be part of the *Furioso*'s false seeming. To call this result "unavoidable" is to suggest the author's helplessness at the hands of his own characters, to accept his own defense of being pressured by their demands for equal time:

> Di questo altrove io vo' rendervi conto;
> ch'ad un gran duca è forza ch'io riguardi,
> il qual mi grida, e di lontano accenna,
> e priega ch'io nol lasci ne la penna.[q]
>
> (xv. 9. 5–8)

The "forza" conveys the sense of pressure, a detour from one narration to fulfill an obligation to another, but the "lontano" and the idea that Astolfo is still trapped "in the pen," reveal, instead, the picture of a poet who enjoys an aerial view of such distances and of a poem whose errant appearance is the highly conscious product of his own hand.

Thomas M. Greene has discussed the way in which the epic

---

[p] "Not more, My Lord, not more of this canto, for I am already hoarse and wish to rest myself a little."

[q] "Of this I intend to render you the account elsewhere; for I must attend to a great duke who calls to me and signals from a distance and prays that I will not leave him in my pen."

hero's control over his environment is an imitation of the expansiveness of the epic genre itself;[15] but just as in the Virgilian or Homeric epic the writer must finally have more control than his heroes, who are subject, often tragically, to inescapable limitations, so in Ariosto's romance the narrator's confessions of a share in his characters' weaknesses only partly cloak the fact that he is very much in control of his text. To note this is simply to repeat what many commentators have already observed, that Ariosto pretends to a formlessness more apparent than real. In relation to the question of the poet's self-conscious adoption of the romance form, however, this picture of a will which presents its own knowing choice as a kind of compulsion ("è forza che . . .") is most revealing. The conclusion can only be that the narrator is willingly led astray, conscious of the implications of such "error," both morally and on the level of an erring genre.

The fact that the parallel between action and narrative form should be so closely drawn suggests that Ariosto, far from being an unwitting victim, is deliberately exposing the fictional principle of romance, uncovering the anatomy of potentially endless error. The Gospel's contrasting of the narrow way of salvation with the broad road to Hell had its inevitable romance descendants, long before Ariosto's description of the roads to Alcina's and Logistilla's. But what in the other *romanzi* might be simply a romance *donnée*, Ariosto makes so insistently explicit that it becomes virtually a lesson in etymology. "Error" and its companion "deviation" are among the most common of spatial metaphors for spiritual facts, so that "errore," as Ariosto reminds us, can be "di via o di mente"[r] (xxxi. 66. 3-4). When Orlando, on the quest for Angelica that St. John is later to reveal as the hero's "error," strays more literally from his path, the poet provides the appropriate etymological gloss: "e sì come era uscito di se stesso, / uscì di strada"[s] (xii. 86. 3-4). One canto later, the narrator refers to his own digressions as just such a deviation:

[r] "of road or mind"
[s] "and just as he had gone out of his mind, he went out of the road" (trans. mine)

Chi fosse, dirò poi; ch'or me ne svia
tal, di chi udir non vi sarà men caro:
la figliuola d'Amon, la qual lasciai
languida dianzi in amorosi guai.[t]

(XIII. 44. 5-8)

just as he earlier had delighted in playing with the problem
presented by a fork in the road: "Da quattro sproni il destrier
punto arriva / ove una strada in due si dipartiva"[u] (I. 22. 7-8).
Ariosto exploits the manifold "errors" of romance—moral
and narrative—just as he edges towards parody all of its customary *materia*, from Astolfo's horn and fantastic flight to the
contest of magics, the enchanted weapons, and a series of
episodes so varied that few readers can be expected to remember the plot. This relentless exposure is, finally, part of
the way in which Ariosto completes, or goes beyond, Boiardo's unfinished poem. The *Orlando innamorato* is archetypally
and allegorically more dense,[16] but its "error" remains more
strictly the state or static moral category, whether it is the
"falso errore" of the Saracen faith (I. xvii. 36. 8) or the fixed,
linear logic of successive romance zones. In comparison with
the *Furioso*, where the lightest of allusions accumulate to per-
meate the entire poem and become, precisely because more
free-floating and unattached, more enigmatic and powerful,
Boiardo's enchanting "errori" are more frequently tied to
place and therefore more easily left behind.[17] Ariosto's very
lack of clear allegorical or iconographic identification, combined with his continual punning play upon the errancy of
both characters and narrative, paradoxically make "error" in
his poem at once subtler and more pervasive. The *Innamorato* is
filled with a series of amazing "libri," from the book Orlando
forgets to consult for the riddle of the Sphinx-like monster (I.
v. 76) to the one which reveals the topography of Falerina's
mysterious garden (I. xxiv. 20ff), but they too remain objects

---

[t] "Who he was I shall tell later; because now she whom you will not be less
glad to hear of takes me away from him: the daughter of Amon, whom a
while back I left weary in her amorous woes."

[u] "Pricked on by four spurs, the charger comes where one road forked into
two."

with a defined and predictable function. The *Furioso* contains fewer references to actual books, though the one given to Astolfo by Logistilla in canto xv combines perhaps all of them into that true Renaissance marvel, the encyclopedia with an index. The references which do exist, however, have enough resonating power to extend this clue to enchantment and its "error" to the act of reading itself. When the secret of Alcina's enchanting illusion is pierced by the "ring of reason" in canto vii and the beautiful seductress is revealed to be an ugly hag, Ariosto describes this uncovering as a kind of interpretation, or "reading":

> Giovane e bella ella si fa con arte,
> sì che molti ingannò come Ruggiero;
> ma l'annel venne a interpretar le carte,
> che già molti anni avean celato il vero.ᵛ
>
> (vii. 74. 1-4)[18]

The "error" of romance, far from being simply assumed, is something the reader is continually being invited to "see," and the topography to be revealed is here that of the book itself.

Fictional Deviance and the Problem of Closure

So deliberate is this exposure of romance "error" that we may begin to suspect that Ariosto is at least in part turning the constant divagations of the romance form into a metaphor for fiction itself. And this suspicion invites speculation on a less obvious but ultimately more revealing sense of "error" in the *Furioso*. For La Fontaine over a century later, human error and instability, if a cause for despair in the moralist, were nevertheless the very source and substance of fable, the reason why "La feinte est un pays plein de terres désertes"ʷ (*Fables* iii. 1. 5). Already in Ariosto, however, these subjects of the moralist's lament are very subtly related to the life of fiction, or at

---

ᵛ "By means of art she makes herself so young and beautiful that she deceived many as she did Ruggiero; but the ring came to interpret the pages that had for many years before concealed the truth."

ʷ "Feigning is a land full of yet-uninhabited spaces." (trans. mine)

least to the fictive genre of romance. When Rodomonte, after
Doralice's betrayal, pledges his undying enmity to
womankind and then quickly changes his mind at the sight of
Issabella, the author makes this "unstable and infirm" mind
the subject of a whole *exordium*:

> O degli uomini inferma e instabil mente!
> come siàn presti a varïar disegno!
> Tutti i pensier mutamo facilmente,
> più quei che nascon d'amoroso sdegno.
> Io vidi dianzi il Saracin sì ardente
> contra le donne, e passar tanto il segno,
> che non che spegner l'odio, ma pensai
> che non dovesse intiepidirlo mai.[x]

(xxix. 1)

The opening lines present this instability in the form of an
exclamatio upon human weakness. The verb used, however, is
"variare," accurate enough in its description of Rodomonte's
change, but also the most common of the narrator's words
for his own technique: "così mi par che la mia istoria, quanto /
or qua or là più varïata sia, / meno a chi l'udirà noiosa fia"[y]
(xiii. 80. 6-8).

To see the link between Rodomonte's erring from his firm
resolve and the poem which is, in its own way, always
"presto a varïar disegno" is to begin to see that the errors the
poet rails against in the famous *exordia* are also, paradoxically,
the elements which keep his story going. Canto ii opens with
a complaint against Love and the fountains whose opposite effect makes for such endless frustration: "Ingiustissimo Amor,
perché sì raro / corrispondenti fai nostri desiri?"[z] (1. 1-2). The

---

[x] "O shifting and unstable minds of men! how ready we are to vary our
plans! We easily change all our intentions, chiefly those that rise from the
anger of love. A little while ago, I saw the Saracen so violent against women
and going so beyond bounds that I thought that not merely would he not get
rid of his hate but would never even cool it."

[y] "so it seems to me that my story, when it is more varied now in this way
and now in that, will be less wearisome to him who listens to it."

[z] "Most unjust Love, why so rarely do you make our desires corre-
spondent?"

counterpart of these fountains in the story of Ruggiero and Bradamante is the seemingly endless series of distractions which make the "sentiero" prophesied by Merlin as early as canto III into a very long and winding one. But if desires did correspond, if these distractions did not exist, the poem would be a very short one indeed; Angelica and Medoro find just such a correspondence, and their story is effectively over. The suggestion seems to be that fiction by its very nature feeds upon frustration, that the real interest begins only when things go wrong. Orlando and Issabella travel for many days without mishap, "Senza trovar cosa che degna sia / d'istoria"aa (XIII. 44. 1-2). And when Ariosto confides to his female readers that the objectionable twenty-eighth canto is perfectly skippable ("Lasciate questo canto, che senza esso / può star l'istoria, e non sarà men chiara,"bb XXVIII. 2. 1-2), he points not only to the digressive nature of his romanzo but to the complicity of the reader in its deviance.

The fundamental connection between "error" and fiction is confirmed by the kinds of events which become metaphors for the particular structure Ariosto adopts. Ruggiero's tangled laces get in the way of simple forward movement towards a desired goal as effectively as the many strands of the author's "varia tela" (II. 30. 5), and "Fortuna" and "Discordia" in Ariosto's hands become, like "error," fictional principles. "Fortuna" often keeps events in the poem from reaching their expected end but is as transparently the agent of the author as that Turpin who demands that he include the twenty-eighth canto. "Discordia" enters the Saracen camp in canto XXVII and the long list of accounts to be settled and the problem of ordering them according to priority are described in terms strikingly similar to the narrator's comments on the ordering of his many stories. Ariosto's "Discordia" may look like her Virgilian counterparts—the guardian of Orcus in *Aeneid* VI and the Fury who stirs up Turnus' troops—but she has, narratively, just the opposite function. In Book VII of the

aa "without finding a thing worth relating"
bb "Skip this canto, for the story can hold together without it and will not be less clear."

Aeneid, Juno calls up the Fury Allecto from Hell in order to disrupt the peace between Latinus and the Trojans, to begin in effect the epic *agon* of the second half of the poem. In the *Furioso*, the arrival of Discordia in the Saracen camp is the centrifugal force which breaks up the concerted action of epic and sends the "cavallieri erranti" back to more accustomed pursuits. Her disruption of the careful schedule of priorities parallels the narrative principle of romance, the virtually endless erring and digression in which any exercise of poetic closure becomes a literary *tour de force*.

It is this problem of closure which haunts a fiction so wedded to *varietas* and complication that it literally loses its way. Luigi Pulci, throughout the wonderful *exordia* of the *Morgante maggiore*, constantly prays to his "Signor" to lead him safely through to the completion of his labyrinthine journey, whose constant and devious windings threaten the very continuation of the poem.[19] The *Orlando innamorato* breaks off when the jarring noise of real war intrudes upon the delights of amorous adventure and bequeaths to its successor the problem of how to resolve events it leaves forever suspended.[20] Ariosto signals his awareness of the potential limbo in which the story had been left by echoing precisely those elements in Boiardo's poem which make closure virtually impossible. The *Orlando innamorato* abounds in images of endlessness—the "fate" who can never die, Balisardo's progressive metamorphoses, and the giant who in dying multiplies,[21] a romance theme on which Spenser's story of Priamond, Diamond, and Triamond provides only one among many variations. The most revealing image of Ariosto's exercise of closure on Boiardo's suspensions is the seemingly indestructible Orrilo who continually reassembles his dissevered parts. Boiardo's Grifone and Aquilante are unable to terminate his infuriating career, but Astolfo, in canto xv of the *Furioso*, discovers the secret of his deathlessness in Logistilla's book, and quickly puts an end to it.

The task of killing the seemingly deathless Orrilo in the *Innamorato* is set for Aquilante and Grifone by the "fata bruna" and the "fata bianca" as part of a strategy to defer the

brothers' fated death in France (III. ii. 42-43). That the strategy of the two fairies is to defer the prophesied end of the
brothers is revealing, for it is just such deferral that is exposed
throughout the *Furioso* as the reason for the *romanzo*'s seemingly endless erring. Ariosto repeatedly uses the word "differire" for the suspension of one narrative by another,[22]
suggesting that the romance multiplication of differences in
space is at least partly the consequence of a temporal deferral.
Atlante's subterfuges, aimed at circumventing Ruggiero's
conversion and inevitable death, become an important structural device; characters put off one objective when interrupted
by another; and "differire" marks the suspension of narration
at the end of too many cantos to name.

Such a suspension of end or closure is the romance equivalent of the intellectual problem of Buridan's ass or of the
popular Renaissance *exemplum* of Hercules at the Crossroads,
where the counterpart of aimless wandering would seem to
be a state of perpetual irresolution. One image of Orlando
"sospeso" between the demands of love and duty in Book II
of the *Orlando innamorato* ("Stando sospeso e tacito a pensare, /
Ché il core ardente e le voglie amorose / Nol lasciavan se
stesso governare,"[cc] ix. 46. 4-6) suggests that this state of indecision is the reason for the constant alternation between
epic and romance themes in both this and its successor poem.
Ariosto calls attention to this irresolution by the very speed of
his alternations, the mode of "meanwhile" which creates the
illusion of suspending linear time. The actual period traversed
in the action of the *Furioso* is unclear, though the central event
of the siege of Paris provides, among other things, a way of
telling time. This technique of narrative *espacement* is also a
kind of deferral in which the reader has the sense of time
traversed because the reading itself is so time-consuming. The
continual shifting from one story to another often provides
what is virtually the cartography of a single moment, like the
extended space of the Renaissance illustrations where the
whole plot is revealed at once. The author alone can see the

[cc] "Undecided and in silence, thinking that his ardent heart and amorous
desires did not permit him to rule himself" (trans. mine)

warp and woof of the "cloth" he weaves (xiii. 81. 1-2), the sum of the frequent romance tapestries which reveal the form of an action before it happens and thus mediate between plot and person, the lofty authorial view and the character or reader still immersed in the process of time.[23] The reader comes to this simultaneous perspective often only in the act of interpreting what he has read, and the discovery of the shortness of actual elapsed time, when it had seemed so long, is truly a revelation.[24]

Ariosto does indeed exercise closure on Boiardo's suspended narrative, and the reader who comes to the *Furioso* from the *Innamorato* may have a sense of things coming full circle, like the amazing ring which in finally returning to Angelica evokes in little the major stations of Boiardo's story. So constant is the play on deviation and digression in the *Furioso* that we begin to expect it, as if there were indeed no ending. When Aquilante boards the ship for Antioch in canto xviii, we expect the now familiar tempest to appear and, with it, yet another change in narrative direction. But nothing does happen on the way and his successful coming to port is at least partly a joke on the reader. What is true of this one episode is also true of the course of the poem and its return to port. Just when he has the reader accepting and even expecting endless digression, Ariosto exercises his own kind of closure, and the "errar sempre" of the stanza which anticipates the completion of his labors (xlvi. 1. 6) is both a reminder of the danger inherent in this errant genre and a subtle index of his achievement.

The only definitive ending to human error in real life is conversion, or death. The first was already such a venerable romance *topos* as to receive Pulci's repeated imitation and parody throughout the *Morgante*, and occurs frequently enough in Boiardo to begin to suggest that it too is a kind of "conclusion."[25] Ariosto concentrates all the implications of this theme on the baptism of Ruggiero, the one conversion missing from Boiardo but essential in bringing the narrative to a sufficiently epic close. The counterpart of conversion in romance, as in the novel, is disillusionment; and the elimination of "incanti" required before the story of Orlando can proceed to its end is at least in part the result of Ariosto's transformation of Boiardo's Astolfo, the "buffone" and "vantatore" who last appears in the *Innamorato* as the fool-hardy victim of Alcina's enchantment but enters the *Furioso* as a literally transformed, and disillusioned, myrtle, prepared by bitter experience to proceed, from this point, more cautiously.[26]

The other definitive ending which seems oddly out of place in romance is death. We are shocked by Issabella's death when it occurs (xxix. 25). Its finality stands in such sharp contrast to the deathlessness of the poem's enchanted knights that it jolts us, momentarily, back into the world of waking reality. And the very fact that we experience her death as a shock reveals our own complicity in the enchantment of romance and its "oblio." Ariosto's wry observation, "Era a periglio di morire Orlando, / se fosse di morir stato capace"[dd] (xxiv. 11. 1-2), suggests that the difficulty of bringing the *Innamorato*'s stories to an end is almost inevitably the consequence of the deathlessness of its enchanted heroes, and his exercise of closure on his predecessor poem takes the form of a literal series of deaths. Agramante and Gradasso both die in battle, an end to the campaign begun in the first book of the *Innamorato*, and Boiardo's two most sympathetic figures, Brandimarte and Fiordelisa, meet their deaths in the *Furioso*. One by one the pagan heroes of Boiardo's poem are killed off, just as the range of enchantments is exposed, and both movements marshal the narrative towards its ending.

To perform a *reductio ad absurdum* on romance is to remind the reader that its plenitude *is* endless error, and that there really is no way to end it except by fiat, the poet's intervening "voglio." The enchantment of romance is in the constant Ovidian metamorphosis which keeps its fiction going and defers, like the storytelling of Scheherazade, the fateful moment of truth. Orrilo has his cycle of revival terminated when Astolfo learns the secret of the enchantment, and its revelation is one of a series of such broken spells, not all of which are greeted with such relief. Some of the inhabitants of Atlante's

---

dd "Orlando was in danger of dying, if he had been capable of death."

castle prison are dismayed to find themselves released from its "incanto"; something pleasurable, which seemed deathless, has come to an end (IV. 39. 7-8). And what applies to this enchantment may apply as well to Ariosto's bringing an end to his own "incantevole" romance. As it is Logistilla's book or the "ring of reason" (VIII. 2. 1-2) which most frequently brings an end to enchantment and illusion in the Furioso, it is not surprising that Ariosto's own exercise of closure on his errant poem should take the form of a movement back towards epic, the genre which Renaissance critics as readily assimilated to reason in the hierarchy of the faculties as they accused romance of pandering to the erring senses. Not only, therefore, does the theme of a guiding providence start to sound again as the end of the poem approaches, but the epic echoes become much clearer and suggest now not deviation from the epic model, as earlier echoes often did, but rather deliberate imitation. Orlando's wits are restored and the one epic action—the war against the Saracens—ends with a victory for Charlemagne and Christendom. Ruggiero, the often frustratingly reticent center of the other epic theme, is finally baptized in canto XLI, and the remaining five cantos surround him with echoes of Aeneas, from Melissa's intervening to save him from death to the abrupt ending of the poem in his single combat with Rodomonte.

The movement towards epic sets a limit to the potentially endless error of the romanzo and Ariosto seems to be leaving Boiardo for the more authoritative models of Dante and Virgil. Even this, however, is not entirely the case, and this fact brings us to the final aspect of our consideration of Ariosto and "error"—the poem's relation to all literary counterparts of the authorized version or "true history." Ariosto's constant punning on "errare" and "errore" pushes to an extreme the qualities of romance most frequently condemned, and his exercise of closure on the poem's enchantment suggests a studied emulation of a more revered poetic genre. But other, more submerged, elements of his poem tend in a more subversive direction, towards the deconstruction of the very idea of a fiction without "error," of an authoritative or privileged literary genre. The *Furioso* reveals, through its complex use of echo and allusion, a pattern of deviation or "error" in literary history itself and exposes the contingency or "erring" of all poetic language, including that of the very authorities with which it was so unfavorably compared. It is to this revelation, this crucial "error," that we finally must turn.

The Authorized Version

READERS struck by the way in which Ariosto, unlike Virgil, produces the effect of a number of actions existing simultaneously often cite the poet's image of himself as the weaver of his "gran tela" (XIII. 81. 2). But what may not at first be quite as apparent is the fact that Ariosto is equally a weaver of echoes from other texts and that the very multiplicity of these echoes undermines the priority of a single literary authority or source. The multiple echoes of Virgil, Dante, Boiardo, and the *romanzi* in the first stanza of the *Furioso* alone subtly qualify even his own claim to treat of "cosa non detta in prosa mai né in rima"[ee] (I. 2. 2). And when he combines echoes from several different writers on the same theme, as he does with the metamorphosed Astolfo of canto VI, with the Harpies in canto XXXIV, and with the recalls of Virgil and Seneca in the cured Orlando's "Solvite me,"[27] the effect is to demonstrate that the subject is the property of no single author and that the new writer is therefore free to provide his own variation. Thomas M. Greene has spoken of the gap Michele discovers between the authorized or heavenly version of society and the actual state of affairs.[28] The parallel on the more strictly literary level to the *Furioso*'s skeptical view of all such authorized versions may be the suggestion that there is more than one story and one story only. Ariosto says to his audience both "You know this story as well as I do" (XI. 5. 3-4) and, on occasions, "Here are the variations; choose your own" (XXIX. 7. 7), slyly challenging the claim of any one version to a monopoly on "truth."

[ee] "something never said before in prose or rhyme"

Renaissance critics often excused Ariosto's irregularity on the basis of his ignorance of epic norms, but a careful study of the context of echoes of one poetic authority—the *Aeneid*—suggests that the "Ferrarese Virgil" was not failing in his imitation of the model but rather quite consciously marking his own departure from it. The great epic action of the siege of Paris is filled with echoes of Virgil's poem, but Ariosto, having raised these epic expectations, explicitly frustrates them in the name of "varietà," a most un-Virgilian principle ("Ma lasciamo, per Dio, Signore, ormai / di parlar d'ira e di cantar di morte,"[ff] xvii. 17. 1-2), and turns to the more Odyssean exploits of Grifone, Aquilante, and Astolfo in the East.[29] When Orlando, angry at being deprived of Angelica, tosses and turns in his bed in the besieged Paris (viii. 71), the simile used to describe him is borrowed from Book viii of the *Aeneid* (20-25), where Aeneas, worried by the approaching war in Latium, casts his mind back and forth between alternatives. But whereas Aeneas finally awakens from his dream of promised victory to seek help for the beleaguered Trojans, Orlando, frightened by his dream of Angelica lost to him forever (viii. 83), rises in the night to go in search of her and thus deprives Charlemagne of his much-needed aid. The common simile makes only too clear the difference between the two heroes.

This use of Virgilian echoes both to mark his own "deviation" and to point up the reduced or diminished context of romance occurs throughout the *Furioso* and calls attention to an important aspect of the "erring" genre. Diminution seems almost the necessary result of romance multiplication and fragmentation, just as all such secondary imitation seems inevitably second hand. Dante's Francesca may see herself as part of the procession of romance heroines (*Inf.* v), but her constant reference to her literary models suggests that she is only an imitative and diminished Dido; Spenser's tawdry version of a latter-day Troy features the literal diminutives of a "Hellenore" and a "Paridell." Ariosto uses Virgilian echoes

[ff] "But for God's sake, My Lord, let us now leave off speaking of rage and singing of death."

to set off the romance complication of more simplified epic episodes,[30] but he also uses them to indicate a context diminished both morally and in scale. Two Virgilian similes, in reversed order, are used for the "empio gigante" (xi. 19. 4) Ruggiero thinks he sees carrying off Bradamante, and the fact that their Virgilian context is Turnus' attack on the Trojan battlements serves to remind us that Ruggiero is not where he should be in regard to his epic duty, either to Agramante in the siege of Paris, or to the destined cofounder of the Este line, whose attractions he has just forgotten (2. 5) at the sight of the naked Angelica. In a more amusing vein, the similarity between the dwelling of the giant Caligorante in the Furioso (xv. 49) and the cave of Cacus in Book viii of the Aeneid points up just such a difference in dimension. In Virgil's eighth book, the long description of Hercules' victory over the fire-breathing monster Cacus serves to prepare for Aeneas' shield and its depiction of Augustus as slayer of the Egyptian queen and her "monstrous gods" (viii. 698) at Actium. But Caligorante is not Cacus, whatever their common connection with the God of Fire,[31] and Astolfo is certainly not Hercules.

If echoes of Virgil point up Ariosto's deliberate deviation from him, other echoes in the poem reveal an awareness of such "error" as the dynamic of literary history, the way in which poems could be said to challenge the authority, or priority, of earlier poetic models. In the prophetic "show" of Bradamante's descendants in canto iii (20-62) of the Furioso, the principal literary model is Book vi of the Aeneid, the genealogical review which was to become a standard feature of Renaissance epic. But there are also, as Renaissance commentators saw, unmistakable echoes in this canto of the much more qualified praise of Augustus in the Metamorphoses and of precisely that part of the poem where Ovid appears most clearly to be straying from or correcting the authority of Virgil.[32] Scholars are uncertain how to interpret Ovid's incorporation of the events of the Aeneid into the last two books of the Metamorphoses; but Ariosto's one Ovidian allusion not only serves to qualify his own praise of the Estes but suggests that he might have seen in this particular part of Ovid's poem a specifically literary kind of "metamorphosis." The rapid summary of the events of the *Aeneid* in a single section of the *Metamorphoses* is virtually a *reductio ad absurdum* of epic, insofar as this genre's overriding narrative concern tends towards chronicle at the extreme. Ovid not only rushes over the most crucial Virgilian events in order to have more time to enlarge upon the parts which interest him,[33] but he also gets out from under the authority of Virgilian closure by taking the story of Aeneas past the point where Virgil left off, opening the poem up by treating it as if it were unfinished, and writing what is in effect the *Aeneid*'s thirteenth book.[34]

If echoes, in the *Furioso*, of Ovid's modification of Virgil suggest a pattern to literary history other than that of faithful imitation, other echoes suggest a precedent for such deviation in Virgil himself. The alternation of epic and romance episodes was the element in the *Orlando furioso* most frequently cited in *Cinquecento* criticism as proof of Ariosto's departure from Homeric and Virgilian authority, and the orthodoxy of strict generic lines. In Orlando, now not just "innamorato" but "furioso," it presents an epic figure lost in the world of romance, woefully out of place in its fluidities,[35] while in Ruggiero it pictures the almost chronically distracted "cavalliero errante" who fulfills his epic destiny only when taken firmly into hand. Its epic conventions—the similes and genealogical review, the night raid and the descent from heaven—stand side by side with an abundance of stock romance themes. Some of the echoes of Virgil, however, manage to suggest not only the authority of a model to be followed but the *Aeneid*'s own place within a specifically literary form of "error." In canto XXXIX of the *Furioso*, Astolfo casts his leaves upon the sea to produce ships, and this "stupendo miracolo" (26. 7) inevitably recalls the "mirabile monstrum" of the *Aeneid* (IX. 120) where the Trojan ships turn into nymphs. But what this recall points to is the fact that the *Aeneid* itself had already deviated from the model of its most famous epic predecessor, the *Iliad*.

Commentators from Servius to the present have noted the

way in which Virgil's poem incorporates not just the epic
agon of the *Iliad* but also the "errores" of the *Odyssey*, the
poem customarily assimilated by Renaissance critics to romance.[36] Astolfo's production of ships out of leaves is thus, in
one respect, only a pushing of the "romantic" elements of
Virgil's poem a little further in the same direction, just as the
"demonio" Gradasso who baffles Ranaldo in the *Orlando innamorato* (I. v. 46) is the logical romance extension of the "imago" Aeneas who draws Turnus away from the epic action in
Aeneid x. It is therefore not surprising that one of the ways in
which Ariosto uses echoes from the *Aeneid* is to push the
Odyssean elements of Virgil's poem just far enough to con-
vert them to a new context. "Errare" in the first half of the
Aeneid, for example, conveys the sense of wandering and
exile which enables Dante to interpret the journey of Aeneas
as another Exodus.[37] But whereas in Virgil and in Dante,
such wandering is only a stage between the no longer and the
not yet, in a journey whose end has been promised, in Ariosto
it becomes the powerful centrifugal tendency which suggests
the impossibility of marshaling the "cavallieri erranti" to any
end whatsoever. Aeneas, "oblitus fatorum," as he ponders
the decision whether to stop, in Sicily, short of his goal (v.
703), has his counterpart in the whole mode of oblivion
which rules the labyrinthine "selva" of romance, and occa-
sionally, Ariosto suggests, the narrator himself (xxxII. 1).
There is even a subtle grammatical shift: whereas in Aeneas'
account of the "Iliad" events in *Aeneid* II the conditional
"would have" points to the tragic difference between what
might have been done with the wooden horse and what was
(54-56), in Ariosto the conditional becomes the poem's mode
of being: his "istoria" is more "variata" (xIII. 80. 6-7) than the
single action of epic precisely because what might have happened so rarely does.

   The catalogue of Virgilian echoes should be sufficient by
now to suggest what seem to be contradictions in Ariosto's
relation to this epic model. On the one hand, by enlarging
upon the Odyssean or romance elements in the *Aeneid* itself,
Ariosto not only recalls Ovid and other poetic encounters

with Virgilian authority but hints at a precedent in the "altissimo poeta" for such deliberate "erring." On the other, the most clearly recognizable Virgilian similes and conventions, if they suggest a knowing deviation from epic's "dritta via," also serve to indicate just how reduced their new romance context is. This departure from the Virgilian model at the same time as he exposes the "errors" of romance may at first seem to leave us nowhere, with a poet who displays his skill at drawing upon both the heroic world of epic and the enchantments of romance, but belongs, finally, with neither. And yet there is at least one other possibility, that in exposing the aberrance of romance, Ariosto is revealing something about all literature, including epic; and this may help to account for the curious way in which epic and romance elements in the *Furioso* seem to act as foils for one another. In this respect, the little allegory of Time and the Poets witnessed by Astolfo on his journey to the Moon in canto xxxv is at once the place where the poem's challenges to the authority of both Dante and Virgil converge and the center of Ariosto's poetic revelations.

The True History

ONE of the most frequently cited "errori degli scrittori de' Romanzi" was their desertion not only of the epic's stricter narrative line but of its higher "truth," founded not on fables and lies but on the authority of history. Antonio Minturno, in the *Arte poetica*, invokes Aristotelian authority for his conception of epic's greater "verisimilitudine,"[38] and Tasso, in the first of the famous *Discorsi dell'arte poetica* (Venice, 1587), makes a distinction with particular resonance for the *Furioso*:

> La materia, che argomento può ancora comodamente chiamarsi o si finge, ed allora par che il poeta abbia parte non solo nella scelta, ma nella invenzione ancora; o si toglie da l'istorie. Ma molto meglio è, a mio giudicio, che da l'istoria si prenda; perché dovendo l'epico cercare in ogni parte il verisimile (presupongo questo, come principio notis-

simo), non è verisimile ch'una azione illustre.

> . . . Per questo, dovendo il poeta con la sembianza della
> verità ingannare i lettori, e non solo persuader loro
> che le cose da lui trattate sian vere, ma sottoporle in
> guisa a i lor sensi, che credano non di leggerle, ma di
> esser presenti, e di vederle, e di udirle, è necessitato
> di guadagnarsi nell'animo loro questa opinion di
> verità; il che facilmente con l'autorità dell'istoria gli
> verrà fatto: parlo di quei poeti che imitano le azioni
> illustri, quali sono e 'l tragico e l'epico; però che al
> comico, che d'azioni ignobili e popolaresche è imita-
> tore, lecito è sempre che si finga a sua voglia l'ar-
> gomento.[gg39]

A closer look at Astolfo's journey to the Moon, however, suggests that Ariosto anticipated even this criticism. St. John's revelations there of the "errors" of Virgil and Homer cast doubt upon the very concept of "verisimilitude" and this episode may provide us with the most telling insight into Ariosto's relation to all such literary authorities, both as models from which deviation means failure and as in some sense the "vera istoria" or "true" account.

The episode of the journey is the poem's most sustained parody of Dante, and this in itself raises the question of the priority of a single great literary model. Astolfo descends like

---

[gg] "The matter, which can still conveniently be called the 'subject,' is either imagined, and then it seems that the poet has a part not only in the choice but also in the invention of it, or else taken from history. But it is much better, in my judgment, for it to be taken from history, because the epic poet must seek verisimilitude in all parts (I presuppose this to be a well-known principle) and only an illustrious act shows verisimilitude. . . . For this reason, since the poet has to deceive his readers with the appearance of truth, and not only persuade them that the things treated by him are true but also submit these things in such a way to the senses of his readers that they believe that they are not reading but are present, and are seeing and hearing them, it is necessary to gain in their minds this opinion of truth, which, with the authority of history, can easily be done. I am speaking of poets like those who write tragedies or epics, who imitate illustrious acts; because it is always permissible for the comic poet, who imitates ignoble and popular actions, to invent as much of the subject as he wants." (trans. mine)

a sky-god upon the afflicted kingdom of Senapo in Nubia, insists that he is only human, and soon proves it against the Harpies.[40] When he finally succeeds in chasing the Harpies back to Hell and hears from its mouth the sighs of its inmates, the more specifically Dantesque journey begins, from Hell to the Earthly Paradise, and from there to the sphere of the Moon. The journey to Hell, however, provides the opportunity not for a "fatale andare" like Dante's but for yet another story of "Amor." The dialogue which in Dante reveals in a short space the reason for a character's particular place in Hell becomes in Ariosto's hands Lidia's extended story of her cruelty in love, less a confession in the *Commedia*'s sense than a reminder that all true confessions tend towards the genre of romance. Ariosto is as quick to leave this Hell once the joke has been had as Astolfo is to escape its thickening smoke (XXXIV. 44. 8), and the paladin's decision not to follow the Dantesque inferno "fin al centro" is matched by his author's eccentric treatment of yet another literary model. The Ovidian sense of a *reductio* of an authoritative poetic model is furthered when Astolfo, after cleansing himself like the pilgrim at the opening of the *Purgatorio*, manages to reach both the Earthly Paradise and the first sphere of the *Paradiso* within a single canto, only one episode in a long and very different poetic voyage.

The most important moment in the entire journey, for our purposes, however, comes when Astolfo visits the Valley of Lost Things on the moon. This Limbo of Vanities and its echoes of other visions of universal folly[41] are already too familiar subjects of critical attention to bear rehearsing here. What is more crucial to note is the fact that this vision has its literary, and epistemological, counterpart in the other revelations of "san Giovanni." When Astolfo is unsure what to make of the old man who throws names into the turgid Lethean stream, the birds of prey who retrieve some of the more beautiful names only to drop them again, and the sacred swans that bear some of the names safely to the temple of Immortality, St. John explains that the first is "Time," the second "procurers, flatterers, buffoons, libertines, accusers,"

and the third "poets" who rescue the worthy from "oblivion,
more piteous than death" (xxxv. 12-22). St.

John's moral
seems to be that all modern princes should follow the example of Augustus to ensure poetic immortality, but he soon
undercuts his own purpose by revealing the distortions of
public poets, including Virgil:

> Non sì pietoso Enea, né forte Achille
> fu, come è fama, né sì fiero Ettorre;
>
> . . . .
>
> ma i donati palazzi e le gran ville
> dai descendenti lor, gli ha fatto porre
> in questi senza fin sublimi onori
> da l'onorate man degli scrittori.[hh]
>
> (xxxv. 25. 1-2, 5-8)

> Non fu sì santo né benigno Augusto
> come la tuba di Virgilio suona.[ii]
>
> (26. 1-2)

> Da l'altra parte odi che fama lascia
> Elissa, ch'ebbe il cor tanto pudico;
> che riputata viene una bagascia,
> solo perché Maron non le fu amico.[jj]
>
> (28. 1-4)

and at last unwittingly implicates himself in the history of poetic untruth with his reference to the "reward" given him by
his "lodato Cristo" (29. 3).

The play in this passage depends upon the commonplace of
poets as licensed liars, but this in itself is a kind of revelation,
spoken, appropriately enough, by "the author of the mysteri-

[hh] "Aeneas was not so pious nor Achilles so strong nor Hector so valiant as
rumor makes them . . . but the palaces and the great villas given by their
descendants have caused the honored hands of the writers to bring them to
these high and endless honors."

[ii] "Augustus was not so holy or so merciful as the trumpet of Virgil
sounds."

[jj] "On the other side, hear what reputation Elissa leaves behind her, whose
heart was so chaste, who is reputed a strumpet merely because Maro was not
friendly to her."

ous Apocalypse" (xxxiv. 86. 2). Many commentators have
observed that this disclosure of an Augustus different from
the one perpetuated by Virgil reflects in turn upon Ariosto's
own praise of his patrons. But this is obvious enough and
hardly worth repeating if meant only as yet another proof of
this poet's ironic "sorriso." St. John's revelation of poetic
error goes much deeper than a joke at the Estes' expense.
What it suggests is that romance may be not an aberration in
literature but rather a revelation of its very nature, of the fact
that all fictions "stray." His indication that literary characters
have a life of their own may remind us of the complaint of
Helen of Troy in *Faust* ii: the "Immortality" conferred by the
authorial version is so powerful that no one thinks to question
its truth.[42] The "revelation" turns on its head the assumption
of the higher authority or greater "truth" of epic, since fame
here is claimed to be assured not by the priority of history but
by the perpetuation, and social authorization, of poetic fictions. But if the revelation of the fictiveness of epic tends to
blur strict generic lines it also sends us back to the *Aeneid* to
see how frequent are its "vanus" and "inanis" and to wonder
again about the end of Book vi and the hero's return through
the ivory gate of deceptive dreams. One of the "lost things"
on the moon may well be a truth about all poetry.

St. John's disclosures implicate all literary counterparts of
the authorized version; but not even this episode is the
Furioso's final word. "San Giovanni" brings his revelation to
an end, his eyes glowing like "two fires" (xxxv. 30. 6). But
the author himself is anxious to return to his other characters
and explains that he cannot sustain so high a poetic flight (31.
1-4). Lucian begins one of his tales with the revelation that all
poets lie and then hastens to recount his "True History."
Ariosto swears faithfulness to Turpin and his "vera istoria,"
admits the reader to St. John's disclosures, and then gets on
with his poem. Astolfo's journey to the Moon becomes in
retrospect only one episode among many, as Renaissance illustrations of this canto so masterfully suggest.[43]

The fact that the poem does continue past St. John's disclosures may mean that Ariosto, like Lucian, is educating us in

what not to expect from fictions. Certainly the reader who returns to the *Furioso* after this episode must now be knowingly participating in its "error." The way in which the poem does continue suggests, as we have already noted, that Ariosto is leaving behind the divagations of romance for the stricter rhythm of a more epic dignity. But even epic's strong "sense of an ending"[44] has been made, by St. John's revelations, irreparably contingent, a form no less fictive than its digressive inferior. The correction of the wayward will may be a greater act of will, but both remain within the realm of error, and their narrative counterparts in romance and epic are still just different kinds, or "genres," of fiction.

The punning play upon "error" is so constant throughout the *Furioso* that it may at first obscure other signs that its author is aware of the more serious implications of the choice of the romance form. Dante begins his *Commedia* in the "selva oscura" usually associated with the locus of romance, but he soon leaves it, and the poem becomes at least partly a critique of romance and its mystifications. Ariosto echoes Dante's "alta fantasia" in order to indicate that his genius is of a different kind,[45] and there is no more certain a sign that he is consciously adopting the "errori de' Romanzi" than his echoes of the *Commedia* at precisely those points where this "error" is most in evidence. In canto VII, the revelation of the enchantress Alcina's true ugliness is described with unmistakable echoes of the stripping of the Siren in *Purgatorio* XIX, but with one important difference. The crucial revelation of Dante's canto is of enchantment as a process of self-mystification: the old hag of the pilgrim's dream turns into a bewitching siren only after he has gazed in wonder upon her. Ariosto returns this tripartite structure to the simpler romance progression of enchantment and disillusion, where the initial step, though suggested by the Dantesque echoes, is remystified,[46] and this return is matched by another. Dante's Dream of the Siren occurs on the terrace of Sloth, the midpoint of Purgatory as it is of the pilgrim's Exodus. The *Purgatorio* is the poem's middle *cantica*, typologically the wilderness of wandering between two fixed abodes, just as it is a mediate and temporal realm destined to disappear when the promised end arrives. The revelation and destruction of the potential impasse of the Siren provides one of the poem's many contrasts between the pilgrim's "fatale andare" and the "wanderings" of Ulysses, which end, in Dante's poem, in shipwreck. Ariosto's description of his own return to port despite the dangers on the way may be another deliberate deviation, a correction of Dante's version of the end of Ulysses' Odyssey by a pointed return to the Odyssean, or romance, original.[47]

This sense of a deliberate play with Dantesque authority is strengthened by the many echoes, in the *Furioso*, of canto v of the *Inferno*, whose procession of "donne antiche e' cavalieri" may well be one of the echoes intended in the opening line of Ariosto's poem. Francesca presents her own error as the result of the power of "Amor," as irresistible as the magic potions of the romances she reads. But if Romantic readers of Dante's poem saw in her the tragic heroine of a *Liebestod*, the careful diction of the canto reveals that she is as much in control of herself as Chaucer's Criseyde, who after the most elaborate staging of her first glimpse of Troilus, still asks "Who gave me drink?" The pilgrim's acceptance of Francesca's version and his involvement with the lovers' plight—"caddi come corpo morto cade"[kk] (*Inf.* v. 142)—is echoed by Ariosto in his description of Atlante's magic shield and its Medusa-like effect—"cada come corpo morto cade"[ll] (II. 55. 7)—with the implication that Ariosto's reading of the *Inferno*'s canto of romance was as lucid as its author's.

To emphasize the highly conscious way in which Ariosto embraces the "errors" of romance in the face of an authority both Virgilian and Dantesque and then extends this revelation to include other, more respectable, forms of literature, may sound like yet another version of the stereotype of this author as the poet of "l'art pour l'art," but it has a more serious intent. Critics following the influential judgments of Hegel and De Sanctis have spoken of the strikingly literary and errant nature of the *Furioso* as if it emptied the poem of any serious

[kk] "I fell as a dead body falls" (trans. mine)
[ll] "falls as a dead body falls"

concern. This view so clearly does not account for all that we feel in reading Ariosto that it has, more recently, been taken to task.[48] Its sense of the self-consciously fictive mode of the *Furioso*, however, may be the kind of half-truth that needs to be pushed a little further. It may not be without certain insight that Ariosto has been labeled the poet of "art for art's sake," for it is precisely this later, nineteenth-century phenomenon which has been the source of much of the modern rediscovery of the nature of fiction. Ariosto's exposure of fictive "error" is at once playful and dark, an undercutting of authority which is also a sense of the ineluctable contingency of all human constructs.

As St. John—author of both the Gospel of the Word and the Book of Revelation—leads Astolfo up from the sublunary world to the first stage of a Dantesque "Paradiso," the reader might well expect initiation into a higher sphere of meaning, beyond the "selva oscura" of the romance terrain. But the journey frustrates these expectations by not proceeding any higher than a moon which turns out to be a kind of lunar junkyard, and by its refusal to acknowledge the typology of an anterior set of signs.[49] The Saint ends his revelations by reminding us that he too was a writer with a patron, and the episode which implicates all texts, even the most privileged and authoritative ones, in its refusal to defer to the truth of history or of revelation, ends by threatening to reduce even the Gospel to the status of a literary fiction.

It is this extension of his disclosures beyond the purely secular which suggests how subversive Ariosto's exposure of "error" finally is. Readers who juxtapose the poems of Dante and Ariosto may argue that, in their insistence on the fictive nature of their works, these two seemingly opposite authors are strikingly similar. Dante employs the quintessentially literary device of the acrostic and, like Ariosto, refers to the pages or "carte" of his own text. The *Commedia*'s Heaven of the Moon is, as in the *Furioso*, the place where the nature of poetic mediation is revealed. But to conclude from this that their revelations are ultimately the same would be to obscure the crucial difference in their relation to the problem of authority. Dante, in the *Commedia*, adopts the Augustinian analogy of temporality and syntax in which the central "punto" to which the whole poem tends is at once the end of the quest and the period, or point, of the narrative statement.[50] Ariosto, in terms of this metaphor, repeatedly deviates from a center which seems no longer to hold, and by a technique of delay and deferral suggests that his poem may not have the same "end." The difference is more than a divergence of narrative model. Dante's literary self-reflexiveness is a defense against idolatry, a sign of the purely mediate nature of a poem which constantly points to its own contingency. But the point of reference is still to an anterior and privileged text, and the poem's universe remains, as Kenneth Burke would say, Logological.[51] Ariosto's self-reflexiveness would seem to be, if anything, this process turned inside out, a revelation about his own poem which may suggest a more far-reaching skepticism. The Earthly Paradise where Dante could describe his vision of the Four Living Creatures by sending the reader to Ezekiel or John (*Purg.* xxix. 100-105) is balanced in the *Furioso* by the little allegory of Time and the Poets, a vision glossed finally only in terms provided within the self-enclosed universe of the poem itself.

To approach the *Furioso* from this direction is not to suggest that this is the only way, or even the best way, to see this long and complex poem whole. Much has been left out or slighted and can only be restored, as Ariosto himself might say, by a recourse to other versions. This particular perspective does, however, suggest the historical significance of the Ferrarese poet, and perhaps indicate in passing that Ariosto's poem may illuminate modern theories of narrative and fictionality as much as it is illuminated by them. Much has been written recently on the narrative "sentence" and its metaphysical implications.[52] But Ariosto's poem already deviates from and calls into question that model—both Augustinian and Dantesque—and the "end" or "center" of revelation it presupposes. A definitive endpoint, which would also imply a temporal progression towards presence, *parousia*, or meaning, is studiously circumvented by the detours and divagations of an "errant" plot, and when the poem does finally take on an epic single-mindedness—with all the appropriate echoes of Homer and of Virgil—it is only *after* the lunar revelations of the mendacity of these models. The exercise of closure, under the sign of a guiding Providence, remains a purely literary *tour de force*, a demonstration that the author of this "varia tela" knows as well as the Weaver Fates (xxxiv. 89) how to bring his carefully woven "text" to an end.

The *Furioso* is a critique of romance as rigorous as Dante's, but it lacks the *Commedia*'s metaphysical ground. Astolfo's journey takes us out of the sublunary flux of endless variety and digression in a way which led commentators to gloss it as an allegory of the *via contemplativa*. But there proves to be no privileged point beyond the terrestrial, no final Revelation for characters still confined within "questa assai più oscura che serena / vita mortal, tutta d'invidia piena"[mm] (IV. 1. 7-8). The poet's "lucido intervallo" is partly a lucidity about the nature of poetic fictions, but it is only partly that. The *Furioso* provides an exposure of romance "error," but the skepticism is finally not just aesthetic but epistemological, and it is this that its Renaissance critics could neither condone nor, perhaps, recover from.

[mm] "this much-more-dark-than-light mortal life, full of envy"

II. Spenser

The waies, through which my weary steps I guyde,
In this delightfull land of Faery,
Are so exceeding spacious and wyde,
And sprinckled with such sweet variety,
Of all that pleasant is to eare or eye,
That I nigh rauisht with rare thoughts delight,
My tedious trauell doe forget thereby;
And when I gin to feele decay of might,
It strength to me supplies, and chears my dulled spright.

The Faerie Queene VI

The Dilation of Being

SPENSER's adoption of the *materia* of romance is clear from the
moment he announces, in the Ariostan echoes of the Proem,
his intention to "sing of Knights and Ladies gentle deeds."[1]
Our focus will therefore be not on the substance of this material and its Spenserian transformations, but rather on a clue to
the more subtle delights and dangers of the form he adopts—
its characteristic "dilation"—and its relation to the problem of
narrative structure and the differing strategies of the poem's
several "Legends." At the climax of the *Cantos of Mutabilitie*,
the creatures assembled upon Arlo Hill await the judgment of
Nature upon the power and extent of Mutabilitie, a judgment
which after "long suspense" is given by Nature "in speeches
few":

> I well consider all that ye haue sayd,
> And find that all things stedfastnes doe hate
> And changed be: yet being rightly wayd
> They are not changed from their first estate;
> But by their change their being doe dilate:

And turning to themselues at length againe,
Doe worke their owne perfection so by fate:
Then ouer them Change doth not rule and raigne;
But they raigne ouer change, and doe their states
    maintaine.

(VII. vii. 58)

The upstart Goddess Mutabilitie is by this judgment literally
"put downe," subordinated within the structure she had chal-
lenged by her ascent, as Nature's "doome," though admitting
the extent of Change, converts it to a contributor to order and
"perfection." The stanza is the climax of the *Cantos*, but it is
also a summation of Spenser's works, from the cycle of
months in the *Shepheardes Calender* to the Garden of Adonis in
The Faerie Queene, where Adonis is less the sun god wounded
by the boar of winter than he is the cycle itself, "eterne in
mutabilitie."[2] Mutabilitie is contained within a framework of
recurrence, and the final limit to her power will be another
kind of "doom." Nature's last word is of apocalypse, that
most definitive of endings:

Cease therefore daughter further to aspire,
And thee content thus to be rul'd by me:
For thy decay thou seekst by thy desire;
But time shall come that all shall changed bee,
And from thenceforth, none no more change shall see.

(59. 1-5)

Nature's judgment is succinct and, it would appear, definitive. But it is not the poem's last word. If the "perfection" to
which all things tend is matched by the certainty of a final
rest, the two stanzas which Spenser's editor labeled "The VIII.
Canto, vnperfite" offer a somewhat different perspective on
the certainty of this ending, and on the power of Mutabilitie:

When I bethinke me on that speech whyleare,
Of *Mutability*, and well it way:
Me seemes, that though she all vnworthy were
Of the Heav'ns Rule; yet very sooth to say,

In all things else she beares the greatest sway.
Which makes me loath this state of life so tickle,
And loue of things so vaine to cast away;
Whose flowring pride, so fading and so fickle,
Short *Time* shall soon cut down with his consuming sickle.

Then gin I thinke on that which Nature sayd,
Of that same time when no more *Change* shall be,
But stedfast rest of all things firmely stayd
Vpon the pillours of Eternity,
That is contrayr to *Mutabilitie*:
For, all that moueth, doth in *Change* delight:
But thence-forth all shall rest eternally
With Him that is the God of Sabbaoth hight:
O that great Sabbaoth God, graunt me that Sabaoths sight.

Unlike the vision of Chaucer's Troilus or Dante's pilgrim, or that of Urania in Spenser's own *Teares of the Muses*, the vision with which *The Faerie Queene* concludes is from the perspective of this world. If the end of history and of mutability is both envisaged and earnestly prayed for, it is remarkable chiefly for its distance. "The mongrel Titaness," as Thomas M. Greene observes, "is the true victress of the poem, and the time of her fall is not yet."[3]

The end of Spenser's poem remains characteristically open-ended. Criticism has divided on the question of how definitive Nature's judgment really is, and the problem is only complicated by the more strictly textual question of whether the *Cantos* themselves constitute an ending to *The Faerie Queene*, despite the larger projected form of the letter to Raleigh. The difference in critical opinion has to do with the question of what is subordinated, a problem which is never easy to resolve in Spenser's poem, even at the level of syntax. The subordination of Mutabilitie by Nature has its counterpart, in Book I, in the defeat of Duessa by Una, but the sequence of the motto to that Book's final canto is suggestively ambiguous:

Faire Vna to the Redcrosse knight
betrouthed is with ioy:

> Though false Duessa it to barre
> her false sleights doe imploy.

The secondary and subordinate position of the clause in which Duessa appears suggests that the victory is Una's; but the betrothal of Una and Red Cross is not the final consummation of marriage, and Duessa, though thwarted and unmasked in Book I, returns to wreak havoc long after Una has disappeared.

The terms of the debate on the ending of the *Cantos* are well known, and need no rehearsing here.[4] There is, however, one aspect of Nature's judgment which has not been fully explored, though it provides a fruitful entrance into the form of Spenser's romance. Nature's "doome" is a statement not simply about the end of change, but about the middle term between beginning and end, the "dilation" of being: "They are not changed from their first estate; / But by their change their being doe dilate." "Dilate" is appropriate within the context of the stanza, a simple description of the process by which being comes full circle. It also carries, however, a resonance which, though lost on modern ears, would have suggested a rich variety of meaning to the learned Renaissance reader. *Dilatio* is the Neo-Platonic term for the "Emanation" of being, its procession out from, and its return to, the Source or the One.[5] The idea, familiar to the Renaissance through the commentaries of Ficino, has one of its most complete statements in the *Consolation* of Boethius, which Spenser almost certainly would have known in Chaucer's translation:

> Alle thynges seken ayen to hir propre cours, and alle thynges rejoysen hem of hir retornynge ayen to hir nature. Ne noon ordenaunce is bytaken to thynges, but that that hath joyned the endynge to the bygynnynge, and hath maked the cours of itself stable (*that it chaunge nat from his propre kynde*).[6]

The conventional Neo-Platonic doctrine is a fitting ending for a poem whose centerpiece is the "first seminarie" of the Garden of Adonis. But "dilation" has a Christian resonance as well, and only the two together begin to suggest the complexity of Spenser's image for the variety and mutability of Creation before its final end. Spatial "dilation" is linked, etymologically, with temporal "deferral" through a complex association with the Latin roots *differre / dilatare*, a connection which survives in the English word "dilatory." *Dilatio* is the term used by Patristic writers as the etymology of Rahab, a figure for the Church, "opening" to gather in its fullness before the final end, or *parousia*.[7] The time between First and Second Coming is itself a respite or "dilation," an interval in which the eschatological Judgment is held over or deferred, a period of uncertain duration when the "end" already accomplished in the Advent is, paradoxically, not yet come, when, though the Promised Land has been conquered, the spiritual Israel still wanders in the wilderness. The deferral of the promised end is, in the phrase of Alanus de Insulis, the "dilatio patriae,"[8] the delay of the coming of the "Sabbath" which is the extended interval of time itself. As the threshold before the final separation of good and evil, this period is also a problematic middle, just as Rahab herself is both harlot and *figura* of the Church before the final, apocalyptic, destruction of Jericho, the city which Spenser's older contemporary, John Jewel, glossed as the city of "Error."[9] The woman who is both Church and whore may seem a characteristically and exclusively Blakean Emanation, but the tension in this figure is already implicit in the close of one of Donne's *Holy Sonnets*:

> Show me deare Christ, thy spouse, so bright and cleare.
> What, is it she, which on the other shore
> Goes richly painted? or which rob'd and tore
> Laments and mournes in Germany and here?
> Sleepes she a thousand, then peepes up one yeare?
> Is she selfe truth and errs? now new, now'outwore?
> Doth she,' and did she, and shall she evermore
> On one, or seaven, or on no hill appeare?
> Dwells she with us, or like adventuring knights
> First travaile we to seeke and then make love?
> Betray kind husband thy spouse to our sights,
> And let myne amorous soule court thy mild Dove,
> Who is most trew, and pleasing to thee, then
> When she'is embrac'd and open to most men.[10]

To raise the connotations of "dilation" in its spatial and temporal, Christian and Neo-Platonic forms, may seem to take us far beyond the *Mutabilitie Cantos*, where the word is used almost unobtrusively. Once noticed, however, this term and the etymological complex which includes not only "deferral" and "dilation" but "difference" provide a revealing perspective on the structure of Spenser's romance.[11] The Neo-Platonic concept of Emanation—the "dilation" of being and its return to perfection—has its Spenserian counterpart in the procession of knights out from and back to the court of Gloriana, which remains, throughout, offstage. The Christian "respite" in the wilderness before the Sabbath rest becomes, in the purgatorial space of "faerie," the interval of "wandering" between vision and fulfillment, between the initiation of the quest and its end, in both senses. The tension implicit in the figure whose "dilation" is that of both Church and harlot is reflected in a poem in which the crucial problem is to separate the poet's craft from that of Archimago and the "dilation" which is the extension of the poem from the "dilation" of the Bower of Bliss:

> Much wondred *Guyon* at the faire aspect
> Of that sweet place, yet suffred no delight
> To sincke into his sence, nor mind affect,
> But passed forth, and lookt still forward right,
> Bridling his will, and maistering his might:
> Till that he came vnto another gate;
> No gate, but like one, being goodly dight
> With boughes and braunches, which did broad dilate
> Their clasping armes, in wanton wreathings intricate.
>
> (II. xii. 53)

This Wood of Mystery, its animated trees dilating "broad . . . / Their clasping armes," looks back to the spreading branches of the Wandering Wood in Book I and forward to Acrasia herself, the romance harlot whose embrace holds knights in thrall. The "Porch" it adorns is that of Dame Excess, a suggestion perhaps of one of the dangers of romance itself and its "vision of plenitude," and the proper response of the temperate knight is that of the Resolved Soul amid the abundance of

Created Pleasure. Guyon, guided by the Palmer, walks straight forward to his mission's end, in spite of the temptation to his "wandring eyes" (II. xii. 69. 2).

"Dilation" here is an invitation to Guyon to stay his forward movement, to delay forever the end of his pursuit. But "dilate" is also used in another sense in *The Faerie Queene*, for the activity of telling or narrating:

> Ne rested they, till that to Faery lond
> They came, as *Merlin* them directed late:
> Where meeting with this *Redcrosse* knight, she fond
> Of diuerse things discourses to dilate . . .
>
> (III. iii. 62. 1-4)

> With that he gan at large to her dilate
> The whole discourse of his captiuance sad . . .
>
> (V. vi. 17. 1-2)

> Tho gan that shepheard thus for to dilate . . .
>
> (VI. x. 21. 1)

The last of these is the introduction to Colin Clout's story of the "pleasaunce" of Venus and the Graces on Mt. Acidale, and the association of "dilation" with the poet's own "signature" here may extend the analogy of *dilatio* to the process of narrative expansion as well. The journey to Acrasia's Bower is filled with echoes of the act of Creation as described in Genesis, a kind of *Hexameron*, though in chaotic sequence. Guyon's "forward" movement in this canto turns Odysseus' wanderings into a pilgrim's progress; but early critics who found Spenser himself more "dilatory" than Bunyan[12] have in this episode, at least, a fertile example. The narrative is literally dilated: the canto is the longest in *The Faerie Queene* and the journey, which in the case of Atin (II. v. 25-28) seemed to take almost no time at all, here fills thirty-eight stanzas.

The celebrated Renaissance analogy between the Creation of God and the creation of the poet is that of Tasso in the *Discorsi del poema eroico*.[13] The analogy, however, also occurs in Boethius in suggestive proximity to the concept of the dilation of being:

For ryght as a werkman that aperceyveth in his
thought the forme of the thing that he wol make,
and moeveth the effect of the work, and ledith that
he hadde lookid byforn in his thought symplely and
presently, by temporel ordenaunce; certes, ryght so
God disponith in his purveaunce singulerly and sta-
blely the thinges that ben to doone; but he amynis-
treth in many maneris and in diverse tymes by de-
styne thilke same thinges that he hath disponyd.[14]

Boethius also suggests the possibility of a dilation which may
expand too far from its "beginning," or "rule," the cosmic
equivalent of a wandering which has no certain end.[15] The
controlled "error" which is the project of *The Faerie Queene* is
flanked by two problems, wandering lost with no hope of arrival and a concern for the end which diminishes the delights
to be found along the way, the narrative equivalent of
Guyon's straightforward progress through the Bower of
Bliss. The problem is in Spenser, as in Ariosto, that of giving
shape to a form as potentially endless as that of romance,
without reducing it. Tasso's *Gerusalemme liberata*, the other
inheritor of the *Furioso* pledged to "overgoe" it, begins with a
pointed reference to the "erring" of Ariosto's poem, the *cause
célèbre* of so much criticism in the period between the two:

> e in van l'Inferno vi s'oppose, e in vano
> s'armò d'Asia e di Libia il popol misto.
> Il Ciel gli diè favore, e sotto a i santi
> segni ridusse i suoi compagni erranti.[a]

"Ridusse" is the promise of a direction to be given to the
"compagni erranti" and by implication to the errant nature of
the romance form, but it also raises another question, the extent to which Tasso's poem, in relation to Ariosto's, is "reduced."[16]

Thomas Rymer accused Ariosto of leading Spenser astray,

---

[a] "In vain 'gainst him did hell oppose her might, / In vain the Turks and
Morians armed be; / His soldiers wild, to brawls and mutines prest, / Reduced
he to peace; so heaven him blest."

from the nobler path of epic into the deviant ways of the
romanzo.[17] A look at *The Faerie Queene*, however, suggests
that Spenser was quite consciously engaging the delights as
well as the dangers of this form. Delay and deferral as moral
categories are in Spenser's poem almost uniformly bad, a version of the dangerous and enervating sin of sloth. Red Cross's
dalliance with Duessa in Book I is a type of *accidia*, the sin
which, for Aquinas, was the dangerous double of the Sabbath
"rest."[18] The "cooling shade" under which he lies for refuge
"against the boyling heat" (vii. 4. 3) of the noonday sun is the
locus of the *demonium meridianum*,[19] the midday demon of
stasis, and the tale of the nymph who stopped "in middest of
the race" (5. 4) and was turned by Diana into a fountain "dull
and slow" (5. 8) looks forward to the Idle Lake of Book II and
the invitation of Phaedria to take no thought for the end of the
quest. Artegall's time wasted as a slave of Radigund in Book
v is a deferral of his mission as dangerous as its classical
analogue, the sojourn of Aeneas in Carthage.

Deferral as temporizing is directly opposed to the "truth"
which never swerves from its end or "troth," an identification which makes the whole of *The Faerie Queene* into a
Legend of Constancy, a "stedfastnesse" at the opposite extreme to the time-serving of Sir Burbon in the Legend of
Justice:

> when time doth serue,
> My former shield I may resume againe:
> To temporize is not from truth to swerue,
> Ne for aduantage terme to entertaine,
> When as necessitie doth it constraine.
> Fie on such forgerie (said *Artegall*)
> Vnder one hood to shadow faces twaine.
> Knights ought be true, and truth is one in all:
> Of all things to dissemble fouly may befall.
>
> (v. xi. 56)

Yet Spenser himself, at the end of the poem's last complete
Book, defends his own version of temporizing, the round-
about way which diverts the knight from the single purpose
of his "first quest":

Like as a ship, that through the Ocean wyde
  Directs her course vnto one certaine cost,
  Is met of many a counter winde and tyde,
  With which her winged speed is let and crost,
  And she her selfe in stormie surges tost;
  Yet making many a borde, and many a bay,
  Still winneth way, ne hath her compasse lost:
  Right so it fares with me in this long way,
Whose course is often stayd, yet neuer is astray.

For all that hetherto hath long delayd
  This gentle knight, from sewing his first quest,
  Though out of course, yet hath not bene missayd,
  To shew the courtesie by him profest,
  Euen vnto the lowest and the least.
  But now I come into my course againe,
  To his atchieuement of the *Blatant beast*;
  Who all this while at will did range and raine,
Whilst none was him to stop, nor none him to restraine.

(VI. xii. 1-2)

The very delay which in Book v took Artegall from his quest
is in this Book a property of the narrative, and Calidore's "delay" (VI. x. 1) among the shepherds, linked as well to Aeneas'
lingering with Dido, is here virtually indistinguishable from
the author's own kind of "straying."

Spenser's more digressive method here is a form of the medieval and Renaissance concept of *dilatatio*, another of the de-
rivatives of *dilatare* applied to a specifically narrative style. As
the opposite of the ideal of *brevitas*, this stylistic *amplificatio* or
dilation was long recognized, and defended, as the characteristic feature of romance, a way in which it was not aberrant
but simply different.[20] In Spenser's romance, however, it
takes on a particular resonance, as part of the tension between
the forward movement towards an ending and the delightful,
and seductive, dilation which is also the poem itself. To engage this problem is to participate in a tension implicit for any
Christian poet in the act of writing, an *imitatio* of the divine
act which may become a fascination in itself. It is part of
the technique of "symbolic parody" that the dilation of

Spenser's poem in this sense should engage its own darker double, just as Arthur—or "Magnificence"—enters the poem for the first time as the enemy of the simply magnified, or dilated, Orgoglio.[21]

Spenser frequently plays upon the link between such dilation and the variety and inconstancy of his own creation. The proliferation of the word of man, the process by which Chaucer's "spirit" passes, "through infusion sweete" (IV. ii. 34. 6), into Spenser's, is included in the same canto as the story of Priamond, Diamond, and Triamond, the brothers whose life is extended by a process of "traduction" (iii. 13. 6), and Spenser, commenting on the folly of prolonging life in this way, echoes the earlier arguments of Despair (IV. iii. 1; I. ix. 43). Nature's "doome in speeches few" (VII. vii. 57. 9) is in significant contrast to Mutabilitie's elaborate and lengthy testimony. And the tension persists in the verse itself, between the sense of "staying" or dilation Warton blamed on the repetition of so few rhymes, the tendency to *pleonasmus* or the "fault of too ful speech,"[22] and the straightforward, linear, syntactic movement towards the final period.

Nature in the *Mutabilitie Cantos* uses "dilate" from the perspective of the end, the perfection of being come full circle. But the circle of Spenser's poem is not finally closed and we remain within the period of *dilatio* as exile, or process. Continual deferral or postponement is part of the sorrow of wandering, the prospect of a Sabbath which remains very distant indeed. But it is also part of the "delightfull land of Faery" (VI. Pro. 1. 2), its potentially endless variety, and it is this tension, in its various implications, that the different Legends of Spenser's romance invite us to explore.

The Defeat of Error and the Reveiling of Truth

THE deferral, or undermining, of a seeming ending is prepared for from the very first canto of the poem—as Una and Red Cross enter into the shelter of the Wandering Wood and defeat the Monster "Errour." The Wood presents immediately the archetypal locus of romance, the *selva oscura* "Whose loftie trees yclad with sommers pride, / Did spred so broad, that heauens light did hide" (I. i. 7. 4-5). Perception of this fact, however, is delayed and the reader, like Una and Red Cross, moves first in a landscape of only potential significances and disjunctive signs,[23] where "shroud," "shade," and "pride" (i. 6-7) are polysemous attributes, and the problem, from the beginning, is learning how to read:

> Enforst to seeke some couert nigh at hand,.
> A shadie groue not far away they spide,
> That promist ayde the tempest to withstand:
> Whose loftie trees yclad with sommers pride,
> Did spred so broad, that heauens light did hide,
> Not perceable with power of any starre:
> And all within were pathes and alleies wide,
> With footing worne, and leading inward farre:
> Faire harbour that them seemes; so in they entred arre.
>
> (I. i. 7)

Each tree in this "faire harbour" has a context or qualifier which expands its range of meaning, and the forest is a plenitude whose description both reflects and invites a human reading. The list of trees conscripted to human use ("The sayling Pine," "The vine-prop Elme," "The builder Oake," the "Aspine good for staues") reaches its final cadence in the "Cypresse funerall" (8. 9), which both continues the catalogue of human industry and marks its "fall." The stanza which begins with the outward sign of an already accomplished glory—the "Laurell, meed of mightie Conquerours / And Poets sage" (9. 1-2)—ends in a disquieting intimation of a weakness within, of something yet to be found out ("the Maple seldom inward sound").

The straying of Red Cross and Una in this plenitude (10. 3-9) frequently prompts a purely moral interpretation, the kind of approach that begins by asking "What did Red Cross do wrong?" Yet what seems more crucial here is the romance experience of not knowing where lines are until they have been violated or crossed. Except for the random hint to the wary reader, the famous catalogue of trees does not suggest anything but the "delight" with which "they thus beguile the way" (10. 1), until its meaning is perceived too late and something seemingly innocent suddenly entraps. Augustine speaks in *The Confessions* of the way in which wandering at will (*deviasse sponte*) may suddenly be frozen into "error" as punishment (*poena errare*),[24] and the straying of Una and Red Cross into a place where "They cannot finde that path, which first was showne" (10. 4) introduces early into Spenser's poem the danger of potential trespass, of a wandering past a point of no return. It is true that the significance of the crossing can be "read" only from beyond this point, retrospectively: the word "read" is used as "advise" when Una finally identifies this forest as "the wandring wood" (13. 6–8). But "reading" in this canto is also a process in which a certain *kind* of recognition may simultaneously circumscribe. To ask what Red Cross *did* wrong would imply that the answer might be supplied by a specific act, something which would make the episode wholly explicable in moral terms. Yet the canto in which a seemingly innocent and ineluctable wandering leads to such serious consequences reveals the question itself to be limited, or capable at this point of only partial answers, even as it provokes the reader to ask it. Yeats thought that the moralizing in Spenser got in the way of the romance.[25] But it may be instead that the poem's very opening canto already anticipates the possibility of mere moralizing, that it demonstrates the process whereby meaning may be limited by the very act which seeks to define it. Red Cross and Una move from a spontaneous "wandering" to "error" in its fixed, or moral, sense as "wrong": the process of the reduction of meaning is dramatized as a movement within the possible meanings of "errare" itself.

There is yet another way in which this episode and its aftermath provide an entrance into *The Faerie Queene* and become part of its reflection on itself. The Monster "Errour" is described as dwelling amid "desert darknesse" (16. 8), and Red Cross's armor makes, in her "darksome hole" (14. 3), only "A litle glooming light" (14. 5). But there is a sense in which she is already brought to light, simply by virtue of being named. The long involved sentences and serpentine syntax which take the reader into the heart of the episode also lead to a kind of freezing, a process which Blake called clarifying the Body of Error, reducing it by making it appear. Spenser's Errour is at once embodied and curiously reduced, and the episode's almost comic-strip character results at least partly from its well-defined outlines and clear sequential frames.

This serpentine progress inward and fixing with a name or identity provides, in little, an introduction to an important aspect of Spenser's mode, and exploration, of allegory. In the allegorical figure of "Errour," meaning is both concentrated and confined: the potential significances raised by the ambiguities of the opening stanzas are focused in a figure whose description is a kind of compendium iconography, a distillation of several monsters into one. Spenser's pictorial qualities were observed from the earliest criticism of the poem, the most frequent comparison being with the allegorical pictures of Rubens.[26] Spenser himself, however, already provides an indication of the way in which the clarity of both picture and allegorical "meaning" is also a kind of immobility:

> Much daunted with that dint, her sence was dazd,
> Yet kindling rage, her selfe she gathered round,
> And all attonce her beastly body raizd
> With doubled forces high aboue the ground:
> Tho wrapping vp her wrethed sterne arownd,
> Lept fierce vpon his shield, and her huge traine
> All suddenly about his body wound,
> That hand or foot to stirre he stroue in vaine:
> God helpe the man so wrapt in *Errours* endlesse traine.
>
> (18)

Alliteration in the opening line conveys the sense of stupefaction, the temporary forestalling, in repetition, of all forward movement; but when the monster regains momentum, the stanza ends in a different kind of stasis, an *exclamatio* ("God helpe the man . . .") which suggests at once an emblem-book illustration and a romance Laocoön. "*Errours* endlesse traine"

comes at the end of a stanza in which the monster is graphically visible, but the phrasing (and the moralizing) also im-
press upon us the sense of an actualized figure of speech, of
the inward personified or made outward. The final alexan-
drine abstracts us momentarily from all narrative movement,
just as Red Cross himself is, for the moment, effectively
fixed. The picture is frozen in its stanza-frame, at the very
point where "Errour" the Monster is made coequal with her
abstract allegorical sense.

Naming is properly *apotropaic*: it allows something to be
placed at a distance, outside the self. But Spenser's language
remains ambiguous about the relation of inside and outside,
in words which, like "errour," refuse to submit to the
dichotomy, retaining instead, in their very history, the joining, or blurring, of subjective and objective. The reduction of
"wandering" to "error" at once simplifies and, at least potentially, short-circuits. Along with the demand to "read" goes
the danger of a false or premature reading; and the subversion
of Errour's defeat as a definitive narrative ending also involves the deferral of fixed or reliable meaning, a reentering
of the space of ambiguous signs. For Red Cross as for the
reader, objectification, as a distancing from the self, may be
both victory and delusion. Externalization, we are told, is related to the phenomenon of daemonization; and the knight
soon moves from this seeming victory to the encounter with
Fradubio, not only a projection or double but a daemonized
tree and an animated text.[27]

In one respect, the beginning of Red Cross's quest would
seem to be identical with its end. His final battle—the end and
purpose of his questing—is to be with the Dragon laying
waste the kingdom of Una's parents. In terms of the archetypes within which the Legend moves, the Monster Errour and the Dragon surrounding Eden are, metaphorically,
one. The episode of Errour contains, *in ovo*, the whole theme
of the emergence of the dragon-killer—a Theseus who
threads a labyrinth and kills a monster, a Perseus who escapes
"stonifying," and an Apollo who begins by killing the
Python.[28] But what metaphor would unite, the narrative

keeps apart. What is crucial in Spenser's narrative is not the identity but the space in between, the interval in which the archetypal clarity of the Body of Errour dissolves into the temporal process of "erring." Archetypal criticism may help us to regain the identities we need in order to recognize the structure of Red Cross's quest—in this respect its tendency is "apocalyptic"—but the poem moves away from this clarity as soon as it is introduced, from concentration of meaning to a more centrifugal process.

The movement away from the victory over Errour is literally this kind of decentering. Red Cross may seem to be moving forward from his "first aduenture" (27. 8), but the next verse specifically tells us that he moves "backward" (28. 2), a direction which, if the only way out of the deadly center of the labyrinth, is also a retrograde step. This movement has its moral implications, as the victor over visible Error falls immediately prey to its invisible counterpart, "Hypocrisie," and "error" is not defeated but multiplied, as the knight, deceived by Archimago, begins his separate wanderings. There is also, however, another way in which the error of the opening episode is multiplied. The Cheshire cat in Alice's Wonderland exits leaving only his smile. Spenser's "Errour" disappears, leaving her trace in the serpentine progress of the poem itself, the *vestigia* the reader must follow in order to thread the labyrinth. Embodied Errour, like Mutabilitie, can be "put downe." But just as the disappearance of the personified Mutabilitie leads to a testimony to the extent of its power in the closing stanzas of the poem, so the Body of Errour, defeated in the opening episode, "dilates" to fill out the remainder of the narrative. One of the Renaissance meanings of "dilate" is "to carry apart or disperse" (*OED*), and there is a kind of *sparagmos* of the Body of Errour through Book 1 and beyond. The trees of the Wandering Wood become the "two goodly trees, that faire did spred / Their armes abroad" (I. ii. 28. 3-4), the metamorphosed Fradubio and Fraelissa of canto ii. The "beaten" path (i. 11. 3) which leads into the labyrinth of Errour prefigures the "broad high way" (iv. 2. 8) which leads to the House of Pride. The dangerous "shade" (i. 7)

which seems to provide a welcome respite is echoed in the
"cooling shade" (vii. 3. 1) where the unarmed Red Cross is
surprised by Orgoglio. The nether regions of the female
monster Errour resemble those of Duessa, the stripped hag
(viii. 46).

To stress the narrative rather than the moral implications of
the defeat of Errour and its aftermath may seem to be a focus
far from the main intent of the Legend of Holinesse. The
motto for the dangerous proliferation of lookalikes through
"Faerie lond"—"Worse is the daunger hidden, then descride"
(II. xii. 35. 5)—is reflected in the education of Red Cross, his
training through experience to recognize the signs of a danger
he failed to perceive in his first victory. But it also provides an
insight into the way Spenser's narrative is effectively "dilated," by repetition and doubling, by the proliferation of the
fragments of one episode into others, so that the reader
becomes a kind of Isis, looking for the relics of this first
emblematic episode scattered like clues through subsequent
cantos. The poem's dilation by episode and digression stands
in marked contrast to the straightforward linear progress of
the pageants and "triumphs" with which it is filled, and the
reader must frequently seek understanding by more indirect
routes. Narrative *entrelacement* is a fertile error, a labyrinth
which generates a multiplicity of meanings: explication proceeds first by implication, or "infolding."[29] The *rationes
seminales* of the Garden of Adonis have their narrative counterpart in the seeds planted in the form of image or idea which
grow almost imperceptibly as the poem continues, "grace" in
the early Books emerging finally as the three Graces of the
Legend of Courtesy. Keats said that the purpose of the long
poem is to allow the reader to wander and forget.[30] Spenser is
perhaps closer to the Miltonic view of the long poem and its
educative function, but it may be that the structure of *The
Faerie Queene*—several times longer than *Paradise Lost*—
allows the reader to wander and remember, to recall what he
has wandered from.

The fertility of Spenser's Errour is of a particularly literary
kind, beyond the narrow allegory of the Roman Church.

Within the frame of the Legend of Holinesse, the redeemed counterpart of Errour's "bookes" (I. i. 20. 6), steeped in ink, is Fidelia's sacred book, "with bloud ywrit, / That none could read, except she did them teach" (x. 19. 1-2). But Spenser's own book is like the monster "Errour" in that it, too, has swallowed a multitude of books and recognizing them is part of the devious process of "reading." Hallam's complaint that the catalogue of trees in canto i is an unnatural assemblage from all soils and climates[31] can only be answered by the observation that the combination is a deliberately literary one. The set-piece of the catalogue is remarkable for its straightforward progress: each line is marshaled by rhythm and syntax into one of the poem's first pageants. But the resonances within it of earlier texts subtly disperse this progress in several directions, and allusion itself becomes a form of exfoliation, a specifically literary metamorphosis. The catalogue of trees in *Metamorphoses* x (90-104) occurs, significantly, in the midst of the story of a poet—Orpheus—and generates, in characteristic Ovidian fashion, the further stories of Cyparissus (Spenser's "Cypresse funerall") and Myrrha ("The Mirrhe sweete bleeding in the bitter wound"). Spenser's catalogue, like Ovid's, works backwards from the legends hidden in trees, to the stories behind the simple names. But the recall of previous texts is also part of this *selva*, as the range of allusion expands to include not just Ovid, but Boccaccio and Chaucer as well.[32] The movement of the catalogue itself is straightforward, but the dilating and regressive movement of its allusions is potentially as distracting to a straightforward reading as the natural "delight" by which Red Cross and Una are beguiled.

Dilation by expansion, or doubling, begins as early as the poem's second canto: the romance begins over again, with a knight and a lady looking for shelter in a wood, but this repetition is now an ironic parody of the first, as the knight who began by escaping an externalized Wandering Wood is now himself "amazed" (ii. 5). Doubling also involves reversal, a through-the-looking-glass exchange of properties: the now brutish Red Cross is replaced by the protector Lion; Una is

left with only her donkey to guide her (iii. 44) while Red
Cross, led on by Duessa, is making an ass of himself. Even
words are transformed, through this looking glass, into their
antithetical meanings, as the knight faithful and true of the
opening stanzas becomes the knight "too simple and too
trew" (ii. 45. 7) following "Fidessa."

The exchange seems almost literally to beget Red Cross's
double, Fradubio (*dubitare*, "to be of two minds"), and the
story of the foul witch who transformed him. Red Cross
himself seems to see in this metamorphosis only the strange-
ness harped upon by the verse (ii. 33. 4; 34. 1), but even an
unrecognized doublet has its assimilating effect, as he too is
rooted to the spot (31. 9). Doubling here seems to be part of a
kind of blindness. The deforming of his own lady by Duessa's
"foggy mist" (38. 5) is not perceived, and is therefore repeated, in the case of Fradubio. And the Red Cross who does
not see the hidden affinity of his own situation with that of the
"Brother" caught "between" becomes yet another victim of
the characteristic romance obscurity, with the suggestion,
perhaps, that if he did perceive his double it would disappear.

Such repetition becomes, as the poem proceeds, increasingly a function of the words themselves. The rhymes have a
kind of agglutinative quality which extends the level of sound
to the level of meaning, as Red Cross and Fradubio, in the
internal and end rhymes of a single stanza—"dwell," "well,"
"spell," "well" (ii. 43)—are inextricably linked both in their
common error and in the clue to its relief. The Protean metamorphosis of the language proceeds through what could only
be called the "floating" quality of Spenser's puns. Syllables
join, splinter and recombine, as the entire movement of Book
I is presented in the rhyming *stichomythia* of a single exchange:

> Despaire breedes not (quoth he) where faith is staid.
> No faith so fast (quoth she) but flesh does paire.
> Flesh may empaire (quoth he) but reason can repaire.
>
> (vii. 41. 7-9)

Red Cross and Una "diuorced in despaire" (iii. 2. 8) have cantos ii to vi divided, or "pa(i)red," between them.[33] "Dis-

mayed" constantly picks up the resonances of fashioning and unfashioning in "dismade" and of the maid unmade, "dismaid" (iv. 49. 1). The "guiltie sight" of Red Cross (ii. 6. 2) hovers between external—what he sees—and internal—his power of vision—and raises the question of the extent to which the false sprites conjured by Archimago from an underworld of dreams are part of his own "subconscious," an identification which would mean that in fleeing from the necromancer's den he is also "flying from his thoughts" (ii. 12. 3). Red Cross, "busying his quicke eyes" upon Fidessa (ii. 26. 6), is not only actively engaged but, ironically, dead, passively yielding to sensation, and it is a passivity which has its effect on the allegory as well, as the reader, like the spectator Red Cross in the House of Pride, becomes, as it were, more passive before the staged pageant of the Seven Deadly Sins. Red Cross's series of apparent victories is, once again, an activity which turns into its opposite, the counterpart, perhaps, of an allegory now no longer "covert" and "dark" but only too obvious.

One of the results of such doubling in Book I is its disappointment of hoped-for endings, in a series of false starts and frustrating false conclusions. Dawn is a revelation repeated every day (iii. 21), but Una, like "that long wandring Greeke" (21. 5) remains long within a darkness which recalls the Wood of Errour ("Then furthest from her hope, when most she weened nie," 21. 9). Her reunion with the knight of the red cross in canto iii raises expectations of a passing from the "shadow" of night to the "light" of day (27. 8-9) and of the coming of the "beaten marinere" (31. 1) to shore, but it proves to be only the parody revelation of a disguised Archimago. The series of frustrations is finally gathered towards an ending in the House of Holinesse, where Red Cross is converted and set upon the completion of his quest, but even this single-mindedness, or sense of "conclusion," is deceiving.

The priority of one Book is being established in the Legend of Holinesse, where wholeness and health are singular virtues, and variety—as in the catalogue of trees—may be ultimately a form of "Error." Book i, however, is only one Legend among many and it is precisely the echoes of other books—or within Spenser's poem, of other Legends—which help to qualify this singularity. Sir Walter Scott's complaint that Spenser, after Book i, "suffered his story to lead him astray from his moral,"[34] though not strictly accurate, contains an important insight. *The Faerie Queene* is virtually a tour of romance forms, but of forms whose tendencies are significantly different, and the prior placing of Book i does not necessarily establish its priority. The simile of the Nile which in the Legend of Holinesse is an image of monstrosity—Errour's "vomit" of "bookes and papers" (i. 20-21)—is, for example, in the very "errant" and Ariostan Book iii, an image of the "infinite shapes" of natural fertility (vi. 8), the spontaneous generation of Amoret and Belphoebe.

The defeat of Errour in canto i is an apocalyptic motif, but succeeding cantos move instead towards diffusion. The Legend of Holinesse multiplies its images of apocalypse as it proceeds towards its end. Arthur's overthrow of the Castle of Orgoglio is linked, by the sounding of the horn,[35] to the final fall of Jericho, the City of Error. The stripping of Duessa, the "scarlot whore" (i. viii. 29. 2), is the romance equivalent of apocalypse, a reminder that the opposite of such "uncovering" or revelation is the enchantress Calypso. The "blessed sprites" (viii. 36. 6) calling from beneath the stone of Orgoglio's altar in canto viii recall the martyrs of Revelation 6. The wounding of Duessa's beast by Prince Arthur recalls the routing of the Beast from the Sea. The victory of the Red Cross knight over the Dragon laying waste the kingdom of Una's parents recalls the Knight Faithful and True of Revelation 19 and Christ's victory over the Great Dragon of the Apocalypse.

Because of these echoes, Josephine Waters Bennett and others have argued that Revelation not only provided Spenser with the details for particular passages but also largely determined the structure of Book i, leading up to the feast in Eden in the final canto.[36] The wanderings of Una after her separation from Red Cross are linked through image and allegory to the biblical prophesies of the paradoxical "erring" of Truth in

the period between First and Second Coming, the time when
men will be "turned back unto fables and lies" (II Tim. 4:4),
when "even the chosen, if it were possible, shall be brought
into error" (Matt. 24:24).[37] Part of the historical allegory of
the trials of the Reformed Church is Abessa and Corceca's
wish for Una—"that in endlesse error she might euer stray"
(iii. 23. 9). Una's retreat into the wilds recalls the Woman
clothed with the Sun of Revelation 12, and her exile in the
wilderness until the defeat of the Great Dragon. From this
perspective, the final canto might seem to promise an end to
all wandering. The "heauenly noise" heard at the betrothal of
Red Cross and Una (xii. 39. 1) suggests the voice of the
"great multitude" at the marriage of the Lamb. Una's gar-
ment, "All lilly white, withoutten spot, or pride" (22. 7),
links her with the Bride of Canticles and of Revelation 19.
And her appearance finally before Red Cross without her
"vele" recalls the prophecy of Isaiah 25:6-8, that at the Messianic banquet the stigma of Israel will be taken away and the
veil of mourning be removed.

All suggests conclusion and consummation, like the *topos*
of the poetic voyage Spenser borrows from the end of the *Orlando furioso* for the opening of his final canto (xii. 1). The crucial phrase in this coming to port, however, is "a while" (1.
8), as Spenser's poem "overgoes" Ariosto's by continuing
beyond this *topos*. The combination, in Red Cross's account-
ing of his adventures to the King and Queen of Eden (xii. 15),
of an echo of Aeneas recounting his "errori" in the court of
Dido[38] with the echoes of the Apocalypse, suggests that this
seeming end is only a way-station, like that of Aeneas in
Carthage. Even the description of Una and Red Cross
"swimming in that sea of blisfull ioy" (41. 5) tends to ally this
stopping-place with other more dangerous "ends" in *The
Faerie Queene*, as if Eden itself could be a Carthage, and its
delights the potential *oblio* of the classical hero. In the very
Book most remarkable for its sense of an ending, the end
turns out to be less like the Apocalypse than the romance
Odyssey, where Ulysses, after twenty years of wandering, returns to tell Penelope that he must set out again.

The Faerie Queene shares in the romance theme of reunion

and reconciliation—the Odyssean *nostos* and the return to
Eden—but even here it employs the romance strategies of deferral and delay. Red Cross is successful but he does not
thereby get rid of the place of wandering. Even the exact extent of "Eden" in the poem is uncertain. At first we are told
that it is a kingdom which stretches over all the world, "from
East to Westerne shore" (I. i. 5. 5) and the defeat of the Dragon would seem to promise a return to its original dominion.
But in the final, culminating, canto, it shrinks to a much more
limited locus. Like the allegorical persons tied to particular
places—Phaedria or Malecasta[39]—it seems to be left behind
precisely because it does not participate in the poem's essential
movement, its shape-shifting process. The landscape of *The
Faerie Queene* is broad enough to contain Eden as only one of
its many prospects. The very immensity of Spenser's poem
seems to subvert the monopoly of such loci, just as the
characteristic syncretism of its imagery undermines the priority of a privileged "source."

Una, though unveiled in the last scene of Book I, is, as it
were, reveiled when Red Cross takes leave of her and returns
to "Faerie," when Archimago the arch-imager is released and
Duessa is once again "covered." Both enable the poem to go
on and this regression from Apocalypse, whatever it may
mean for the scheme of the Virtues or for the relation in the
poem of "nature" to "grace,"[40] suggests once again the affinity between fiction and "error." Spenser's plan, as enunciated
in the *Letter to Raleigh*, is one in which the beginning and the
end of each quest is also the poem's center—the court of the
Faerie Queene. Bishop Hurd defended the unity of *The Faerie
Queene* from its common origin and end.[41] The poem as we
have it, however, is all middle: Gloriana's court, beginning
and end of all movement, never appears. The respite period of
"dilation" is figured in a poem where the end of wandering is
more envisioned than attained—Britomart and Artegall still
only betrothed, the consummation of Scudamour and
Amoret still to be enjoyed, Arthur both still in the making
and still in search of the original of his dream.

This radical openness even distinguishes, within the poem,

between the kinds of romance. The almost cartoon character of the Book of the Apocalypse is a feature of romance dialectical in its tendency. The traditional function of Apocalypse is to portray the enemy as already defeated, in a vision of the end which places us outside the monsters we are still inside— as Job at the end of his trial is shown the externalized forms of behemoth and leviathan—and, by this act of identifying or naming, proleptically overcomes them. Spenser gives us this kind of romance at the end of Book I, a form which presents evil in its most monstrous shape and thus reduces it. His menacing and fire-breathing Dragon also bounces on the "brused gras" (xi. 15. 3) for joy and comically claps his "yron wings" (31. 9). This is not, however, Spenser's only mode, and the rest of his long romance is more indefinite. The poem, indeed, leaves its most important endings open, as if what could be defined would also, therefore, be limited, and "romance" becomes part of the leftover or uncontained, the "inescapable" or "uncontrollable mystery"[42] which makes Spenser the common precursor of Keats, Yeats, and Stevens. "Troynovaunt" is only suggested as the hopeful opposite of the tawdry and reduced "second Troy" of Paridell, its character only the hoped-for transformation of cultural late-coming into the promise, in England, of something genuinely new.[43] Purely schematic representations in the poem seem to appear at either the macro or the micro level, the scheme of Virtues for the order of the Books or the pageants inserted at points in the story when its own development is suspended, as if such schemata were either too large or too reduced to represent the poem's more dilatory, or indirect, movement.[44] "Romance's visionary impulse, its radical hunger for certainty and divinity," is tempered, in Spenser, by its "mystery and melancholy," its acceptance of "less than total knowledge."[45]

The Vale of Vision

C. S. Lewis tells us that Spenser is of all English poets closest to the symbolism of the New Testament, with its antitheses of Light and Dark, Life and Death; and Northrop Frye re-

minds us that the black and white characterization of romance
is part of its dialectical separation of opposites.[46] But whatever the dualism of Spenser's imagery and the clear preference
for "Day" reinforced in the repeated descriptions of dawning
through the poem's several books, *The Faerie Queene* remains
within the realm of the veiled. Arthur's great tirade against
Night in the fourth canto of Book III depends for its force
upon the New Testament imagery of the Children of Light
and the Children of Darkness ("Dayes dearest children be the
blessed seed, / Which darknesse shall subdew, and heauen
win," 59. 5-6), and the ensuing apostrophe to Day—"O
when will day then turne to me againe, / And bring with him
his long expected light?" (60. 1-2)—is perhaps the closest of
anything in the poem to the poet's own closing prayer for the
final end or "Sabaoths sight." The progress of the syntax,
however, is instructive: "Which darknesse shall subdew" can
be read as a victory for the Children of Light only if it is in-
verted, and this inversion is, syntactically, a temporal process.[47] The realm of wandering remains finally not that of an
apocalyptic, or Manichaean, Day or Night but, in the frame
of the poem's temporal imagery, that of the Evening Star, the
gem which only "figures" Gloriana on the baldric of the
knight who seeks her (I. vii. 30. 1-4).

If the motive power of *The Faerie Queene* is, as Frye
suggests,[48] the cynosure or centripetal gaze, the poem itself is
always just a little off center, making the visible a little bit
hard to see. Center and apocalyptic end are conflated in the
elaborate courtly pun of the final lines of the *Cantos of
Mutabilitie*:

> For, all that moueth, doth in *Change* delight:
> But thence-forth all shall rest eternally
> With Him that is the God of Sabbaoth hight:
> O that great Sabbaoth God, graunt me that Sabaoths sight.

The "Eli-sabbath," God of the Sabbath, is also, in the English
Renaissance compliment, the etymology of "Elizabeth,"[49] so
that Spenser manages once again both to conceal and to reveal
his sovereign within the "covert vele" of his poem. But just

as the end is distanced or deferred, so this central presence is
only obliquely "figured." Spenser's opening invocation to the
Muse in Book I ends with an address to the "Goddesse
heauenly bright, / Mirrour of grace and Maiestie diuine, /
Great Lady of the greatest Isle" whose "beames," like those
of the sun, are to illumine his "feeble eyne" (i. Pro. 4). The
language of biblical *figura* and poetic figure which Boccaccio
and others combined[50] is borrowed by Spenser for the allegorical person of Gloriana as the sovereign's "glorious
type" (i. Pro. 4. 7), an image which is expanded in the Proem
to Book ii:

> And thou, O fairest Princesse vnder sky,
> In this faire mirrhour maist behold thy face,
> And thine owne realmes in lond of Faery,
> And in this antique Image thy great auncestry.
>
> The which O pardon me thus to enfold
> In couert vele, and wrap in shadowes light,
> That feeble eyes your glory may behold,
> Which else could not endure those beames bright,
> But would be dazled with exceeding light.
>
> (ii. Pro. 4. 6-9; 5. 1-5)

The language is taken from the description of the "veil" over
the face of Moses in ii Corinthians 3, and the figure whose
"glorie" is too bright for feeble eyes suggests an apocalyptic
presence, "Glory" in its full theological sense. Spenser's
poem thus becomes a kind of "old testament," a text still
within the realm of the "figure," like Andrew Marvell's punning "mosaic . . . book" ("Upon Appleton House," 582-84).
The implication is that the veil is there for the reader to pierce,
as Spenser suggests in the Dedicatory Sonnet to Lord Bur-
leigh, where the metaphor of the veiled "testament" is combined with the common Renaissance concept of the veiled
surface of allegory protecting truth from the eyes of the vulgar.[51] "Reading," then, becomes part of the process of revelation, of moving from "magic to miracle,"[52] like the moments
of revelation, of the lifted veil of Una or the raised vizor of

Britomart, in the poem itself. Once again, however, the apocalyptic movement towards revelation is countered by a movement towards multiplication and refraction.

The Proem to Book III provides us with an instructive example. It too is a compliment to Elizabeth, with the "shadow" of *figura* now modulated into the "shadow" of artistic representation, but the tendency of the compliment is somewhat different. Spenser begins by saying that he has no need to "fetch from *Faery* / Forreine ensamples" (Pro. 1. 3-4) when he comes to write of Chastity, since it is enshrined in his "Soueraines brest" (1. 5), but he goes on to talk of the "error" of all representation:

> But liuing art may not least part expresse,
> Nor life-resembling pencill it can paint,
> All were it *Zeuxis* or *Praxiteles*:
> His daedale hand would faile, and greatly faint,
> And her perfections with his error taint . . .
>
> (2. 1-5)

"Daedale" is, in the context of the single line in which it appears, simply a commonplace epithet for the artist; in combination with "error" in the next line, however, it suggests an analogy with the labyrinth, created by the figure whom Renaissance mythographers both praised and blamed for his "variety."[53] The *topos* of modesty here might seem the apex of Spenser's courtly compliment, an inability which leads him to "shadow" his sovereign's "glorious portraict" in "colourd showes" since he cannot figure it "plaine" (3. 5-9). In this sense the stanza simply echoes the *Letter to Raleigh*, with its division of "the most excellent and glorious person of our sovereign the Queene" into her public and private "persons," and the reference to "mirrours more then one" is a fitting description of a poem in which Elizabeth is figured variously in Una, Belphoebe, Britomart, Mercilla, and Gloriana. But the poem itself complicates the image: "shadow" is often suspect,[54] multiplicity is often the source of potential variance, and refraction into "mirrours more then one" may be the centrifugal counterpart of "erring."

This erring or interplay of differences is one of the evasions made possible by the "shade" or ambiguous "foreshadowing" of allegory itself. Spenser's schoolmaster, Richard Mulcaster, wrote that poets "couer a truth with a fabulous veele, and resemble with alteration."[55] In Spenser's romance, "alteration," or the not-quite-complete coincidence of word and thing, is part of the poet's avoidance of idolatry and profession of weakness, the inability of his "rusticke Muse." It is also, however, a gap left open for the act of interpretation. The veiling of Elizabeth in *The Faerie Queene* is, one suspects, less a result of the Neo-Platonic conviction that truth must be veiled from the vulgar understanding or of the Christian concept of the Mosaic "letter," than it is an opportunity to play one "shadow" of her identity off against another, the technique of the poetic *eiron* of "Colin Clouts Come Home Againe," who always manages to say more than one thing at once. Refraction and multiplication can also be forms of evasion, and none of the "figures" can finally be marshaled into a single truth.

One aspect of the "alteration" in the allegory is the poem's temporal disjunction: Arthur is Gloriana's contemporary and Elizabeth's ancestor, but Elizabeth and Gloriana are allegorical alter egos. Part of this disjunction is a kind of praise in the optative: the false glory of the courts of Lucifera and Philotime are as much a warning to the poem's patroness as they are a species of symbolic parody, a distortion of the standard she is supposed to embody. "Moniment" is often used by Spenser as both "monument" and admonishment, as in the opening lines of "The Ruines of Time,"[56] and *Briton Moniments*, the chronicle of British history which Arthur surveys in the House of Alma, is at once a genealogy and a warning. Elizabeth is not coincident with "Glory"; she is also the successor to a line very much subject to error. The chronicle of British history, as Harry Berger, Jr., suggests, "presents history as a series of beginnings, of backslidings and renewals,"[57] and the relation to Elizabeth remains equivocal. The canto opens with an echo of Ariosto's more openly ironic prelude to the praise of his patrons:

Who now shall giue vnto me words and sound,
Equall vnto this haughtie enterprise?
Or who shall lend me wings, with which from ground
My lowly verse may loftily arise,
And lift it selfe vnto the highest skies?
More ample spirit, then hitherto was wount,
Here needes me, whiles the famous auncestries
Of my most dreaded Soueraigne I recount,
By which all earthly Princes she doth farre surmount.

(II. x. 1)

Spenser's irony is not the mordant wit of the Italian poet (*OF* III. 1), but neither is it a sober and straightforward incorporation of the other's stanza without its subtlety. The final line— "By which all earthly Princes she doth farre surmount"— may be simply a statement of how far she may rise above her history; but it is also a reminder that she too is of earthly origin, within the realm of Mutabilitie.

C. S. Lewis laments the fact that our understanding of *The Faerie Queene* is limited by the absence of the "allegorical centre, the union of Arthur and Gloriana."[58] But whether or not the poem is finished, the courtly compliment remains oblique. Prince Arthur's union with the Faerie Queene would be the union of prophecy and history, idea and reality. The Elfin History read by Guyon in the House of Alma begins with Elfe and Fay, an unfallen Adam and Eve, and ends with Gloriana. The cycle of disruption and disorder in the *Briton Moniments* contrasts sharply with the undisturbed succession and order of the chronicle of Faerie. The histories are parallel—the isolation of Guyon and Arthur as each reads is stressed—and as such, like the parallel lines of Marvell's "Definition of Love," they may, short of apocalypse, never meet. The suggestion is that Arthur will not reach his Faerie Queene until the realm of history coincides with that of Faerie, a synapse the poem is not prepared to cross.

The Faerie Queene as a whole remains on the threshold of a posited presence, a kind of poetic Book of Deuteronomy.[59] Dante distinguished between Limbo and Purgatory, the place of eternal suspension on the threshold or "lembo," from the wilderness of the Exodus, of certain, though delayed, progress to the Promised Land of a *Paradiso*. In the landscape of Spenser's Faerie, however, all is potentially a region of unlikeness or place of exile, and "limbo" is one of the dangers of wandering itself. "Wandering" and "Limbo" are linked as early as the second canto of the poem, when Red Cross, astonished by the voice within the tree, cries out:

What voyce of damned Ghost from *Limbo* lake,
Or guilefull spright wandring in empty aire,
Both which fraile men do oftentimes mistake,
Sends to my doubtfull eares these speaches rare,
And ruefull plaints, me bidding guiltlesse bloud to spare?
(I. ii. 32. 5-9)

The paralysis of the spell "Fra-dubio" is under is partly a reflection of the mental state of *dubbio* in its root sense of looking two ways at once, like the Janus-figure of "Doubt" who guards the Temple of Venus in Book IV. Limbo, however, is also traditionally the place where Adam and Eve are imprisoned before the Harrowing of Hell, and the parallels between this episode and the picture of Una's parents held captive in the tower of canto xi are too numerous to be accidental.[60] The "brasen towre" (I. xi. 3. 2) is "harrowed." But the presence of these paralyzed trees en route to the final vision, and the return of Red Cross to Faerie after the release of Adam and Eve, help to establish "Faerie lond" itself as a potential *terre gaste*, a place where wandering never ends.

This possibility is further suggested by the tale which provides one of the sources for Arthur's dream of the Faerie Queene. Chaucer's "Tale of Sir Thopas" is a burlesque not only of the form of the metrical romance but of its potential endlessness. It ends only when it is interrupted by the Host. The "Tale of Sir Thopas" may be Spenser's native *Orlando innamorato*, the unfinished predecessor whose example bespeaks the difficulty of bringing this errant form to any satisfactory ending. Chaucer's Tale could be said to go around in a circle,[61] and the relay race succession of quests in *The Faerie*

Queene, together with the suggestion that the bear baby of Book VI will grow up to experience his own adventures (VI. iv. 38), gives to Spenser's poem the potential form of the cycle of generation, a reminder of the connection between romance and the continually turning Wheel of Fortune.

This possibility is raised by the echo chamber of the poem itself. As if to heighten the sense of potentially irredeemable "error" even in the poem's central quest, Spenser surrounds Arthur's dream of Gloriana with more doubtful echoes:

> For-wearied with my sports, I did alight
> From loftie steed, and downe to sleepe me layd;
> The verdant gras my couch did goodly dight,
> And pillow was my helmet faire displayd:
> Whiles euery sence the humour sweet embayd,
> And slombring soft my hart did steale away,
> Me seemed, by my side a royall Mayd
> Her daintie limbes full softly down did lay:
> So faire a creature yet saw neuer sunny day.
>
> Most goodly glee and louely blandishment
> She to me made, and bad me loue her deare,
> For dearely sure her loue was to me bent,
> As when iust time expired should appeare.
> But whether dreames delude, or true it were,
> Was neuer hart so rauisht with delight,
> Ne liuing man like words did euer heare,
> As she to me deliuered all that night;
> And at her parting said, She Queene of Faeries hight.
>
> (I. ix. 13-14)

"Whether dreames delude, or true it were" is the first clear echo of an earlier, more sinister dream, the "fit false dreame, that can delude the sleepers sent" (I. i. 43. 9) which Archimago's messenger brings from the "Yuorie dore" (44. 6) of the Cave of Morpheus to the sleeping Red Cross. But once it is heard, other echoes crowd in to complicate or qualify the reading of Arthur's vision. The "louely blandishment" of the "Queene of Faeries" echoes the "gentle blandishment and louely looke" (i. 49. 8) of the false sprite which Archimago fashions in the image of Una. Arthur's "slombring soft" upon the grass recalls the "slumber soft" (i. 41. 1) of Morpheus himself. "Me seemed" is suggestively close to the constantly repeated "seeming" of the visitation to Red Cross. "Rauisht" and "steale away" may be both the *ecstasis* of the medieval dream vision and the secular analogy of the Christian knight's vision of "glory,"[62] but they also suggest a more dangerous *raptus*. The Romantic reading is already implicit in Spenser's verse. "Dearely sure," in its placing of "sure," is at least potentially as ambiguous as Keats's "Belle Dame Sans Merci" ("And sure in language strange she said— / 'I love thee true' "). Most subtly of all, the final line of the first stanza ("So faire a creature yet saw neuer sunny day") suggests, in the careful inversion of the syntax, the possibility not only that she is the fairest creature ever seen by "sunny day" but that she herself may be one of the creatures of the ambiguous dark, like the spirits brought from Morpheus' house, "where dawning day doth neuer peepe" (i. 39. 5). The parallel between Arthur's vision and that of Red Cross could, once again, be simply one of the poem's instances of symbolic parody, a crucial separation of similitudes. But symbolic parody assumes the certainty of a fixed standard, and the relation of real form to parody in Spenser's poem is often no more predictable than that of fable to its allegorical meaning.

Arthur's account of his dream of Gloriana and her disappearance occurs in the same canto as the episode of Despair, a coincidence which is not without significance though it is rarely interpreted. The figure of Despair would seem, in the first instance, to have nothing to do with Arthur: his potential victim is Red Cross and the episode is prefaced by a parting of the ways, as Red Cross goes to fight with "*Vnaes* foe" and Arthur continues "on his way / To seeke his loue" (ix. 20. 1-3). But Arthur's pallor (ix. 16. 1) is echoed by that of Despair's victims and Sir Terwin, like Arthur, absent from the object of his desire, falls victim to the enchanter's soothing words. Despair is one of the dangers of the threshold state and his locus is not inappropriately a wilderness like that of

Dante's Wood of the Suicides. Arthur meets his own "Despair" in the figure of Maleger in Book II, the specter of melancholy (xi. 22) which haunts any quest for a presence which is "there" and not "here."[63] Later editions describe Arthur's antagonist as "*this* lifelesse shadow" (xi. 44. 3), but the 1590 edition reads "*his*." "Praysdesire," the *anima* figure Arthur meets in the House of Alma, is, in this respect, not just "desire of praise" but the more urgent "prays for desire," a counter to the spectral death wish.[64]

The rhetoric of Despair gathers up all the images and *topoi* of the wilderness of wandering which fill the poem:

> Who trauels by the wearie wandring way,
> To come vnto his wished home in haste,
> And meetes a flood, that doth his passage stay,
> Is not great grace to helpe him ouer past,
> Or free his feet, that in the myre sticke fast?
>
> (I. ix. 39. 1-5)

The argument for suicide is an appeal for *quies* where the "travel" of continued wandering is inseparable from its root meaning of "travail." Despair's contention is that time simply condemns, that "wandering" cannot be anything but "error" (ix. 43. 8-9: "For he, that once hath missed the right way, / The further he doth goe, the further he doth stray"). But Arthur in his explanation to Una of his dream of the Faerie Queene invokes an image of time which might be emblematic of the way in which the poem is a species of *dilatio* in its incompleted sense:

> Most goodly glee and louely blandishment
> She to me made, and bad me loue her deare,
> For dearely sure her loue was to me bent,
> As when iust time expired should appeare.
>
> (ix. 14. 1-4)

The "iust time" is the period of his "labour," and the antidote to Despair in the Legend of Holinesse is the ministration of Speranza and Fidelia, both betrothed to a distant consummation (x. 4).

The Demon of Possession

IN the Legend of Temperance, the equivocal nature of this middle time or dilated interval informs the temporal structure of the Book itself. If Book I of *The Faerie Queene* is its purest example of the romance quest—the killing of the Dragon— Book II explores the *activity* of questing, the difficult process of moving towards an envisaged end. Maleger's companions are Impotence and Impatience, parodies of the dialectical *festina lente*, the "royal" proverb which underlies Spenser's "Book of the Governor."[65] Castiglione's *Cortegiano* takes the form of a symposium in order to avoid the monotony of a single point of view, but this variety is also a potential conflict, an interplay of discourses from which no single form emerges. In *The Faerie Queene*, the temporal equivalent of multiplicity is the process of error as the education of its ",cyropedic heroes."[66] "Wandering" rather than proceeding by the shortest route seems to be for the sake of something else in the meantime, the mean-time of the romance's characteristic mode. The opposite of the premature or precipitate end is the process leading to *maturitas*, the "tryed time" (85-90) of the *December* eclogue. Temperance is for Spenser, as for Milton, inseparable from the notion of "triall" and after the crucial tempering of Guyon in the Cave of Mammon, the final destruction of the Bower of Bliss is almost an anti-climax. Even the story taken from Ariosto for the episode of Phedon and Philemon is transformed into a fable of the wrong kind of questing, an antitype of Guyon's quest for revenge. What is in Ariosto a digression which leads yet another knight away from his mission (*OF* v) becomes in Spenser's hands part of the romance motif of the demonic hunt, Phedon's chase through "woods and plaines" (II. iv. 32. 2) until he himself is overtaken by the demon "Furor." Questing in this episode is a potential form of dis-ease or disease, an image of the reduction of the human to the elemental quester, like the physical elements to which the figures of this Legend are reduced.

Deferral of the end is often, in *The Faerie Queene*, something like the Freudian *Aufschub*, a delay of gratification for the sake of a consummation which may never come. Spenser's vision thus shares in the Virgilian melancholy, the sense of an end as elusive and distant as the ever-retreating Ausonian shores. Yet however powerful this melancholy, it is perhaps more than matched by a sense of the danger of the premature or reductive end. The journey to the center in the opening canto of the poem turns out to be a journey to the monster at the center of the labyrinth, and avoidance of this fixity is paradoxically a strategy of "error," of taking the long way round. The "carelessness" and "care" of Phaedria and Mammon in Book II are partial ends constructed into reductive *cosmoi*, parodies of the *"frame* of Temperance" (II. xii. 1, my italics).[67] Spenser frequently expresses the desire for rest in architectural metaphors, images which turn the temporal process into an edifice, or edification. The constantly reiterated quality of "stedfastnesse" is an index of the wanderer's constancy. But the "stedfast state" (II. xii. 51. 2) of the "Heauens" in Acrasia's bower is a sign of the wrong kind of end, the opposite of the temperate *krasis* or mixture.[68] And the sleeping "Verdant," though at first a fitting emblem of this *locus amoenus*, is also a symbol of its paralysis: the faintly sexual "idle instruments / Of sleeping praise . . . hong vpon a tree" (80. 1-2) are also an echo of the suspended instruments of the Psalm of exile (Ps. 137: 2), and transform its pensiveness into a romance limbo, suspension "in the middest of the race." The "stedfastnesse" of Red Cross is enjoined by the allusion, in the first canto of the poem, to Ephesians 6:16: "Take unto you the whole armour of God, that ye may be able to withstand in the evil day, and having done all, to stand." But the standing fast of constancy has its suspect double in the Renaissance meaning of "standing" as "stagnant." Spenser's "Idle Lake" and its enchantress (II. vi) recall Tasso's "steril lago,"[69] a reminder that all premature *loci amoeni*, like the biblical Sodom, stand upon some form of a "Dead Sea."

Each of the Legends of *The Faerie Queene* provides a variation on the tension between premature end and indefinite extension. In Books III and IV, the form the reductive impulse takes might be characterized as the quest for "possession."

Britomart, complaining of the "shade and semblant of a knight" (III. ii. 38. 3) she has seen in Merlin's prophetic mirror, does not find comfort in her nurse's assurance that her love is more worthy than that of Biblis, Pasiphae or "th'Arabian Myrrhe" because these at least were able to "possesse" the object of their desire:

> Beldame, your words doe worke me litle ease;
>   For though my loue be not so lewdly bent,
>   As those ye blame, yet may it nought appease
>   My raging smart, ne ought my flame relent,
>   But rather doth my helplesse griefe augment
>   For they, how euer shamefull and vnkind,
>   Yet did possesse their horrible intent:
>   Short end of sorrowes they thereby did find;
> So was their fortune good, though wicked were their
>   mind.
>
> (III. ii. 43)

The trajectory of questing in this Book is the romance equivalent of the "endless torment" of the *Amoretti* sonnets, the Petrarchan dialectic of absence and presence in which the seeking subject is always *en route* towards an elusive object of desire. The image of wandering lost with no hope of reaching the end (Sonnets XXIII and XXV) and of despair at finding no nourishment for the "loue-affamisht hart" (Sonnet LXXXVIII) appears, in Britomart's lament, as a folly even greater than that of Narcissus:

> But wicked fortune mine, though mind be good,
>   Can haue no end, nor hope of my desire,
>   But feed on shadowes, whiles I die for food,
>   And like a shadow wexe, whiles with entire
>   Affection, I doe languish and expire.
>   I fonder, then *Cephisus* foolish child,
>   Who hauing vewed in a fountaine shere
>   His face, was with the loue thereof beguild;
> I fonder loue a shade, the bodie farre exild.
>
> (III. ii. 44)

Narcissus is the patron saint of courtly love[70] if only because all dialectics of subject and object depend upon some kind of projection, a relation in which a subject is literally "subjected" to an object or end. The image of Narcissus as applied to Britomart's lovesickness, however, is twofold. The limbo-like situation of the *Amoretti*, where the lover is suspended before the goal of his desire, is suggested by the image used for the "torment" of Britomart in canto ii: "She shortly like a pyned ghost became, / Which long hath waited by the Stygian strond" (52. 5-6)—the classical image of the threshold before "rest." Narcissus' love was an unfruitful one: he starved and died. The emphasis, throughout Britomart's quest, is on its potential fruitfulness, or "issue." To this end, she must go through the looking glass and this first image of crossing a difficult threshold—the "hard begin, that meets thee in the dore" (iii. 21. 8)—is repeated through Books III and IV in a series of such thresholds, from the ring of fire which Scudamour, unlike Britomart, fails to cross to the Janus-figure of "Doubt" in the Temple of Venus.

The contrast established in the lament of Britomart, between the "short end" (ii. 43. 8) of possession and the potential endlessness of her wandering, becomes the polarity within which this Legend moves. Spenser adopts Ariosto's story of Fiordispina and Bradamante (*OF* xxv. 26-70) for Malecasta's frustrated effort to possess Britomart, but pointedly omits the happy solution of a twin brother. The potentially endless course of Britomart's desire is repeated in the lament of Timias "wounded" by Belphoebe (v. 42. 7-9) and in Arthur's tirade against the darkness which separates him from the end of his quest (iv. 55-60). The little myth Spenser employs to surround the story of Merlin seems to be included simply to provide one more image of this endlessness: the magician's "sprights," having been ordered to continue their work until his return from the "Ladie of the Lake," now labor endlessly, ignorant that their master has been taken prisoner (iii. 10-11). The radical perspectivism of romance[71] is extended to the prospect of history, the "issue" of Britomart's quest. In Merlin's prophecy of the history to come, the "euer-

lasting woe" (iii. 42. 1) of the Britons seems to be given a
"terme" (48. 1) and the long years of exile brought to a fruitful end with the advent of Elizabeth. But Merlin ends his
prophecy with the words "But yet the end is not" (50. 1), and
a caesura highly unusual in Spenser's verse marks the gap
which is the opening of the poem onto an uncertain present
("There *Merlin* stayd, / As ouercomen of the spirites powre, /
Or other ghastly spectacle dismayd, / That secretly he saw,
yet note discoure," 50. 1-4).[72] This vista of openness and
open-endedness, and the shift of historical perspective it implies, renders somewhat ironic Britomart and Glauce's "hope
of comfort glad" (51. 3) and their plan, in that stanza, of how
"to possesse the purpose they desird" (51. 7).

The problem raised by this potential endlessness has its reflection, in Book III, in the proliferation of substitute ends or
objects of desire. Venus, wandering through the earth in
search of the truant Cupid, takes one of the twins of
Chrysogone as a substitute and consolation (vi. 28. 8-9: "And
in her litle loues stead, which was strayd, / Her *Amoretta* cald,
to comfort her dismayd"). The witch who cannot detain the
fleeing Florimell—the Book's chief figure for the object of
pursuit—creates False Florimell as a substitute for her griev-
ing son (vii). Even the Hyena, deprived of his prey when
Florimell escapes into the fisherman's boat, transfers his
wrath to a more proximate object (vii. 28). Each of these sub-
stitutions is a species of sublimation as reduction: Amoret is a
repetition and a diminutive of Cupid; the counterfeit
Florimell finally proves redundant beside the real one; the destruction of Florimell's horse leads Satyrane to jump to a
premature conclusion. Substitution both offers a more immediate "end" and paradoxically complicates the narrative.
Venus's finding of Amoret leads to a protracted series of "errors" which extend the original wandering of Eros. The creation of a double for Florimell generates the subplot of Brag-
gadocchio and the rival knights which continues into the next
Book and becomes part of the centrifugal effect of "Discord."
Satyrane's error leads to the multiple discords of the Tournament in Book IV where the substitute object of Florimell's

girdle suggests the reduction of the quest for all such objects to a form of fetishism.[73]

The opposite of the pole of potential endlessness is the extreme of "possession." In the Legends of Holinesse and Temperance, the end to which the quest is directed is the knight's *religio*, an end to which he is simultaneously "bound" and "bond" (I. i. 3. 1). Browning's " 'Childe Roland to the Dark Tower Came' " is perhaps the most powerful late Romantic vision of the way in which the quest itself can imprison or "frame"; but even within *The Faerie Queene*, questing may be a form of compulsion, and objective be reduced to mere object. The quest in Book III is shadowed by the motif of the hunt or chase, where narrative error is paradoxically the creation of rigidity, each single quester, as in Ariosto's "palazzo incantato" (*OF* XXII. 17), pursuing his projected end. The bonds of friendship and of wedlock become the "bonds" of possession—the "eternall bondage" of Argante's young men, the "Dongeon deepe" into which Proteus casts Florimell, and the enclosure of Amoret in the House of Busirane.

Images of a realized possession seem to be provided in Books III and IV only as a contrast to the human, whether that possession is monstrous and subhuman or divine. In the Garden of Adonis, Psyche, whose wanderings in Apuleius' fable are a version of romance "errori," is finally "reconcyld" (III. vi. 50) with Cupid, and Venus is in possession of Adonis (46. 8-9): "But she her selfe, when euer that she will, / Possesseth him, and of his sweetnesse takes her fill"). But even here, there may be, in the echo of Venus and Adonis in the tapestry of the Castle Joyeous (i. 34-38), a hint of possession as "possessiveness," an allusion which colors the end or objective of "possession" just as hints of apocalypse in the uniting of Red Cross and Una are qualified by echoes of a more dangerous kind of rest. The ending which is deferred at the end of Book I becomes in Books III and IV at once a temporal deferral and a maintenance of separation or difference. In the original 1590 ending of Book III, Scudamour and Amoret are united in an image of possession which moves Britomart to envy:

Had ye them seene, ye would haue surely thought,
That they had beene that faire *Hermaphrodite*,
Which that rich *Romane* of white marble wrought,
And in his costly Bath causd to bee site:
So seemd those two, as growne together quite,
That *Britomart* halfe enuying their blesse,
Was much empassiond in her gentle sprite,
And to her self oft wisht like happinesse,
In vaine she wisht, that fate n'ould let her yet possesse.

Scudamour and Amoret are, in the 1590 ending, united as the "Hermaphrodite."[74] In the second installment of *The Faerie Queene* in 1596, however, their union is indefinitely deferred. "Scudamour" and "Amoret," like "Britomart" and "Artegall," are, as joined names, the verbal equivalent of the androgyne, literally the analogue of the "Hermes-Aphrodite." But the deferral of this union preserves their difference and extends their story. Significantly, in the changed version, it is not Amoret but Ate or "Discord" that Scudamour first meets, as the Ariostan principle of *Discordia* becomes, in Book IV, the embodiment of fictional complication and extension. The "preposterous"[75] ordering of the narrative of Scudamour and Amoret—the curious fact that their first meeting, in the Temple of the Hermaphrodite Venus, is the last event to be related—involves a reversal of beginnings and endings which marks their distance from this "heauen," from a place where lovers already "their loues desire possesse" (IV. x. 28. 3-6). The end or climax of the narrative play on "possession" through Books III and IV is the vision of the Hermaphrodite and its aftermath, the climactic marriage of the Thames and the Medway. But the episode in the Temple of Venus is only the beginning, for Scudamour, of a series of frustrations and deferrals, and the final scene of Book IV is not marriage but, as in Book I, a betrothal.

This deferral of consummation in the case of Scudamour and Amoret is repeated in the case of Britomart and Artegall. As a *Venus armata* or "martiall Mayd" (III. ii. 9. 4), Britomart would seem to come closest to the self-enclosed compound identity of the androgyne. She literally "divides" herself in order to bring concord out of the exclusiveness of the custom of the castle which demands that either she or the knight she has defeated be locked out (IV. i. 11. 7-9): as "Knight" she claims her right to Amoret, and as lady she chooses as her mate the excluded knight. The moments in which she is revealed are revelations of this dual nature, of her "manly terrour" and "amiable grace" (III. i. 46. 1-2).[76] But revelation in this Book, too, is qualified. The only real Hermaphrodite figures in the poem—Venus and Nature—both remain veiled. Britomart still seeks a mate outside herself, and if this distinguishes her from Narcissus it also keeps her within the romance world of "quest." From the very first episode in which she appears, she is defined by an essential lack (III. i. 60. 5-7), and even the union with Artegall is never, within the poem, realized.

This technique of deferral and delay is partly the Ariostan exploitation of romance "error" in the two Books which most insistently recall the *Furioso*. Critics who speak of Spenser's relation to romance often note his intention to "overgoe" Ariosto, a comparison from which Spenser often emerges as both less flexible and more sage and serious than the Ferrarese ironist. Such a view falls victim to the *eiron* of *The Faerie Queene* who speaks incessantly of his "fraile wit" and "ragged rhymes" and whose irony is often less that of the Continental master than of "Dan Chaucer," the English one; Spenser's best jokes frequently pass unnoticed because they are a species of deadpan, like the inclusion as well as the overgoing of Chaucer in the "Legend of Friendship." Even a cursory glance at the poem reveals that Spenser mastered Ariosto's technique of interweaving; Paul Alpers has shown the way in which scattered allusions to the *Furioso* itself provide a *sotto voce* commentary on the incidents of *The Faerie Queene*.[77] But Spenser also overgoes his Italian model by incorporating it as only one mode of romance among many, just as he includes the *ottava rima* within the longer form of his own stanza. *The Faerie Queene* is virtually a tour of romances, from the biblical quest and the classical "wanderings" of Odysseus and Aeneas in Books I and II to the "social banditry"[78] of Book V and the pastoral interlude of the Legend of Courtesy. And Books III and IV incorporate the "errori" of Ariosto's poem by beating the master at his own game, including the first three cantos of the *Furioso* within the opening episodes of a single Book.[79]

Spenser even uses the Ariostan "differire" for one of his canto endings (IV. vii. 47. 9). His use of difference and deferral in these two Legends, however, goes beyond its significance as a metaphor of narrative complication. At the Tournament of Satyrane in Book IV, Cambell and Triamond—the Legend's titular heroes—both put the other's claim to victory before their own, "So that the doome was to another day differd" (iv. 36. 9). The image of a suspended "doom" recapitulates several images in the Book where deferral of a resolution Either-Or is connected with an image of Concord. In the original fight between Cambell and Triamond, the "doubtfull ballance" (iii. 37. 1) in which the battle stands is not resolved by the victory of one over the other. Instead, the forward progress of their strife is interrupted by the arrival of Cambina with her "rod of peace" (42. 1) and the cup of Nepenthe (42. 9). Spenser specifically says that this drink is of "more gratious powre" (45. 1) than the Fountain of Hate in Ariosto ("that famous Tuscane penne") which, as in Boiardo, is also the fountain of fictional discord and complication. The "resolution" of Friendship is not so much a resolution as a suspending of resolution, ending their battle in a kind of draw.

This concord is reflected in the suspended ending of Book III and its carryover into the Legend of Friendship. The absoluteness of the *Amoretti* is balanced, in Spenser's canon, by the Wedding Hymns and their recognition of separate identities. Delay, in the middle of *The Faerie Queene*, is part of the restraint involved in love which incorporates friendship, just as betrothal is a form of delayed gratification. In order to fulfill Gloriana's behest, Artegall must harden himself against the attractions of Britomart and go on his way (IV. vi. 42), while Britomart is bound by friendship to help Scudamour find the lost Amoret. Such deferral is opposed simultaneously to possession and to an exclusive *égoïsme à deux*, and this acknowledgment of otherness is, in Spenser's poem, a tempering of the violence from within and without which another romance poet, Wallace Stevens, calls a fruitful dependence.[80]

This maintenance of difference is essential to the Legend of Concord. The "golden chaine" of Concord (i. 30. 8) which keeps "this worlds faire workmanship" (30. 6) from being destroyed is a descendant of the golden chain in Homer from which Zeus suspends all creation. It is an image of "resolution" not as apocalypse but as *discordia concors*, the tempering of opposites which holds this Creation in being. Primaudaye, in *The French Academie*, introduces the virtue of temperance with a passage praising the organization of the cosmos:

> The divine excellencie of the order, of the equall and wonderfull constancy of the parts of the world, as well in the goodly and temperate moderation of the seasons of the yeare, as in the mutuall coniunction of the elements, obeying altogether with a perfect harmony the gracious and soveraigne government of their Creator, was the cause that *Pythagoras* first called all the compasse of this universall frame by this name of *World*, which without such an excellent disposition would bee but disorder and a world of confusion.[81]

"Constancy" here is a function not of singularity but of *krasis* or mixture. "Harmony" is traditionally the child of Venus and Mars, an image of concord and discord in one. Ate or Discord threatens to reduce the world of Spenser's poem to chaos, and the comparison of the rival knights in Book iv to warring elements is followed by a vision of potential dissolution (ix. 23). Yet "discord" is also part of the mixture: "dischord oft in Musick makes the sweeter lay" (iii. ii. 15. 9). Ate is described as "double" (iv. i. 28) and her companion is "Duessa." Duessa in this Book, however, is opposed not by Una and the singular virtue of "Holinesse" which works by exclusion, but rather by Concord, who comprehends *varietas* and forestalls the collapse into oneness. In the Temple of Venus, Concord is the figure who, in mediating between the Empedoclean principles of "Love" and "Hate," keeps Hate from being overcome (x. 32-35). The emphasis there is not on a final end but on a continuing process, and the alternative to the potential chaos of atomistic selves is not an all-embracing unity in which identities blend but an accord which recognizes the equilibrium of differences. In the very Book in which "difference" seems simply disruptive, it becomes an essential part of Spenser's *Concordia*.

Creation, in the biblical account, proceeds by a process of differentiation, and the six-book poem is in many ways Spenser's *Hexameron*. Images of a premature collapse of differences parallel premature and reductive ends. Spenser anticipates the horror of Pope's "uncreating word" in the "gross fog" on the way to the Bower of Bliss, where "all things one, and one as nothing was, / And this great Vniuerse seemd one confused mas" (II. xii. 34. 8-9). Each of the Deadly Sins in the House of Pride participates in the dissolving of difference or discrimination. Sloth does not know whether it is "night or day" (I. iv. 19. 6); Gluttony cannot separate "friend" from "fo" (23. 5); Lechery loves all that he sees (26. 1); Avarice weighs "right and wrong ylike" in his "ballaunce" (27. 9); Envy reduces everything to "bad" (32. 5); while Wrath vents himself without distinction on all (33. 6). Their counterpart in the Legend of Justice is the Egalitarian Giant, who significantly echoes Spenser's own complaint, in the Proem to that Book, that everything has gone astray.

Spenser's image of completeness is the mixture of elements which is opposed by A-crasia and her premature eternity. His opposition to Chaos within the poem is not a reduced cosmos but what Joyce called a "Chaosmos," containing but not reductively so, not without loose ends. Thomas Roche, Jr. sees Spenser's *discordia concors* as primarily a movement towards union, the resolution of conflict in a final end.[82] But the union of Scudamour and Amoret, Britomart and Artegall, is indefinitely deferred and the narrative, like the poem's own ambiguous play of "double senses" (III. iv. 28. 8), is not re-

stricted to a *sens unique*: the movement towards solution or
resolution is matched by the movement of dissolution, or disillusion. The constant reminder of mutability—that "Nothing is sure, that growes on earthly ground" (I. ix. 11. 5)—has
its counterpart in the way in which the poem undermines its
own certainties. Spenser characteristically takes away with
one hand what he gives with another, a technique which
leads, in a later version of romance, to Yeats's image of the
interlocking gyres, each dying each other's life, living each
other's death. The continuous *va-et-vient* of romance is also
part of what Harry Berger, Jr. calls the "Spenserian
dynamics," the poetic *discordia concors* in which "no moment
of union or reconciliation, of relief or triumph, is to be con-
strued as absolute—absolute either in the sense of being final,
or in the sense of being totally one-sided."[83] Even the dialectics of characterization yield to this pressure. One reader of
the poem speaks of the way in which the characters "reveal
themselves to be members of One Man, One Hero, or of his
Enemy."[84] But this apocalyptic terminology will not wholly
work. Characters shift according to context. Proteus is the
villain in the story of Florimell, where, despite his many
changes of shape, he is, for narrative purposes, reduced,
placed on the level of the lecherous old man he substitutes.
But he is also the host of the marriage of the Thames and
Medway, an emblem for its boundless promise of fertility.[85]
For such figures, no single moral label will hold.

This leads us finally to one other kind of "possession" in
the poem. Books III and IV are filled with "signes" which do
not have any immediately apparent meaning. Britomart is
unsure how to read the signs which appear above the doors of
the House of Busirane. Amoret, ignorant of Britomart's identity, does not know how to interpret her ambiguous speech,
so full of "many things so doubtfull to be wayd, / That well
she wist not what by them to gesse" (IV. i. 7. 5-6). Satyrane
misreads the "relique" of Florimell's girdle to be a "signe"
(III. viii. 49-50) of her certain death. Marinell's mother, trying
to possess the future of her son by prophecy, is, ironically,
blind to a crucial error in interpretation. The problem of

"possession" in the quest for meaning comes to a focus in the story of Malbecco and his reduction to an allegorical abstraction. Possessiveness is the driving force of the *fabliau* of Malbecco and Hellenore, where jealousy is both the demon of possession and the demon by which Malbecco is finally possessed. Its conclusion is that species of symmetrical reduction called poetic justice: Malbecco reappears as the figure of "Gealousie" while Hellenore becomes the satyrs' "commune good" (III. x. 36. 9).

The tale also provides a reflection on the relation of fable to allegory. Angus Fletcher speaks of allegory's "compulsive teleology."[86] Allegorical meaning, like apocalyptic "identity," can be a premature or preemptive end: Talus in the Legend of Justice nails up Munera's allegorical extremities and throws the rest away.[87] In the story of Malbecco, the moral literally coincides with the exhaustion of the fiction: the allegorical abstraction "Gealousie" is a phenomenon absolutely coincident with, or possessed by, its meaning. If demonology is the only exact science (Lawrence Durrell), the demon of allegory in *The Faerie Queene* has as its potential end this kind of exaction, or rigidity. Malbecco is left behind because he does not participate in the poem's process: his transformation is, in Paul Alper's brilliant remark, "not a change in him, but a terrible remaining what he is."[88] He becomes, as it were, a Lunatic of One Idea.

This collapse of phenomenon and meaning reveals by contrast the more devious ways of signification in Spenser's poem. Meaning too has a meantime, a gap which provides a fertile field for "error." Editions which provide the reader with the identity and name of each character as he appears could not be further from the phenomenology of Spenser's poem, where "identity" is less an endpoint than a process of discovery.[89] "Meaning" is deferred in order to leave room for the crucial act of reading, which does not necessarily lead to a single end. Spenser speaks ironically in the Proem of Book II of those who, faced with the "signes" of "Faerie lond," cannot "without an hound fine footing trace" (4. 1-5), and the "hunt" for meaning becomes, like other hunts in the poem,

part of a potentially compulsive teleology, a concern for
definite and defined ends which the poem will not satisfy.
Talus in Book v is a hunter for truth who binds the Protean
Malengin and threshes out falsehood ("in his hand an yron
flale did hould, / With which he thresht out falshood, and did
truth vnfould," i. 12. 8-9). But the threshing metaphor, if it
suggests Apocalypse, also suggests, in the very figure of
Talus, a process which is perhaps only a mechanical operation
of the spirit.

In Book iv, Spenser alludes to the story of Menenius
Agrippa, the "prudent Romane" whose Fable of the Belly
"reconcyld" a divided populace (ii. 2. 7-9). The immediate
context of the allusion is the power of words to heal "wicked
discord" and Agrippa joins the examples of Orpheus and
David. The fable itself is a tale of the uses of diversity, the
order over which the "belly" presides, and it links the Book
of Concord to that of Governance. But there is a sense in
which, as we move to Book v, the female figure of Concord
and the male figure of the Artegall-like Maker who governs a
world gone astray are in conflict.[90] Little has been written on
the difference and potential tension between the Pauline
metaphor of the Body and Agrippa's Fable of the Belly,
though Shakespeare's treatment of the latter in *Coriolanus*
may suggest the possible perversion of a metaphor of difference into a rigid and literalizing defense of hierarchy.[91] Flank-
ing the dialectic of the *discordia concors* are the extremes of
chaos and rigidity, and the description of Concord's tempering in Book iv contrasts with Artegall's description of the
"Maker":

> He maketh Kings to sit in souerainty;
> He maketh subiects to their powre obay;
> He pulleth downe, he setteth vp on hy;
> He giues to this, from that he takes away.
> For all we haue is his: what he list doe, he may.
>
> (v. ii. 41. 5-9)

The "making" of creation is almost inseparable here from the
"making" of compulsion, and this difference between the two

Books is perhaps what makes Book v, despite its recent de-
fenders,[92] less immediately attractive or, we might almost
say, less familiarly Spenserian than the other Books. The
metaphor of hierarchy is a difficult one, and not only for
modern ears: the Celestial Hierarchy Dante borrows from the
pseudo-Dionysius is said not to be a hierarchy in the earthly
sense, but Milton's Satan reads it somewhat differently. In
Book v of *The Faerie Queene*, "difference" and its play run the
risk of being frozen into something more rigid. The extreme
situation described in the Proem—the flight of Astraea and
the degeneration of the earth from the Golden Age—seems to
call in this Legend for extreme measures. It may be argued
that these extremes are necessary to the Book's central
paradox of Justice and Mercy, and to a justice which avoids
the blurring of "pity" which Spenser abhorred as much as
Blake. But finally not even the force embodied in Talus
works, and the indefinite deferral of union or ending in Books
III and IV becomes, in the Legend of Justice, a darker sense of
the impossibility of final solutions in a world which has
"wandred farre" from its first course (Pro. 4. 7). The careful
counterpoint of Artegall's adventures with those of Hercules
only serves to reveal that, in Spenser's version, these "labors"
are not ultimately completed.[93] "Irena," whose name
suggests the "irenic" peace of the millennium or Sabbath, is
ironically chosen for Ireland. Artegall is recalled to Faerie
Court before he can "reforme that ragged common-weale"
(v. xii. 26. 4) and to the end of the journey is defenseless
against the Blatant Beast. And this interrupted ending continues into the final Legend of Courtesy, where the Beast is
both the object of the quest and that which undermines it, and
where the darker background of this earlier Book makes romance now at least partly a form of escape.

The Romance of Romance

READERS frequently have sensed, in reading Book VI, that the
poem, if not demonstrably ending, is beginning, retrospectively, to explore its own implications. Humphrey Ton-

kin finely remarks in it a tension between two types of romance—the chivalric and pastoral—which is finally a tension between *The Faerie Queene*'s two archetypes, quest and circle, forward movement towards end or accomplishment, and the bower, or embowered moment, along the way.[94] The task of the knight of Courtesy is the accomplishment of the end Artegall does not reach—the subduing of the Blatant Beast. But just as in the Legend of Friendship the resolution of end, conflict, or "travail" is suspended in favor of a *discordia concors*, so in the Legend of Courtesy, the emphasis falls not only on the completion of the quest but on the delights—and discoveries—of the "way." The opening stanzas of the Proem extend this dwelling upon, or dilation of, that middle space to the delightful "wanderings" of the poem itself:

> The waies, through which my weary steps I guyde,
>   In this delightfull land of Faery,
>   Are so exceeding spacious and wyde,
>   And sprinckled with such sweet variety,
>   Of all that pleasant is to eare or eye,
>   That I nigh rauisht with rare thoughts delight,
>   My tedious trauell doe forget thereby;
>   And when I gin to feele decay of might,
> It strength to me supplies, and chears my dulled spright.
>
> (VI. Pro. 1)

This stanza seems to gather up and remove the sting from images and phrases which earlier in the poem suggested more dangerous kinds of delay. The "delightfull land" of Faery echoes the solace of the Wood of Errour ("Led with delight, they thus beguile the way"), while "Exceeding spacious and wyde" inevitably recalls the Bower of Excess and its more suspect dilation. "Rauisht," if it picks up echoes of Arthur's dream of the Faerie Queene ("Was neuer hart so rauisht with delight," I. ix. 14. 6), also recalls the false Una brought to Red Cross ("So liuely, and so like in all mens sight, / That weaker sence it could haue rauisht quight," I. i. 45. 4-5).

Similarly, the bowers encountered as this Legend proceeds seem now to be not dangerous temptations, but rather part of the inwardness of the Virtue itself. The first enclosed space is that "siluer bowre" which, "hidden" from "view of men, and wicked worlds disdaine" (Pro. 3. 3-4), is "the sacred noursery / Of vertue" (3. 1-2), the growing place of Courtesy. And this bower anticipates the proliferation of desirable *tempes* which, after the social and political concerns of Book v, seem manifestly a form of retreat, and yet one whose leading "inward farre" (I. i. 7. 8) is now not *in malo* but *in bono*. Young Tristram dwells in seclusion "amongst the woodie Gods" (VI. ii. 26. 3), the Salvage Man "Farre in the forrest by a hollow glade" where "foot of liuing creature neuer trode" (iv. 13. 5-8). Priscilla is discovered with Aladine, as Serena with Calepine, in secret "shade" (ii. 43. 2; iii. 20. 3). The Hermit shuns "this worlds vnquiet waies" (vi. 4. 7) and Meliboe the "vainenesse" of the court (ix. 24. 9). The three Graces were begotten in a "pleasant groue" (x. 22. 3), and Courtesy itself seems linked with the honoring of privacy, as Calidore apologizes for intruding upon the bower of Calepine and Serena (iii. 21). *Tempe* indeed proves, as the Book progresses, to be only temporary, and the bower a fragile defense against more threatening intrusions, but the sense which accompanies its loss, in this Legend, is frequently a sense of regret, and not the sense of the priority of the questing or forward movement which overturns the dangerous embowered spaces and suspect "shades" of earlier Books.

From the perspective of a retreat not suspect but delightful, the linear thrust of the quest itself becomes a kind of intrusion, a movement which if it involves the accomplishment of a goal, also breaks up the pastoral *tempe*. The mention of Calidore's armor as he doffs it for "shepheards weed" (ix. 36. 3-4) seems almost inevitably to provoke the comparison to Paris and Oenone (36. 7), to an entry into a retreat which finally meant its doom. The potentially problematic nature of questing is raised earlier in the poem, in the elemental questers of Book II and the end-stopped or possessive pursuits of Books III and IV. But here it seems curiously to be reflected in the Blatant Beast itself—both the quest's ostensible object and a monster which like Malory's Questing Beast seems at least

partly to embody the restlessness of questing, a pursuit whose
"toile" (x. 2. 2) anticipates that rejected in Marvell's very
Spenserian "Garden." Calidore's choice of the "perfect pleasures, which doe grow / Amongst poore hyndes" (x. 3. 5-6) is
a retreat from his primary objective, and yet is praised by the
poet in contrast with the hunt after "courtly fauour" and its
"shadowes vaine" (x. 2). Indeed, the folly of exclusive focus
on an end or goal is perhaps most evident in the case of
"Courtesy," which must not only follow the quest laid upon
the knight by his Queene (x. 1. 4), but have the leisure, and
occasion, to "shew" what it professes (xii. 2. 4).

Yet this contrasting of desirable retreat and intruding "pursuit" is only one aspect of the complexities of this Legend.
The bower and its cognates, the closed circle and the centripetal gaze, participate in an ambivalence which is created,
as so often in Spenser, by a network of internal echoings, the
unsettling repetition of the same words in several dissonant
contexts. The motif of the cynosure or closed visual circle
links the sight of Pastorella on her "litle hillocke" (ix. 8. 1)
with the vision of the Graces on Mt. Acidale, but it also includes the cannibals staring at the nakedness of Serena (viii.
43) and the merchants' "greedy" gaze (xi. 13. 8). The description of Calidore's "hungry eye" (ix. 26. 7) as he gazes upon
Pastorella may be simply part of the vocabulary of love, but it
is disturbing as well, coming as it does only one canto after
the cannibals' "feeding," and may be a reminder that the
cynosure is always at least potentially a visual gluttony or
embowered fix, a variant of the enchantress feeding her eyes
upon the paralyzed youth (ii. xii. 73).

Similarly, the inwardness of the bower may provide the
privileged site of vision, but it also involves, in this Book, the
ambivalence of what Wallace Stevens later called "evasion,"
the impulse of "retreat" in both senses. Echoes of Phaedria's
bower in the opening stanzas and beyond seem to be presenting the positive side of its appeal, the pastoral retreat where to
take no thought for the morrow is to be open to the grace of
God as well as of nature. Yet Meliboe's honeyed words in
praise of the retired life (ix. 26) have the same effect as De-

spair's (I. ix. 31), and the success of the brigands is at least partly enabled by the passivity of an attitude, or retreat, which neglects to prepare for them. Even at the climax of the pastoral interlude and of the Book itself—the vision upon Mt. Acidale in canto x—the curious juxtaposition within the motto which precedes it suggests that vision itself may be a form of evasion, and in this respect, this center of several concentric rings[95] only intensifies the problematic inwardness of the retreat:

> Calidore sees the Graces daunce,
>   To Colins melody:
> The whiles his Pastorell is led,
>   Into captiuity.

The juxtaposition—however fortuitous[96]—implies that "Pastorell" may be ravished *because* Calidore is rapt in vision, a fixation which, like an earlier one, leaves him without "any will . . . thence to moue away" (ix. 12. 2), at the same time as the destruction of the "pastoral" by the brigands leaves a sense of the melancholy of intrusion, of the sacrifice of circle to line.

This interrogation of both embowered space and that which intrudes upon, or supersedes it, heightens the poem's earlier exploration of both questing and retreat to the point where the Book's subject seems to be becoming the ambivalences of romance itself. In a Legend which seems on the surface so simple,[97] so many contradictions remain as contradictions, juxtaposed but not resolved into any higher meaning. Some of the Book's most important passages are irreducibly ambiguous, capable of saying at least two things at once, and manage simultaneously to suggest both the possible connection and potential conflict between its principal concerns—bower and quest, inward and outward, origin and issue. Several of its passages explore the possibility that the enclosed bower and forward quest might not be antagonists—either in the sense of Resolved Soul and Created Pleasure in Book II or in the sense of the fragile *tempe* violated by intruders—but rather complements, enabling the knight to emerge from the refreshment of retreat while still drawing from its "well" (Pro. 2. 5). Yet the very lines which suggest this fruitful dependence also contain the alternative—conflict rather than complementarity between the Legend's several opposites.

In the Proem itself, the possibility of continuity between inner and outer, bower and emergence, is expressed in the metaphor of "ripenesse," of the "heauenly seedes" in the hidden "bowre" which burst forth into "honour" (Pro. 3). The sense here of a fruitful connection is continued in the imagery of fruition or pregnancy—the process of bringing to birth—which links the "noursery" of "vertue" with the nurture of the Legend's several children, from Tristram whose "bud" of courtesy "At length breakes forth" (ii. 35. 8-9) to the secret pregnancy of Claribell and the final emergence of Pastorella. The Proem, however, also presents a relation of inward and outward which is not continuity, but conflict. The several "buts" of stanza 5 ("But vertues seat is deepe within the mynd, / And not in outward shows, but inward thoughts defynd," 8-9) reflect a tension between the "hidden" (3. 3) and the manifest, between "true curtesie" (5. 1) and the "forgerie" fashioned only "to please the eies of them, that pas" (5. 3-4).

Lewis, Tuve, and others have consistently argued that the eternal in Spenser is the ground as well as the goal of the temporal, that which enables divagation or wandering to be a species of "play."[98] Yet Book vi, for all its happy endings, recovered origins, and miraculous coincidences, seems to admit of some radical doubt, a doubt which involves the questioning of its most central images. The Proem invokes a fruitful or natural connection between origin and issue, in the image of seeds grown to ripeness or of rivers returned to their "King" (7. 4-5), and seems to align with these the "bloosme of comely courtesie" which "brancheth forth in braue nobilitie" (4. 2-4). Yet Courtesy, if it has its hidden origin "deepe within the mynd" (5. 8), may also emerge as mere *bel sembiante*, a contrast to the nakedness of the Graces (x. 24). "Grace" itself embodies a tension between the uncontrollable (the Graces appear and disappear; grace either strikes or does not) and the art of control: there is both continuity and distance between its various meanings.[99] Calidore is the knight through which the hidden virtue is to be made manifest, but the showing forth of his courteous arts is often indistinguishable from calculation. The "kind courtesies" which he "inuents" (ix. 34. 6) for Pastorella echo the too artful courtesy of Blandina in canto vi, and his adaptation of "manner" to occasion (ix. 36. 2) curiously resembles her ability to temper "words and lookes" (vi. 41. 9). His "queint vsage" (ix. 35. 2) and its contrast with the "lowly things" (35. 5) of Pastorell reflect the tension throughout the Book between the virtue nurtured on a "lowly stalke" (Pro. 4. 3) and the "Courtesie" derived from "Court."

This suggestion of both a continuity and a potential gap or "shade" between origin and issue, inward grace and outward sign, also extends to the more general preoccupation of the Book with origins and sources. The poem itself seems to be returning to its beginnings, as Serena recalls Una, Acidale the House of Holiness, the Hermit Contemplation, and the "harrowing" of the brigands' cave the recovery of Eden. The Legend is even generically in touch with origins, in its return to pastoral, a traditional and, for Spenser, actual early mode. But the Book which asks to be shown the source of its own virtue also calls into question the return to origins or the possibility of their recovery, emphasizing the gap as often as the link between origin and issue, including the "origin" which is etymology ("Of Court it *seemes*, men Courtesie doe call . . ." i. 1. 1, my italics). Courtesy itself is not always traceable to a particular source or "birth," and the examples of the gentle Salvage Man and the savage Sir Terpine both question the predictability of its origin and undercut the singularity of its possible "nourseries." Both continuity and discontinuity with origins are suggested through the copresence in this Legend of real and supposed foundlings. Pastorella is returned to, and recognized by, her natural parents, but the bear baby is *"gotten, not begotten"* of Sir Bruin (iv. 32. 7), and the teasing coincidence of names leaves it comically uncertain whether or not an actual homecoming is involved.

This complication of the return to origins also finally extends to the origins of romance itself. Countless readers have recorded the sense in this Book of returning to the roots of the genre, in a Legend whose anthology of romance motifs runs the gamut from Wild Men, faery rings, and secret cells to brigands, mysterious foundlings, and the reunion of parents and children. But there is a sense in which this rehearsal of romance motifs also distances them, these origins like other origins in the Legend both sought and seen as retreating. The Book multiplies its tales of the unexpected or miraculous end, and the venerable romance *topos* of conversion is reflected in the unexpected changes of heart in Briana and Crudor, in Sir Enias, and perhaps in Mirabella. The revelation of Pastorella's birthmark is the romance tale of recognition and restoration in its purest form. But it might also be said that Spenser is deliberately distancing these images. The seeming contradiction between the romance of infinite delay and the romance of happy endings dissolves in this Legend, where the happy ending is itself a form of retreat. A sense of miraculous fortune hovers over Calepine's coming upon the cannibals just in time to save Serena. But "fortune" is here, as in Ariosto, the poet himself, and Spenser seems uncharacteristically at pains in this Book to point to the resultant artifice of its transitions:

> The which discourse as now I must delay,
> Till *Mirabellaes* fortunes I doe further say.
>
> (vii. 50. 8-9)

> But first it falleth me by course to tell
> Of faire *Serena*, who as earst you heard . . .
>
> (viii. 31. 1-2)

> But day, that doth discouer bad and good,
> Ensewing, made her knowen to him at last:
> The end whereof Ile keepe vntill another cast.
>
> (viii. 51. 7-9)

Both the marking of transitions and the careful interweaving of episodes throughout Book vi contribute to this sense of artifice, an impression which Spenser usually mutes.[100] Calidore disappears in canto iii and does not reappear until canto ix, a digression which calls forth another of the narrator's metaphors for his own activity (ix. 1). The happy endings, by their very nature, seem contrived. The story of the foundling Calepine saves is virtually a parody of the fortunate coincidence. The baby who begins as the prey of a "cruell Beare" (iv. 17. 8), is borne by Calepine, and finally, in answer to a prophecy, becomes the heir of "Sir Bruin," seems a *reductio ad absurdum* of the romance tale and its almost perfect circular form. Each of the Legend's images of refuge—of the closed or embowered circle or the fortunate ending—is shrouded by a simultaneous sense of distance and contingency. The happy ending whereby Sir Bruin gets his heir is specifically said to be a miraculous forestalling of a fiend called "Cormoraunt": it is, that is to say, a tale told against time. But canto xi—the canto of the carnage in the brigands' cave—opens with a reflection on the impossibility of any "sure happinesse," "on earth too great a blessednesse" to last.

This sense of the fragility of the enclosed space and happy ending extends finally to the status of words and the power of poetry itself. Book vi is a highly literary legend: "Meliboe" is a name taken from both Virgil and Chaucer; Aladine suggests the printers Aldine; "Colin Clout" is an allusion both to Skelton and to Spenser. "Turning all to game" (iv. iv. 13. 1) is a frequent image, in Book iv, for the *concordia* of gracious speech, its crucial element of "play," and this "play" reaches its climax upon Mt. Acidale. But if words too are part of making outward what is inward, and thus part of this Legend's reflections on the *form* of emergence, there is a sense in this literary legend that words alone are by no means certain good. The "glas" of the Proem (5.5, "Which see not perfect things but in a glas . . .") is both that which separates inward and outward (5.6, "that glasse so gay, that it can blynd . . .") and the shadowy *speculum* of mediation. The vision on Mt. Acidale has to do not only with vision—as in the episode of Contemplation in Book i—but with poetic mediation, as Colin Clout's "dilation" (x. 21. 1: "Tho gan that shepheard thus for to dilate . . .") fills in the gap left by the disappearance of the Graces. This "dilation" is itself a form of emergence or coming-out: it has a Hermes or hermeneutic function in relation to its source,[101] like the "meantime" of procession between origin and end in the Neo-Platonic *dilatio* of Mutabilitie. But it is also a sign of absence, and it is a tribute to the complexity of Spenser's double vision—of the limitation or loss signalled by this "dilation" and yet also of its worth—that readers have tended to stress one *or* the other.[102]

Courtesy, like poetry, depends upon the art of words: Calidore is, for Spenser's knights, untypically short on weaponry and the implication is that words are his substitute. But when, in the fight against the brigands, Calidore finds a "sword of better say" (xi. 47. 5), the suggestion in the *double entendre* is that words have failed him, that the humanist Hercules Gallicus has reverted to the more purely physical hero.[103] His "harrowing" of the brigands' den recalls the descent of Orpheus to regain Eurydice, and Pastorella's restoration seems to be a successful version of that myth. But the happy ending of Pastorella's return is specifically put before the pursuit of the Blatant Beast, and Calidore's victory is only temporary.

Spenser's own claim to be the "Bryttane Orpheus" sounds implicitly through the *Shepheardes Calender* and *The Faerie Queene*: Orpheus in the "October" eclogue (28-30) is the legendary tamer of Cerberus and in the Legend of Friendship (IV. ii. 1) the civilization hero of Comes' description, the singer who calmed the discord of the Argonauts. Spenser's image of himself as an Orpheus draws at least partly on that portion of the myth which celebrates the poet's triumph over time; but the Orpheus of Book VI is more the dismembered and unsuccessful one.[104] The Graces can no more be recalled than can Eurydice. And the descendant of Cerberus, the "fearefull dog" (xii. 36. 9) Calidore leads "in bondage" through "all Faery land" (37. 1-5), escapes to attack even the "gentle Poets rime" (40. 8). The Book in which the possible complementarity of withdrawal and emergence is figured by the simultaneous advance and retreat of the dancing Graces, ends instead with a splitting apart or distancing of directions. The happy romance ending of Pastorella's return retreats from view as the narrator leaves mother and daughter to a joy whose privacy he cannot describe (xii. 20-22), while the Blatant Beast seems in the final stanzas ("So now . . . now . . . of late") to be advancing towards us, breaking through the circle of the poem into the harsh world of the present.

Book vi opens with a petition to be guided in the "strange waies" (Pro. 2. 8) of the "delightfull land of Faery" (1. 2), which "none can find, but who was taught them by the Muse" (2. 9), and the poet asks to have revealed, and to be led into, a "siluer bowre" far from "wicked worlds disdaine" (3. 4). But the gap between hidden bower and the poet's world seems to be widening in the final lines, as "Pastorell" is left behind and Calidore's victory (xii. 38-39) recedes into the past of a Faery Land forlorn. The suggestion through the Legend is that to inquire too closely into origins—or to penetrate a secret "shade"—would be to intrude upon a privacy, like that of a grace which cannot be forced or the Graces who disappear when Calidore determines to question their identity. But here this circumspection seems to be yielding to its other aspect, a sense of being ineluctably excluded from this bower, or unable to find the "way." The shadow which falls between origin and issue, bower and emergence, may finally be that of a retreat whose shade is impenetrable and a "noursery" whose location cannot be "revealed" (Pro. 3), not even by the "Muse."

The duality of judgment surrounding Calidore's pastoral retreat—seen both as a deviation from his "first quest" ("Vnmyndfull of his vow and high beheast," "entrapt of loue, which him betrayd," x. 1. 3, 7) and as refusal to "hunt still after shadowes vaine" (x. 2. 7)—has provoked a critical controversy which seeks to settle what Spenser leaves in ambiguous suspension, and this ambiguity extends to the stanzas which treat of the "staying" or "straying" of the poem itself. The same opening to canto xii which defends Calidore's delay offers a defense of the poet's own digression or wandering ("Right so it fares with me in this long way, / Whose course is often stayd, yet neuer is astray," 1. 8-9). Yet, in the *topos* which connects poetic and actual "feet," the "spacious" ways

and ravishing "delight" of the Book's opening stanza suggest
the possibility that poetry itself may be a siren song, an invitation to oblivion ("forget thereby") as persuasive as Phaedria's; and this voice in Spenser anticipates Romantics and
Romantic critics since who note that *accidia*, the poem's moral
evil, is also part of its poetic vagrancy, or "charm."

Spenser's sixth and last completed Book thus carries a resonance which provides not only a retrospect on romance but a
sense of its prospects, the fortunes of the form from Milton to
the Romantics, and beyond. Coleridge observed in a lecture
"the marvelous independence and true imaginative absence of
all particular space or time" in Spenser's poem, adding "it is
truly in land of Faery, that is, of mental space. The poet has
placed you in a dream, a charmed sleep, and you neither wish,
nor have the power, to inquire where you are, or how you
got there."[105] His remark, however revealing of later concep-
tions of romance, falls short of Spenser's fine distinction between placed and unplaced, history and "faerie." But it does
carry further a suggestion already implicit in the poem's final
Legend, that romance itself is a bower, charm, or region of
wandering, an evasion, and yet one perhaps necessary to the
life of poetry, the only chance for creation in a Mammon
world. If the displaced "faerie" at the opening of Book II anticipates the delights of Wallace Stevens' "Description without Place," the questioning here of both bower and questing,
shady retreat and the demands of the "waking" world, leads
in later versions of romance to a more anxious opposition. To
emphasize the sense in Book VI of romance reflecting upon itself is not to substitute a Romantic reading of *The Faerie
Queene* for a more sensitively historical one, but simply to
suggest what in the poem itself was to make it the romance
poets' poem. Spenser's final Legend seems to privilege neither
the overturning of the bower by actuality nor its own impulse
to retreat; yet if it explores the possibility of a fruitful connection between the two, it also acknowledges its failure, the ap-
prehension of a distance not diminishing but widening. The
"end" of the embowered space in Book VI is as often catastrophe or loss as it is fulfillment, and the simultaneously sus-

pect and protective "staying" of such spaces, including the poem itself, intensifies an element already in the poem and transforms it. *The Faerie Queene* is imbued with a sense of the doubleness of all things, the perception that "some virtues and some vices are so nicely distinguished, and so resembling each other as they are often confounded."[106] But the ambiguities and unresolved contradictions of Book VI seem to participate less in the poem's network of parody doubles and real and counterfeit forms than in a genuine ambivalence, what may be finally not a doubleness of vision but a doubleness of mind.

The sense of both the desirability and the danger of delay or wandering remains in this Book in suspension, just as the final stanzas of the *Mutabilitie Cantos* leave the question open, impenetrable to a critical controversy whose very assumption of a definitive or final reading may not be appropriate to the deliberate, or perhaps, as one reader suggests, simply fortuitous, ambiguity of the closing lines.[107] In the speaker's last reflections on the "doome" of Nature and the extent of Mutability, the ambiguity of "loath" ("Which makes me loath this state of life so tickle, / And loue of things so vaine to cast away," VII. viii. 1. 6-7) leaves finally uncertain which is prized, "mutability" or its ending. The movement of the syntax is not, as so often in Milton, a *correction* of the first line by the second, but, characteristically for Spenser, a *complication* of it. And the closing lines—both the prayer for the final "Sabbath" and the claim that "all that moueth, doth in *Change* delight" (vii. 2. 6-9)—leave finally open the question of which is uppermost, the dilation of a creation he would be "loath" to leave or the precipitation of the fall of all that stands between him and the promised "Eternity."

III. Milton

Truth indeed came once into the world with her divine Master, and was a perfect shape most glorious to look on: but when he ascended, and his Apostles after him were laid asleep, then strait arose a wicked race of deceivers, who as that story goes of the Ægyptian Typhon with his conspirators, how they dealt with the good Osiris, took the virgin Truth, hewd her lovely form into a thousand peeces, and scatter'd them to the four winds. From that time ever since, the sad friends of Truth, such as durst appear, imitating the careful search that Isis made for the mangl'd body of Osiris, went up and down gathering up limb by limb still as they could find them.

Areopagitica

The Vision of Eve

IN Book IV of *Paradise Lost*, in the midst of Paradise, the Mother of Mankind recounts the first moments of her creation:

> That day I oft remember, when from sleep
> I first awak't, and found myself repos'd
> Under a shade on flow'rs, much wond'ring where
> And what I was, whence thither brought, and how.
> Not distant far from thence a murmuring sound
> Of waters issu'd from a Cave and spread
> Into a liquid Plain, then stood unmov'd
> Pure as th' expanse of Heav'n; I thither went
> With unexperienc't thought, and laid me down
> On the green bank, to look into the clear
> Smooth Lake, that to me seem'd another Sky.

As I bent down to look, just opposite,
A Shape within the wat'ry gleam appear'd
Bending to look on me, I started back,
It started back, but pleas'd I soon return'd,
Pleas'd it return'd as soon with answering looks
Of sympathy and love; there I had fixt
Mine eyes till now, and pin'd with vain desire,
Had not a voice thus warn'd me, What thou seest,
What there thou seest fair Creature is thyself,
With thee it came and goes: but follow me,
And I will bring thee where no shadow stays
Thy coming, and thy soft imbraces, hee
Whose image thou art, him thou shalt enjoy
Inseparably thine, to him shalt bear
Multitudes like thyself, and thence be call'd
Mother of human Race . . .

(IV. 449-75)[1]

The obvious literary echo of the passage—noted from the earliest commentaries—is Ovid's description of Narcissus, the figure whose fate Eve suggests and then avoids by turning from self-reflection to the one "Whose image" she is. But, though the association is only indirectly introduced through the possibility of a pun on "Eve," this moment of self-reflection and turning also recalls that interval of decision which Patristic tradition described as "evening" or "twilight" vision. In puzzling over what Genesis intends when it refers to God's separation of the light from the darkness on the First Day, before the creation of the physical sun, Augustine, and Aquinas after him, explained that in the first, "twilight" interval of angelic existence, some of the angels, perceiving within themselves an image or dim reflection of the Creator, turned to the reality above them, to await the eternal morning of the vision face-to-face, while others remained within themselves and sank into eternal night.[2] This separation left no room for a middle ground; indecision, for the angels, was only a temporary twilight and ceased to exist in the final, and definitive, moment of choice.

If indeed, as several commentators suggest, both the Patristic and the Ovidian resonances coexist, Eve's crucial moment of "staying" or self-reflection recalls the structure of the angelic *cogito*; the suspended interval of introspection does not remain static, but moves instead either to acknowledgment of genuine otherness or down into the Narcissistic "shadow" so vividly recalled in the Ovidian coloring of Milton's lines.[3] Raphael will soon arrive to relate to Adam how the recreant angels fell, and Eve's autobiography obliquely prefigures the later narrative. But here the story is not of a fall but of a turning, and the movement of the faithful angels from "evening" to "morning" vision receives its apt poetic reenactment within Milton's other hierarchy, "Hee for God only, shee for God in him" (IV. 299).

The resonances of this wider context, once apprehended, continue to reverberate in the mind. Readers of the poem have frequently sensed that this passage is somehow central within the structure of the epic as a whole.[4] It is echoed in Adam's description of his movement from creation to Creator, prepares for Raphael's account of the War in Heaven, and foreshadows both Satan's later appeal and Adam's turning from the God "Whose image" he is to the reflection of his own image in Eve. Perhaps even more importantly, however, Eve's momentary staying upon her own image becomes within the epic an emblem of all such suspensions, of the pivotal or merely temporary threshold state which may lead either way, up towards dawn or down into night, like the "twilight melted into morn" and "twilight died into the dark" of Tennyson's "The Day-Dream." In the submerged but unmistakable Miltonic pun, the interval of decision before the pool is also, proleptically, the twilight zone of history itself before the final separation of the children of light from the children of darkness, the sixth age of "re-creation" traditionally prefigured by Eve.[5] The image of "evening" unites the threshold state of time with the threshold of choice. If Eve's vision foreshadows the movement of temptation and Fall, it also anticipates the structure of paradise regained.

That "evening" as a figure for the suspended or pivotal might be present here submerged in the momentary irresolution or "staying" of "Eve" is further suggested by the occurrence of this passage within a complex of Miltonic images and puns which link evening with the persistent theme of the pivot or balance, a complex which begins when Satan first sees in prospect this "pendant world" (II. 1052) and culminates in the final event of Book IV, the balancing or weighing of Satan's alternatives in the celestial "Scales." It is not by accident that Book IV, our first view, after Hell and Heaven, of Creation, should be virtually the evening or "even-ing" Book of *Paradise Lost*. Augustine and Aquinas in their descriptions of "vespertinal" consciousness read "evening" in Genesis as the space of creation, that which is distinct both from the complete knowledge of the Creator and from "night."[6] Like twilight, a temporarily suspended middle, or "short Arbiter" (IX. 50) between light and dark, Eden itself not only literally hangs from Heaven but hangs precariously in the balance as Satan approaches it, in the crepuscular or "dubious light" (II. 1042) of a kind of "dawn" (1037).

The first allusion to the advent of evening in Book IV is significantly accompanied by a pun on its pendency. Satan reaches Eden just as the sun is about to set:

> the Sun
> Declin'd was hasting now with prone career
> To th' Ocean Isles, and in th' ascending Scale
> Of Heav'n the Stars that usher Evening rose . . .
>   (IV. 352-55)

"Ascending scale" is a characteristically Miltonic pun, since the "Stars that usher Evening" must now be rising in Libra, the constellation in which Satan's alternatives will be balanced at the end of the Book. But the "scale" of heaven also implies the balancing of light and darkness associated with Libra as the equinoctial sign, "Balance bright, / Equall divider of the Day and Night,"[7] an appropriate preface to the description of a world which is not only, before the Fall, perpetually equinoctial, but at this particular moment precariously "pendant."

We are never allowed, in the midst of this pendency, to forget utterly—though we are allowed and even invited by the verse to forget temporarily—whose gaze we are seeing this poised and fragile world through; but after Satan departs with his ominous warning ("enjoy, till I return, / Short pleasures, for long woes are to succeed," 534–35), what follows is a remarkable series of variations upon the evening, or evensong, theme, as evening itself lengthens out to cover a space of almost three hundred lines. The first of these (the "setting Sun" against "the eastern Gate of Paradise / Levell'd his ev'ning Rays," 540–43) associates evening with "levelling," as the refractive effect of earth's atmosphere creates an apparent slowing down, or staying, of the sun's more precipitous descent. The second ("Thither came Uriel, gliding through the Even / On a Sun-beam," 555–56) combines in its punning play the evening which is both time of day and balance, or suspension, of extremes. Bentley's famous objection to this "Even" ("I never heard but here, that the evening was a Place or Space to glide through")[8] misses the way in which Milton's evening becomes a kind of "even-ing," a dilated and gradual descent. The image transposes time, for a moment, into space; the descent of Uriel is softened, graduated, like the gentler light of evening itself.

The "Sun-beam" here looks forward to the punning "beam"—both light and balance—on which Uriel returns (590–92), and both prepare not only for the final image of the Scales (997–1002) and its resonance of Miltonic puns on physical and mental "weighing" ("pendulous," "pendant," "pensive," "ponderous"), but, more immediately, for the masterfully graduated advent of evening when Uriel departs:

> Now came still Ev'ning on, and Twilight gray
> Had in her sober Livery all things clad;
> Silence accompanied, for Beast and Bird,
> They to thir grassy Couch, these to thir Nests
> Were slunk, all but the wakeful Nightingale;

She all night long her amorous descant sung;
Silence was pleas'd: now glow'd the Firmament
With living Sapphires: Hesperus that led
The starry Host, rode brightest, till the Moon
Rising in clouded Majesty, at length
Apparent Queen unveil'd her peerless light,
And o'er the dark her Silver Mantle threw.

(IV. 598-609)

There is, here, progression without surprise. The nightingale "all night long" keeps Silence from becoming too absolute, just as the appearance of Hesperus, or the Evening Star, bridges the potential moment of darkness between sunset and the rising of the moon. Evening "evens" the passage from Day to Night, into an orderly succession, or gradual fade-in, of lights. No sharp, epiphanic break intrudes. The movement from lesser to brighter light is mantled in a succession of graded steps which, syntactically, almost overlap. The "sober livery" of twilight is followed only by the "silver mantle" of the moon. "Unveil'd," with its epiphanic overtones, is balanced by a kind of reveiling, and "apparent" mutes succession and epiphany, heir-apparent and appearing queen, within a gradual ascent.

The twilight moment which for Eve represents a dangerous "staying," an interval which must be crossed, is here, through a series of such images, both dilated and "stayed." G. Wilson Knight singles these lines out from the more doctrinal pressures which elsewhere crowd the poem, as one of its brief respites, or more pleasing suspensions.[9] But Adam, at the vespers in Eden, is careful to distinguish the features of this evening retreat from its more suspect romance analogues and to explain the function of such "staying" within the larger rhythm of night and day, rest and the resumption of "labour" (610-33). Evening is not in his description a static balance or perpetual retreat but rather precursor or *mediatrix*, part, as in Genesis, of the rhythm of creation. And the theme of preparation sounds again in his explanation to Eve of the lights which prepare for the coming of dawn:

Those have thir course to finish, round the Earth,
By morrow Ev'ning, and from Land to Land
In order, though to Nations yet unborn,
Minist'ring light prepar'd, they set and rise;
Lest total darkness should by Night regain
Her old possession, and extinguish life
In Nature and all things, which these soft fires
Not only enlighten, but with kindly heat
Of various influence foment and warm,
Temper or nourish, or in part shed down
Thir stellar virtue on all kinds that grow
On Earth, made hereby apter to receive
Perfection from the Sun's more potent Ray.

(IV. 661-73)

The function of evening and of the lights which, as it were, extend it until day here again recalls the Augustinian threshold, that middle space which may lead either down into night or to the dawning whose greater light it figures. Evening, then morning, in Augustine's commentary, is the rhythm of Genesis as the repeated structure of conversion from creation to Creator, from the shadowy, dim *speculum* of I Corinthians 13 to the vision of the Sun himself. For those who patiently await the vision face-to-face, there is no night, but only a period of transition, or gradual succession, from evening to morn.[10] Evening, in Adam's description, is both threshold and harbinger, the temporal counterpart of the promise to Eve ("follow me, / And I will bring thee where no shadow stays / Thy coming"). But this image of evening as preparation for dawn is joined, even before the Fall, by its alternative, a "twilight" vision which leads simply down into "night."

The precarious pendency of evening through Book IV both as a space in time and as a figure for the threshold of choice is made even more striking by the way in which Book V, as it opens, both plays with and ominously inverts the previous Book's "even-song," in the dream which moves not upwards, to vision or "enlightening," but down into the very darkness which "Eve" like "evening" stands poised before. Eve's first words on awakening strengthen the implicit anal-

ogy, in the earlier scene by the pool, between the movement
from Eve to Adam and that from evening to dawn, as both
Adam and morning are subsumed within a single object: "O
Sole in whom my thoughts find all repose, / My Glory, my
Perfection, glad I see / Thy face, and Morn return'd . . ." (v.
28-30). The passage which follows is remarkable for its anxious repetition of "night" both as dangerous impasse and alternative direction ("for I this Night, / Such night till this I
never pass'd," 30-31; "offense and trouble, which my mind /
Knew never till this irksome night," 34-35), but even more so
for the subtle twisting of earlier images which begins as Eve
recounts her Satan-inspired dream:

> Why sleep'st thou Eve? now is the pleasant time,
> The cool, the silent, save where silence yields
> To the night-warbling Bird, that now awake
> Tunes sweetest his love-labor'd song; now reigns
> Full Orb'd the Moon, and with more pleasing light
> Shadowy sets off the face of things . . .
>
> (v. 38-43)

The passage is so strikingly an echo, or virtual Satanic quota-
tion, of the advent of Evening in Book IV, with its queenly
"Moon" (IV. 606) and "wakeful Nightingale" (602), that it
more than evokes in the reader Adam's later response (v.
114-16: "Some such resemblances methinks I find / Of our
last Ev'ning's talk, in this thy dream, / But with addition
strange . . ."). The "addition strange" which most pointedly
recalls the earlier discussion of evening and perverts it to
Eve's own self-regard is the conversion of her questioning of
the function of evening lights when none is there to see (IV.
657-58: "for whom / This glorious sight, when sleep hath
shut all eyes?") in the invitation by Satan to the Narcissism of
an involuted or purely self-regarding "eve" ("Heav'n wakes
with all his eyes, / Whom to behold but thee," v. 44-45). The
echo masterfully conflates both parts of Book IV—the explanation of the mediatory role of evening lights and the gazing
of Eve at her own image in the pool—in a way which
suggests that "eve" may be not benign *mediatrix* but the im-

passe or limbo of the *intra nos* or self-regarding vision, and the
echo of the conversion of Eve at the pool to the higher vision
and presence of Adam to which she is called is here both
strengthened and reversed in the line "I rose as at thy call, but
found thee not" (48). Though Eve here, like Eden itself, is
still "pendant" ("Evil into the mind of God or Man / May
come and go, so unapprov'd, and leave / No spot or blame
behind"), the sense of the possible proximity of "Eve" to
"Night" is conveyed syntactically by the characteristically
Miltonic juxtaposition which places them in sequence before
a new line can undo the link:

> Thus Eve her Night
> Related, and thus Adam answer'd sad.
>
> (93-94)

Echoes of both evening visions—the conversion of Eve and
the darker alternative—are gathered in the image which precedes the very narrative of temptation Eve's dream proleptically outlines, as the temporary threshold of evening at the
beginning of Book IX recalls once again the Hesperus of Book
IV but follows it now only by darkness, a "fall" in which the
earlier graduated rhythm is replaced by a precipitate movement from a definitive "sunk" to an already accomplished
"had veil'd":

> The Sun was sunk, and after him the Star
> Of Hesperus, whose Office is to bring
> Twilight upon the Earth, short Arbiter
> Twixt Day and Night, and now from end to end
> Night's Hemisphere had veil'd the Horizon round . . .
>
> (IX. 48-52)

What ensues, in the temptation and fall of Eve, combines all
the cumulative echoes of the moment of self-reflection in the
pool, the images of evening as "balance," and Eve's evening
dream into a *mundus inversus* in which "up" and "down" are
confused and where Eve, sinking into the spiritual darkness
prefigured by the literal fall of night, praises the fruit "of Divine effect / To open Eyes" (IX. 865-66).

Before and after this critical moment, evening and its pendency stand as signs for the interval just prior to decision, or ending: Eve's two visions and Adam's description of evening as precursor, preparation for the greater light of Day, anticipate the alternatives of direction or "turning" in the postlapsarian "twilight." Within the familiar theology of mediation, of Christ as Morning Star or Sun of Righteousness, "evening" is the image of the mediate, the space of creation as the threshold of choice. But as figure for the pendant or the pivotal, a space which may lead down as well as up, this image leads finally into a wider field of Milton's poetics, the problem of all mediation, or middle states, and the relation of that problem to the twilight, or suspended, threshold of "romance."

Shadowy Types: The Romance of Language

AUGUSTINE extends the vespertinal metaphor to the mediation of the "shadowy Type" and accuses of indolence those who "linger in the figure" even after the Light is come:

> Alas for those who abandon you as leader and who stray in what are but your footprints, who love the signs which you show but not yourself, who forget your meaning, O wisdom, most gracious light of a purified mind! . . . Woe to those who turn away from your light and love to linger in their darkness! It is as if they turned their backs upon you, they are held fast in the shadow cast on them by their works of the flesh, and yet what delights them even there they still receive from the brightness shed by your light. But love of the shadow makes the soul's eye too lazy and weak to endure your sight. . . .[11]

The "staying" of Eve upon her shadow gains from this figural context an even greater resonance: the interval of self-reflection is the threshold not only of decision but of meaning. Adam's explanation to Eve of the function of the evening lights thus moves as well within a tradition in which the "heavens" which declare the glory of God in Psalm 19 are the apostles of the Word, and Old Testament *figurae* the stars which prepare for the advent of the Morning Star.[12] The movement from evening to morning is, implicitly, the movement from "shadowy Types" to "Truth."

The spiritual sloth of "staying" or "straying" in the veiled realm of the sign is, of course, by Milton's century, a commonplace of exegesis. Origen begins an extended meditation on the sustenance provided in the wilderness—quails or "flesh" at evening, manna or "bread" in the morning—with the mediation of the Incarnation, the veiled presence of the Word born into the twilight of human history, but soon extends the progression to a theory of reading, the movement from the "evening" of the Mosaic scriptures to the "morning" when Christ taught the disciples how to read. Samuel Mather, in Milton's day, begins his study of the "shadowy Types" with a reminder that the figural language of the Old Testament shares in the ambiguity of all veiled or twilight states. Seen from the proper perspective, the "end" revealed in Christ, "they do exceedingly enlighten." Uninterpreted, they lead down into darkness.[13] For Mather and the Puritan exegetes, the crucial emphasis on interpretation, on the perspective taken from the End, is central to the contemporary warfare between "old" and "new" testaments, the maintenance of the freedom of the Gospel in the face of a Church which has attempted "to dig Moses out of his Grave," to return to the "dark and legal shadows" of Jewish ritual even after "Christ the Substance is come."[14]

Mather is no more concerned with this *agon* than Milton himself, for whom the shadowy realm of the figure, now abrogated, remains only as a dark temptation, an invitation to the siren error of a corrupted church. The whole polemic of *The Reason of Church Government* is, as in Mather, against the prelates' inversion of the Testaments, the substitution of shadow for substance, servile imitation for freedom and Truth. And the continuing temptation to the Son in *Paradise Regained* is to be preempted by his own foreshadowings, simply to succeed or to imitate the figures he came to fulfill.[15]

In *Paradise Regained*, the crucial movement of fulfillment depends upon an essential discontinuity, on the sense of a reality which may be shadowed by, but is not synonymous with, any of its "figures." The notion of *figura* itself traditionally depends upon a crucial element of failure or destruction. Only by an act which destroyed the Garden could the Garden come to be a "type" of the Truth. Only when David "failed" as king could he become a figure for the Kingship of Christ.[16] If Old Testament "figures" were stars which had, as in Adam's description, their ministry to perform, they were also lesser lights to be eclipsed, like the stars in the "Nativity Ode" which wait patiently for the coming of the Light and then depart, their "evening" the "Morning" of a new birth (69-76).

The vespertinal in this tradition was also a figure for mediation, or figuration, in a larger sense, beyond the particularity of the biblical "type." Early Christian writers extended the dynamic of *figura*—its simultaneous continuity and discontinuity—to the "foreshadowings" of pagan myth, at once approximations of the Truth and treacherous deviations from it. In Justin Martyr, for example, the pagan examples of Orpheus, Aesculapius, and Hercules are close enough to the reality of Christ to be at once useful and dangerous. In the first *Apology*, the pagan heroes first form a crucial part of the argument that there is nothing in the new faith that pagan belief does not already acknowledge. When, however, the text moves from defensive to offensive, the sons of Jove are no longer useful analogies to the sonship of Christ but diabolic distortions of the Messianic prophecies. Analogy viewed from the other side becomes parody. And the same pagan example which provides in the first instance a bridge to understanding becomes in the next a dangerous stumbling block.[17] Clement of Alexandria makes use of pagan myths as *exempla*, but he also pictures the multiple "saviours" of the heathen as "the slippery and hurtful deviations from the truth which draw man down from heaven and cast him into the abyss."[18] The concern at once to join and to separate that which is joined is repeated, only more anxiously, by the Puritan mythographers of Milton's day for whom the analysis of myth must move quickly from analogy to difference, to the radical gap between Christian truth and any of its "types."[19]

This central dynamic of *figura*, approximation and difference, becomes, in *Paradise Lost*, the fundamental dialectic of a Christian poetics. But it also involves the poem in its central contradiction. However much his story might be the "original, archetypal story which later history and myth distort," Milton must, as Thomas Greene remarks, "nonetheless employ these distorted fragments to reconstruct for us a living experience of the true."[20] The enterprise is, by definition, "preposterous," and if the reader becomes a kind of Isis reassembling the shattered fragments of Truth, he must also be continually reminded that this "gathering" is not enough, that the whole remains greater than the reassembled parts. Something of what this implies within the poem was captured in Hazlitt's famous remark that Milton's is a genius which "the nearer it approaches to others, becomes more distinct from them."[21] It accounts for the incredible lightness of a learning which "has the effect of intuition," a poetic sense of play not unlike that of the elephant wreathing his "Lithe Proboscis" (IV. 347). But it also accounts for something which moves the poem very far from play, for the constant sense of the ultimate seriousness of the difference.

The assertion of discontinuity in Milton often takes the form of what might be called the syntactic feint, the movement in which line endings become invisible turning points, interstices in which a mistaken continuity is reversed. "Hesperian Fables true, / If true, here only . . ." (IV. 250-51) becomes one of many syntactic mottos, or models, of the description of Paradise, the simultaneous evoking of an image or surmise (here "true") and the redirecting *caveat*, the undertow which reveals that truth to be contingent. If the Narcissistic danger in the figure is that it too, like the image Eve contemplates, can "stay" a coming, the task of the prophetic poet is at once to employ and to subvert its staying power. The "Graces," "Hours," and the "Castalian Spring" come forth to make the unimaginable imaginable, but all are undermined by the Miltonic "greater than," the sense that great things finally cannot be compared with small. Tasso's theory of *asprezza*, of the roughening of poetic line, becomes in Milton a syntactic method in which error, in its ruin, leads to truth.

What may be said of Milton's use of pagan myth may also be said of his dialectical use of all media, including the images of the poem itself:

> The other shape,
> If shape it might be call'd that shape had none
> Distinguishable in member, joint, or limb . . .
>
> (II. 666–68)

The description of Death in Book II is virtually an initiation into a special kind of reading, into the process of imaging, retracting, and reimagining in pure contingency. The poetic line breaks down as it is read. The concrete image of the "shape" is frustrated by the seeming finality of "shape had none"; but "Distinguishable" qualifies the negative by supplying to the eye the images of "member, joint, or limb" at the same time as it restates their absence. The eye returns for focus to the central "call'd," to what is finally, in such a context, the sheer contingency of naming. Milton simultaneously builds the lofty rhyme and undermines the potential Babel of figures, and this movement of construction and deconstruction becomes in *Paradise Lost* part of a poetic *Aufhebung* which suggests how the same poet might be at once image-maker and iconoclast.

William G. Madsen explains this phenomenon by suggesting that Milton telescopes the Joachite age of the Son with that of the Spirit, the "intermediary period" of reading and the Word with the end, or abolition, of all mediation, the "Sabbath" in which *significantia* gives way to *significata*.[22] For Milton, argues Madsen, this passage has already been made in the ascent

> From shadowy Types to Truth, from Flesh to Spirit,
> From imposition of strict Laws, to free
> Acceptance of large Grace, from servile fear
> To filial, works of Law to works of Faith.
>
> (XII. 303–6)

Yet, in another sense, the decisive passage is still to come. Milton's poem participates in the ambiguity of that twilight interval of time in which though "figures," like oracles, have ceased, figuration remains. And if awareness of this tension necessitates a straining of poetic language beyond itself—a movement from the shadow of the figure to the reality it adumbrates—the flow also potentially moves in the opposite direction, back from the high noon of apocalypse or revelation to the attractive *vestigia* of the poem itself. The tension is not unlike that already suggested by the poem's images of evening, the difference between "twilight" as theological figure, or even as that combination of image and structural principle Frye calls the "archetype," and the less directed, almost autonomous description of the "Twilight gray" (IV. 598) which Knight felt escaped the epic's more purely theological pressures. The first is figurally directed, a reminder that all twilight states, like the dark mirror of mediation in I Corinthians 13, exist to be superseded. The second, more relaxed, creates, as Bentley, however obtusely, grasped, a sense of extended space, a place which of itself dilates and lingers.

Milton's greatest poem, then, participates in a tension we have hitherto identified with the uncertain middle realm of "romance." The shadowy and ambiguous realm of wandering becomes, in a sense, the radical instability of linguistic signs and the simultaneous attraction of their variety. Though Milton formally rejected the genre of romance in favor of epic and implicitly the "faerie" example of Spenser for something higher, *Paradise Lost*, within English poetry, takes romance beyond the strictly generic and thus provides a prospect from which to look before and after. "Error," as recent critics have reminded us, becomes the romance of the figure, and the suspended threshold state of "dubbio," of Hercules at the Crossroads, becomes at once the crucial middle space of trial and the activity of reading.[23] Milton makes a quest implicit in all romance into the central one: the knight's quest becomes, as in Bunyan, a pilgrim's progress, but the pilgrim is now the reader himself.

There are, however, at least two possible perspectives on this "romance" in Milton. In the first, Milton, like God, puts his people to the test, or text, and their wanderings, or errors, become a necessary part of the exodus from "shadowy Types" to "Truth." In this respect, Milton's own implicit theory of reading approaches, as Stanley Fish suggests, his description of the oblique pedagogy of Christ:

> . . . the Disciples had bin longer bred up under the Pharisaean doctrin, then under that of Christ, and so no marvel though they yet retain'd the infection of loving old licentious customs; . . . But why did not Christ seeing their error informe them? for good cause; it was his profest method not to teach them all things at all times, but each thing in due place and season. Christ said *Luke* 22, that *hee who had no sword should sell his garment and buy one*: the Disciples tooke it in a manifest wrong sense, yet our Saviour did not there informe them better. . . . Yet did he not omitt to sow within them the seeds of sufficient determining, agen the time that his promis'd spirit should bring all things to their memory.[24]

The interval between the sowing of "the seeds of sufficient determining" and "the time that his promis'd spirit should bring all things to their memory" is the hermeneutic analogue of the space between advent and apocalypse, a kind of "second coming" of recognition. Meaning, as in Spenser, assumes a meantime, an interval which includes the possibility of error. Eve's "staying" upon the shadow in preference for the substance, with its echo of the Augustinian "twilight" of the mediate, becomes a figure for the potentially seductive medium of the poem itself. The "timely" trial of the Lady in *Comus*, waylaid in the "tangl'd Wood" (181), becomes, in *Paradise Lost*, the crucial middle time of interpretation, the pivotal or pendant zone which could lead either way. In a dialectical process which involves, potentially, as much risk as the primal scene of temptation, the judgment on readers who do not "come through" may be not unlike that of Augustine on those who "linger in the figure" and never reach the "End," and Milton's text becomes one of the "Tablets of Stone" which the Spirit, in the process of reading, internalizes and transforms.

The other, less unidirectional perspective unfixes the stable hierarchy of inspired author and ephebe-reader and suggests the ways in which the shadowy attractions of the figure exert their power over even this authority, the unidirectionality of the authorized version. This second view is arguable, perhaps, only by inference, and may be finally, like the problem of Milton's "Satanism," a question which exists only in the realm of speculation; but it does point to something subversive in poetry itself, an error, or deviance, which perhaps cannot be fully "redeemed." Milton very early dedicated himself to the writing of a work not "to be obtain'd by the invocation of Dame Memory and her Siren daughters, but by devout prayer to that eternall Spirit who can enrich with all utterance and knowledge."[25] The separation, however, is not as absolute in practice. Making present may be the promise of prophetic poetry, but its potential stumbling block, its shadow, is representation. In a Romantic rewriting of *Paradise Regained*, the encounter of "shadowy Types" and "Truth," imitation and abrogation, might be recast as a gothic *agon*, a potential victory for the shadows over the new Original. But that tension is already present in Milton. Like Blake, whose final debt to the mediation of the senses only subliminally appears in the ironies of a poem such as "To Tirzah," the poet of *Paradise Lost* may encounter the primal shadow in figuration itself, a representation already preempted by the past, still inextricably wedded to "Dame Memory and her Siren daughters."

The first of these perspectives—the movement from "error" to correction, shadowy type to Truth—makes Milton's poem into what Fish describes as a kind of "scaffolding" which falls away, one of the century's self-consuming artefacts.[26] From this perspective, reading, like liturgy, serves to bring the reader to the point where its mediation is no longer needed, to a revelation beyond its scope. Such a radical theory of reading helps at least partly to explain the peculiar form of Milton's epic. E.M.W. Tillyard saw in *Paradise Lost* what he called a "domestication" of both crisis and epic, the "crisis" of the poem being not that moment in which Eve succumbs to temptation, but the whole of Books ix and x, the disintegration and gradual realignment of the relationship between Adam and Eve.[27] Subsequent readers, however, have found the decentering of the crisis even more striking. Viewed at closer range, the poem seems to have no single crisis or center. Instead, it participates in a radical poetics in which any analogue or image might be the threshold of vision, a "crisis" in the New Testament sense, and every moment within the sequence a potential discontinuity. Leavis's complaint that Milton's verse works by "ritual" may simply be the other side of the realization that every line in the poem is a potential invitation to apocalypse, that the essential revelation or "end" is not the vanishing point in a linear tract of time but an insistently present possibility.[28]

What qualifies Fish's argument—his charting of the implications of the reading process to its end—is that this endpoint is finally discontinuous, or unknowable. This "indécidabilité" is, of course, part of the dynamic of all prophetic poetry. Dante states the insufficiency of poetry to lead to the end to which it points, an end which depends finally on an event within the reader:

> Trasumanar significar per verba
> non si porìa; però l'essemplo basti
> a cui esperïenza grazia serba.
>
> (*Paradiso* i. 70-72)

Dante's insistence on the figural or fictive nature of his own poem is the hole in his linguistic system that warns against its becoming idolatrous, what Blake called the one "Moment in each Day that Satan cannot find." There is, however, nothing intrinsic to the poem itself which would prevent a determined literalist from reading it as a closed circle, with its last line, like that of *Finnegans Wake*, joining its first. Milton's Satan, in *Paradise Regained*, is a legalist and literalist who objects to

Christ's interpretation of the "bread of life" as "allegoric," and the reader fresh from the Satan of *Paradise Lost* and his version of the Celestial Hierarchy might well wonder how he would have read the *Paradiso*. A poem may lead to "revelation," as evening leads to morning, or shadowy type to truth, but the moment of revelation is by definition discontinuous, beyond signs.

One way of approaching the problem of discontinuity in Milton's epic might be through one of the poem's paradoxes, its curious admixture of the gradual and the apocalyptic. The notion of gradual, or graduated, movement, of procession "by degrees," permeates the poem. Each lower form of unfallen creation, "by gradual scale sublim'd" (v. 483), participates in the ascent through "various degrees / Of substance" (473-74) from "body" to "spirit" (478). The process of angelic digestion, as described by Raphael, "transubstantiates" the "grosser" to the "purer" (416), but it differs only "in degree" from the process of mutual nourishment on the lower rungs of the great alimentary Chain of Nature. The descendental counterpart of the *scala naturae* is the sociable angel's "accommodation" of "spiritual to corporal forms" (573), a condescension which enables, on the part of man, a gradual rise:

> Well hast thou taught the way that might direct
> Our knowledge, and the scale of Nature set
> From centre to circumference, whereon
> In contemplation of created things
> By steps we may ascend to God.
>
> (v. 508-12)

Even the approach of Adam to the vision of Eden is "accommodated," or staged. "There is," as Geoffrey Hartman observes, "a stairway even to paradise."[29]

The Fall, then, is, from this perspective, an attempt to hasten the ascent, to circumvent the process of education by degrees, and to repeat the error of the angel who thought that "one step higher" would set him "highest" (IV. 50-51) and who enters Paradise in one "bound" (181). Milton's God vir-

tually equates the space of gradual ascent with the intervening
time of trial, with the testing, in one man, of

> a Race
> Of men innumerable, there to dwell,
> Not here, till by degrees of merit rais'd
> They open to themselves at length the way
> Up hither, under long obedience tri'd,
> And Earth be chang'd to Heav'n, and Heav'n to Earth,
> One Kingdom, Joy and Union without end.
>
> (VII. 155-61)

It is precisely the attempt to foreshorten the period of patience
and "obedience"—to proceed directly to that "Higher degree
of Life" (IX. 934)—which breaks the gradual chain of ascent in
Book IX.

This sense of the graduated, or staged, persists after the Fall
in the new dimension acquired by time. Creation is only "accommodated" to the temporal framework of the six "days";
the work of re-creation proceeds through the six ages of man.
Jonathan Richardson, in his *Explanatory Notes*, remarks that it
is "Delightful to see how Finely Milton observes All the
Growth of the New Man. Creation was all at Once, Regener-
ation is like the Natural Progression, we are Babes, and come
by Degrees to be Strong Men in Christ."[30] The gospel is revealed in stages or, as Michael says, in "scenes," a gradual
process of enlightenment which incorporates the twilight vision of 1 Corinthians 13 into a vision of time itself: "Light
after light well us'd they shall attain, / And to the end persist-
ing, safe arrive" (III. 196-97). The "Shade above shade" of the
unfallen Eden (IV. 141), the mutual "covering" or reflexive
ascent of the scale of nature, becomes, after the Fall, the
typological movement through "shadowy Types," a mediation, or graduation, which now is temporal, the "clothing" of
Adam and Eve in Book X a foretaste of the "covering" of the
Incarnation.

This reflexiveness extends to the graduated "tempo" of
poetry as well. The "Acts of God" are "Immediate," but cannot be told "to human ears" without "process of speech" (VII.

176-78), and this conversion of the instantaneous to the processional also involves some kind of poetic "accommodation." The pun on "due feet" in "Il Penseroso" (155) combines the gradual ascent "by steps" to God and the "measure"
of poetry whose "Harmonious numbers" (*PL* III. 38) move in
time. But there is also in Milton the claim to "unpremeditated
Verse" (IX. 24), a claim in sharp contrast to the century's
more premeditated poetry of meditation and its reliance on
such models as Bernard's *De gradibus*.[31] This coexistence of
modes leads to a paradox inherent in the writing of poetry
and to a contradiction at the heart of *Paradise Lost*. On the one
hand, Milton is the poet of Inspiration, opposed to the
tyranny of mediation and custom as the temporal accretion of
"error" and united with Blake against "Dame Memory and
her Siren daughters." On the other, he is the poet of "due
feet," "measure," and ascent "by steps," of an imagination so
graduated that the theologically discontinuous moment of the
Fall is almost inevitably foreshadowed.

The paradox of graduated continuity and radical discontinuity in *Paradise Lost* is the poetic analogy of the problem of
mediation in relation to what is finally a free act. The crucial
moment of decision is, by definition, beyond language and
enters it only when that discontinuity—the absence of any
necessary prefiguration—is obscured, when an event in the
future is approached as if it were already in the past, already a
foregone conclusion. Satan in the great soliloquies before the
Fall characteristically puts the innocence of Eden, still to be
tried, in the past tense, "thus forlorn" (IV. 374). By the time
Eve speaks of the taste of the fruit "too long forborne" (IX.
747) or Adam says "some cursed fraud / Of Enemy hath be-
guil'd thee, yet unknown, / And mee with thee hath ruin'd"
(904-6), the moment of the decision to fall has already
passed.[32] Poetically, however, the problem of the "foreshadowed fall" involves the problem of the narrative "becoming" of an act which, theologically, has no necessary
becoming, a problem which appears to be, finally, a problem
in language. Waldock observes, "There was no way for Milton of making the transition from sinlessness to sin perfectly
intelligible,"[33] and intelligibility is, poetically, precisely the

problem. Where can the decision "appear"? Dante's Adam
says that the Fall itself consisted in "il trapassar del segno" or
what Milton's Adam carefully terms the "sign of our obedience," which is to say that the transition itself is beyond the
visibilia of signs. Though the process of temptation continues
through a series of gradations (Eve's movement, for example,
from "Not unamaz'd" through "more amaz'd unwary"), the
movement of decision itself is just beyond gradation, beyond
language and its ladder of "degree." This radical gap is crucial
to the Miltonic premise of freedom, to a process in which
causation would be the analogue of mere "imitation," of the
untransformed tablets of stone. But poetically the problem is
more complex. The bias of language—its syntagmatic
curse—is the dominance of sequence and thus of "consequence," the continuous linear chain in which contiguity appears as cause. The problem of presenting, in narrative, the
radical freedom of the Fall from any of its foreshadowings is,
on one level at least, the same as that of separating Christ, in
Paradise Regained, from his *figurae*. Poetry as late in the tradition as Milton's epic is almost necessarily mediated, inseparable from the accretions of "error" and the ministrations of
"Dame Memory." Memory, in the Augustinian division of
the faculties, is the counterpart of the Father,[34] and Milton's
imagination in this sense is Satanic: it does not want to be
fathered. But neither is Milton an anabaptist of the imagination. The objection is limited to poetic fathers; no such radical
a relation is claimed to his other Source. This difference involves Milton in the paradox of being against the poetic doctrine of "translation"—of the history of epic poetry as a
graded series of temporal mediations, the westering of an inspiration from its source—and yet simultaneously for the
theological doctrine of "accommodation," of the final disjunction of human words and divine things. In the first, to be
mediated is to be secondary, dependent on a chain which extends backwards in time. In the second, to be mediated is,
paradoxically, to be initiated, in the only way possible, into
vision, by the descent in divine humility which enables the ascent, "by steps," to God.

This strange duality may explain Milton's somewhat ambiguous relation to his own century's theories of language. On the one hand, he shares both the Puritan and the Baconian distrust of metaphor, the impulse which led John Wilkins to propose a language free of "Synonymous words," "Equivocals" or words of "several significations," and of metaphors, those "infected ornaments" which "prejudice the native simplicity of speech."[35] On the other, however, he does not share his contemporaries' faith in the imminent removal of this error, the apocalyptic union of word and thing. For these commentators, "error" was the gap between signifier and signified, the "difference and disparity" lamented by John Webster and others.[36] But Milton, sympathetic though he might have been to the aims of his contemporaries and to their distrust of rhetorical turns, was unable to share their optimism, largely because it implied, as Allen and others suggest, a kind of impiety and presumption.[37]

Milton's sense of the insufficiency of language is suggested obliquely in his description of the principle of scriptural accommodation:

> It is safest for us to form an image of God in our minds which corresponds to his representation and description of himself in the sacred writings. Admittedly, God is always described or outlined not as he really is but in such a way as will make him conceivable to us. Nevertheless, we ought to form just such a mental image of him as he, in bringing himself within the limits of our understanding, wishes us to form. Indeed he has brought himself down to our level expressly to prevent our being carried beyond the reach of human comprehension, and outside the written authority of scripture, into vague subtleties of speculation.[38]

Though never explicitly arrogating to himself a method exclusive to Scripture, Milton does extend the analogy of "accommodation" to the veil of figurative language and, by implication, to his own poetic method. The conflation is already present in the *Paradiso* of Dante, where the divine "condescension" (IV. 43) is inseparable from the poem's own figurative mode. Since God did not write *Paradise Lost*, the accommodation involved is of a different sort from that of Scripture, but the emphasis still falls upon the gap between "meaning" and "name" (VII. 5), on the necessary discontinuity between language as a limited system of signs and the reality to which it points. The "greater than" formula of its multiple allusions is a pointing "beyond accommodation," a movement which rescues imitation from idolatry. The "to come" dimension of the figure is the mark of its insufficiency but it is also, paradoxically, its hope, the promise of continued movement rather than the Satanic reduction of meaning, the premature collapse of words and things.

Milton's perspective on the "errors" of language is thus significantly different from that of his more impatient contemporaries. Ambiguity and metaphor are, like the "degrees" to be traversed by Adam and Eve, part of an intervening space of trial, and process rather than elimination becomes the crucial focus. The tension this involves is implied in Milton's version of a familiar Renaissance *topos*. Mere "verbal curiosities" and "swelling Epithets thick laid / As varnish on a Harlot's cheek" are part of a medium to be rejected when all oracles are ceased.[39] But figuration remains a necessary bait for readers "of soft and delicious temper who will not so much as look upon Truth herselfe, unlesse they see her elegantly drest," since "Truth . . . ere she can come to the triall and inspection of the Understanding" must first "passe through many little wards and limits of the severall Affections and Desires," putting on "such colours and attire, as those Pathetick handmaids of the soul please to lead her in to their Queen."[40] Milton certainly does make use of the manifold "errors" of language, of what Giamatti calls "the satanic style."[41] The process of reading thus enacts the ambiguous temporal interval of the *sparagmos* of Truth, the wilderness of wandering between Christ's disappearance and the *parousia*. Its tendency may appear to be teleological, like the definitive resolutions of the verse, in which correction follows the brief respite of a false surmise:

                              in Ausonian land
Men call'd him Mulciber; and how he fell
From Heav'n, they fabl'd, thrown by angry Jove
Sheer o'er the Crystal Battlements: from Morn
To Noon he fell, from Noon to dewy Eve,
A Summer's day; and with the setting Sun
Dropt from the Zenith like a falling Star,
On Lemnos th' Ægaean Isle: thus they relate,
Erring; for he with this rebellious rout
Fell long before . . .

                                        (I. 739-48)

Stanley Fish has raised this process of misprision and correction to a dialectics of enlightenment, a movement in which
the function of error is to educate, or bring through. But a
resolutely teleological reading of Milton's poem may be faithful, finally, to only one of its tendencies, and the experience of
the poetry itself leads us back to the problem with which we
began, the question of how single-minded, or unidirectional,
this process is. To answer it we might at first take the long
way round, beginning with the poem's own meditations on
its "suspensions" and "errors."

This Pendant World

BOTH "suspension" and "wandering" share in the Miltonic
critique of "false surmise," the dangers rather than the delights of an arrested middle. As intermission or respite from
final end or certain meaning, both are alike in being potentially endless, a kind of parody of God as *sine fine*. "Suspense"
and "suspended" in *Paradise Lost* carry a full range of association, from expectancy (Satan's "look suspense," II. 418) and
indecision, to a delay or deferral of end or awareness. As a
momentary suspension of movement, their analogue is the celestial *anakuklesis*[42] which Adam invokes in his invitation to
Raphael to "stay":

the great Light of Day yet wants to run
Much of his Race though steep, suspense in Heav'n
Held by thy voice, thy potent voice he hears,
And longer will delay to hear thee tell
His Generation, and the rising Birth
Of Nature from the unapparent Deep:
Or if the Star of Ev'ning and the Moon
Haste to thy audience, Night with her will bring
Silence, and Sleep list'ning to thee will watch,
Or we can bid his absence, till thy Song
End, and dismiss thee ere the Morning shine.

(VII. 98-108)

"Suspense" in this passage means simultaneously "attentive" and "hanging," or "undecided," as if, indeed, there were no difference. The syntactic gap, after "Song," rhythmically enacts the postponement of the "End," and the crucial phrase ("suspense in Heav'n") is itself left hanging, without certain reference. It is a moment later recalled by Adam's own staying upon Raphael's charming voice: "The Angel ended, and in Adam's Ear / So Charming left his voice, that he a while / Thought him still speaking, still stood fixt to hear . . ." (VIII. 1-3). As a prolonging or postponing of end or awakening, it is the inverse of Eve's counsel of suicide because she cannot stand the suspense (x. 974ff) or of Satan's impatience, in *Paradise Regained*, to have his story concluded. As a precarious middle, it is the temporal counterpart of Creation itself, the "pendant world" which Satan views at the end of Book II.

One of the most revealing moments of "suspense" in *Paradise Lost*, and one of the most frequently questioned, comes in the speech of the Father to the Son, after the second day of the War in Heaven:

sore hath been thir fight,
As likeliest was, when two such Foes met arm'd;
For to themselves I left them, and thou know'st,
Equal in thir Creation they were form'd,
Save what sin hath impair'd, which yet hath wrought

Insensibly, for I suspend thir doom;
Whence in perpetual fight they needs must last
Endless, and no solution will be found:

. . . .

Two days are therefore past, the third is thine;
For thee I have ordain'd it, and thus far
Have suffer'd, that the Glory may be thine
Of ending this great War, since none but Thou
Can end it.

(vi. 687-94, 699-703)

The passage carries with it a history of speculation on the
eternity of the world, and the movement here from second to
third day, from dyad to triad, provides to this question Milton's own decisive resolution: the Son intervenes to tip the
balance, to bring an end to a "suspension" that would otherwise remain "perpetual."[43]

The multiple play upon "error" and "wandering" in
Paradise Lost shares this aspect of the potentially endless. The
link between the aberrant motion of the planets (Gr. *planetes*,
"wanderers") and the ubiquity of human error is a medieval
and Renaissance commonplace which Milton echoes and expands in Raphael's warning of the danger of "wand'ring
thoughts, and notions vain" (viii. 187) so soon after the description of the planets' "wandring course" (126). The provision of a limit to "wandering" in Raphael's "be lowly wise"
(173) suggests, by indirection, the possibility of trespass or
transgression and indeed it is Eve's "wand'ring vanity" (x.
875) which leads to the first trespass and the beginning of all
moral error.

"Error" in its many contexts seems, indeed, to be weighted
according to whether or not it has an end, or *telos*. The vain
curiosity of "wand'ring thoughts" that dream of "other
Worlds" (viii. 175) is dangerous only insofar as it approaches
Belial's "thoughts that wander through Eternity" (ii. 148)
and, by extension, the perplexity of the discoursing angels "in
wand'ring mazes lost" (ii. 561). The difference between

"wandering" in Hell and "wandering" in Heaven is suggested in the "mazes intricate" of the cosmic dance:

> That day, as other solemn days, they spent
> In song and dance about the sacred Hill,
> Mystical dance, which yonder starry Sphere
> Of Planets and of fixt in all her Wheels
> Resembles nearest, mazes intricate,
> Eccentric, intervolv'd, yet regular
> Then most, when most irregular they seem . . .
>
> (v. 618–24)

The dance is an integration of the "error" of the planets into
the cosmic harmony, a cosmic prefiguration of the redemption of the "error" of a Fall revealed retrospectively to have
been "fortunate," part of the pattern of good brought forth
out of evil. "Error" is thus subsumed within design, which is
to say that, where recovery is possible, "wandering" becomes
purgatorial, part of the way through.

After the Fall, the pleasant grove of trees in Eden becomes
"these wild Woods forlorn" (ix. 910), a darkened *selva* in
which Adam seeks shelter from his "doom":

> O might I here
> In solitude live savage, in some glade
> Obscur'd, where highest Woods impenetrable
> To Star or Sun-light, spread thir umbrage broad,
> And brown as Evening . . .
>
> (ix. 1084–88)

Eden itself turns into a Wood of Error, like Spenser's, "Not
perceable with power of any starre" (*FQ* i. i. 7. 6), and Adam
desires the shade of "Evening" as an end in itself. It is virtually impossible to separate what actually happens to this
wood from Adam's own projected wish, his need to turn
"Evening" from *mediatrix*, or timely re-creation, into a permanent resting place, refuge from a Presence now too bright
to bear.

Evening, however, is also the time of the Judgment which

is simultaneously an act of Mercy ("The Ev'ning cool, when he from wrath more cool / Came the mild Judge and Intercessor both," x. 95-96), neither the blazing noon of the *sol iustitiae* nor the time when the sun has gone down upon God's wrath.[44] What had been before the Fall an image of the pendency or poised innocence of Eden becomes after the Fall a figure for the middle or the mediated in yet another sense, the twilight zone of history now that the final judgment, the apocalyptic separation of Day and Night, is "Remov'd far off" (211). The uncertainty, at the end of Book XII, as to whether it is evening or morning plays yet once more on the crepuscular ambiguity of the threshold state.[45] As the fallen pair is led out of Eden, the world becomes "pendant" in a more ominous sense ("where to choose / Thir place of rest," 646-47), "wandering" becomes more burdened than the prelapsarian, *penseroso*, mood, and Milton's own sense of the significance of this new threshold emerges in the blending of elegy and prophecy, melancholy and hope which pervades the poem's closing lines.

In passages such as these, it is difficult to decide which is the crucial Miltonic focus, the middle period of suspension, wandering, trial, or the final movement towards resolution and end. The emphasis, certainly, throughout *Paradise Lost*, is on this "pendant" earth, the "well-balanc't world on hinges hung" ("Nativity Ode," 122). Anne Ferry points out that the characteristic figure of the poem is the circle, and the circling of the cosmos around the "opacous Earth, this punctual spot" (VIII. 23).[46] The action of the poem mirrors this concern, proceeding and returning as it does to the earth as focal point: even the War in Heaven, that notorious mythic preemptor of the human, is, in Milton's epic, narrated for the sake of man. The decisive level remains the moral one, the interval of temptation and trial: the dramatic locus of paradise regained is not Paradise but the wilderness, the counterpart of the "woody maze" of romance.[47] The characteristic Miltonic focus is on the process rather than on the product, or end. Instead of a Satan recognizable immediately as the stock devil to be hissed offstage, Milton presents a figure in the process of

his falling, a falling more like the slowed descent of Mulciber
in the fable than like the decisive "Fell" of its authorial correction. The reader is set before events which have already happened as if they were about to happen, still a matter of choice.
And though the action progresses through temptation and
Fall, the reader remains, in a sense, still poised on this
threshold, before a decision whose coordinates may alter but
which still remains "to come."

This focus may explain the frequency, in *Paradise Lost*, of
the thematic hinge, the division of the action into its cardinal
points. Eve's "staying" upon her image in the pool is only
one of the poem's instances of the pivotal moment. Books v
through viii are the hinge of the whole epic, a narrative interval in which movement forward is temporarily suspended,
and Adam, on the threshold of a decision, is provided with a
space for reflection. The center of the epic, the space between
Books vi and vii, turns on the pivot between Fall and Creation, destruction and restoration, and the crucial biblical
hinge time of the Flood becomes, in the opening of Book xii,
Milton's figure for a corresponding narrative transition:

> As one who in his journey bates at Noon,
> Though bent on speed, so here the Arch-Angel paus'd
> Betwixt the world destroy'd and world restor'd,
> If Adam aught perhaps might interpose;
> Then with transition sweet new Speech resumes.
>
> (xii. 1-5)

In a poem as self-reflexive as *Paradise Lost*, the larger world
of the poem's thematic movements is not surprisingly reflected in the little world of the line, and "suspension" has, so
to speak, its answering style. Michael's pause between "the
world destroy'd and world restor'd" is mirrored in a style in
which all the crucial interfaces or transitions are Janus-like,
Milton's version, perhaps, of a common Renaissance "inter-
textual" device. G. Wilson Knight speaks of the characteristic
winding and unwinding of Milton's verse,[48] of the spiral
movement whose syntactic counterpart is the trope of *chias-
mus*:

> A Universe of death, which God by curse
> Created evil, for evil only good,
> Where all life dies, death lives . . .

(II. 622-24)

The verse moves by convolution and involution and the center is the pivot, the hole in the middle of the trope.

Dr. Johnson's complaint that Milton's material, being well known, could afford the reader no suspense, here finds its answer: the suspense is there, and abundantly, in the language. In the description of the fallen angels whose "Song was partial, but the harmony / (What could it less when Spirits immortal sing?) / Suspended Hell . . ." (II. 552-54), the syntactic suspension literally enacts the harmonic metaphor of the delayed "cadence." Words at line endings frequently appear as if momentarily suspended until they are revealed, retrospectively, to have been part of a transition:

> Then feed on thoughts, that voluntary move
> Harmonious numbers . . .

(III. 37-38)

The quintessentially narrative question—"What happens next?"—shifts, in *Paradise Lost*, to the syntax.

The sense of surprise is furthered by Milton's frequent use of the intermediate or pivotal phrase, so placed between two referents as to be capable of referring to both, as if uncertain which of two paths to take and deliberately exploiting the uncertainty.[49] Such ambiguity is a familiar Satanic technique, part of the epic's "satanic style":

> Taste this, and be henceforth among the Gods
> Thyself a Goddess, not to Earth confin'd,
> But sometimes in the Air, as wee, sometimes
> Ascend to Heav'n, by merit thine, and see
> What life the Gods live there, and such live thou.

(v. 77-81)

"The Words *as wee*," as Zachary Pearce remarked, "are so plac'd between the sentences as equally to relate to both."[50]

The question of whether Satan himself can "ascend to Heav'n" as well as dwell "in the Air" is left in the balance, uncertainly poised for Eve, or the reader, to resolve.

Similarly, Adam describes to Raphael his first view of Paradise:

> all things smil'd,
> With fragrance and with joy my heart o'erflow'd.
>
> (VIII. 265-66)

Richardson and other editors since who have noticed that this "fragrance" has two possible referents have hastened to choose one over the other.[51] But the verse leaves the question hanging, and the phrase, if only for a moment, looks both ways at once. Often the stylistic hinge defies certain identification, as in the lines which to Bentley were simply not English grammar:

> No sooner had th' Almighty ceas't, but all
> The multitude of Angels with a shout
> Loud as from numbers without number, sweet
> As from blest voices, uttering joy, Heav'n rung
> With Jubilee, and loud Hosannas fill'd
> Th' eternal Regions . . .
>
> (III. 344-49)

Bentley endeavored to rescue the syntax by adding several crucial main verbs, while Pearce placed parentheses from "Heav'n" to "Hosannas."[52] The point of this suspended phrase, however, its very lack of certain reference, would seem to be neither connection nor sequence, the logical underpinnings of syntax, but heavenly simultaneity, the "accommodated" version of a place where all sounds happen at once.

Often the suspension, or confusion, of logical order opens up an interpretative space, a kind of dilation of possibility. Bentley objected to the Miltonic penchant for saying and unsaying ("The fellows of his crime, the followers rather") and one nineteenth-century Miltonist actually set out to straighten the poem's roughened syntax, to make the reading of *Paradise*

Lost less difficult. But both fail to catch the significance of the movement of misprision, the difference between unsaying and never having said, a movement which, like the rhetorical trope of *occupatio* or *paralepsis*, first creates a poetic space and then negates it.[53] Satan's forces, as yet only half awake to their plight in Hell, are caught in the momentary hesitation, or hovering, of a double negative: "Nor did they not perceive the evil plight / In which they were, or the fierce pains not feel" (I. 335-36). The two possibilities exist at once, before the mind can adjust sufficiently to separate them.

Such techniques, of course, extend in Milton's poetry beyond *Paradise Lost*. In *Comus*, the lines "Bacchus that first from out the purple Grape / Crusht the sweet poison of misused Wine" (46-47), seem to suggest a menace inherent in the wine itself until "misused" is clearly heard. Similarly, the passage in *Lycidas*

> The Willows and the Hazel Copses green
> Shall now no more be seen,
> Fanning their joyous Leaves to thy soft lays . . .
>
> (42-44)

suggests a sympathy in nature which extends even unto death, until the unobtrusive "thy" reveals this conclusion to have been premature: it is, indeed, not the copses which will no longer be seen, but the singer of lays.[54] In *Paradise Lost*, however, the range of poetic "feints" which suggest a momentary uncertainty or provoke a premature conclusion becomes part of a poem whose enterprise is at least partly to reveal the origins of the ambiguity of language itself.

This kind of suspension has particular relevance for the series of allusions in which an image or analogy could, like the threshold of "evening," lead in one of two directions. In the midst of the description of Paradise in Book IV, the reader comes upon one of many provocatively suggestive comparisons:

> Not that fair field
> Of Enna, where Proserpin gath'ring flow'rs

Herself a fairer Flow'r by gloomy Dis
Was gather'd, which cost Ceres all that pain
To seek her through the world; nor that sweet Grove
Of Daphne by Orontes, and th' inspir'd
Castalian Spring might with this Paradise
Of Eden strive . . .

(IV. 268-75)

It contains ostensibly a comparison of places—Enna and
Eden—but the emphasis shifts inevitably, for the reader, to a
comparison of persons, to Eve as a potential Proserpine. But
in coming, perhaps too precipitously, to this conclusion, and
thence, perhaps, to the assumption of an already "fallen"
Eden, the reader must ignore the simile's wider context, the
characteristically Miltonic formula of the "greater than." The
implication, therefore, must remain twofold. Both possibilities, before the Fall, remain open—the continuity of analogy
(as Proserpine, so Eve) or the discontinuity of superiority (as
Eden above Enna, so Eve above the fate of that other
"flower"). The traditional analogy between Proserpine and
Eve is a comparison applied after the fact, but here Eden itself
is still "pendant," and the fact that the detail of Ceres' "pain"
does not quite complete the analogy may not be so much a
weakness in an otherwise impressive homology as an indication of a disjunction within comparison, a possible parting of
the ways.[55]
   The point here, as proponents of the premature "Fall" have
indirectly grasped, is precisely provocation. There is, within
any framework of analogies, a tendency for the reader to
jump constantly to conclusions. The mind seems to need resolutions. Like Eve after the Fall, it often cannot stand the suspense. The reader—like Eve "staying" upon the shadow in
the pool or unable to stand the uncertainty of a deferred
"doom"—faces two opposed temptations: to linger, indefinitely, among the signs or, prematurely, to precipitate a
meaning. Prolepsis, or anticipation, is the poem's key figure,
but it is also, potentially, a form of pre-destination, a figure
for the end before its coming.

Christopher Ricks cites a masterful example of what he
calls "potential syntax" in the description of Eve:

> With Goddess-like demeanor forth she went;
> Not unattended, for on her as Queen
> A pomp of winning Graces waited still,
> And from about her shot Darts of desire
> Into all Eyes to wish her still in sight.
>
> (VIII. 59-63)

The "Darts of desire" are not revealed as innocent until the
final line, and the conclusion the reader might have drawn
remains, as yet, only as potential danger.[56]

A similar provocation exists in the words calculated to
elicit, in the midst of Paradise, the "guilty" response. In such
phrases as "mazy error," "wanton," "wandering," "luxuri-
ant," "oppressed," and even "falling," the mind constantly
tips the balance, weighing down innocent etymologies with
their burdened, postlapsarian meaning. In themselves, however, the words retain a kind of poise, like the active suspension of evening or the "self-balanc't" earth. "Hanging," the
word which Wordsworth found most characteristic of Milton's epic,[57] has in this suspension its linguistic reflection. A
phrase, in Paradise, such as "vegetable Gold" (IV. 220) virtually asks the reader to tip the balance in one direction, to see in
it, for example, a sign of fallen artifice, to mistake an
accident—color—for a substance—gold. But the phrase itself
hovers between the possibilities of meaning, as the earth still
hovers between Heaven and Hell.[58]

Even the most provocative of the descriptions in Eden implies no necessary conclusion:

> close the Serpent sly
> Insinuating, wove with Gordian twine
> His braided train, and of his fatal guile
> Gave proof unheeded . . .
>
> (IV. 347-50)

"Sly" and "insinuating" repeat earlier examples, in Book IV,
of the need to separate the etymological from the ethical:

neither dexterity nor winding movement has, as yet, its pejorative shade. Even "fatal guile" escapes necessity: "proof" is the key term, and the emphasis shifts from nature to observer, to Adam and Eve who, unfallen, do not "heed" its implications and finally to Satan who soon will see in the serpent a fit shape for his own designs. "Fatal" retains its implicit future tense, "killing" not as completed act but as pure potency.

This hovering of word and image in Milton removes them from all necessary reference, a situational or contextual poetics in which meaning remains decisional, a matter not of categories but of choice.[59] "Orient," for example, turns upon its context, from the "Orient Colors" of the banners of Hell (I. 546) to the Sun's "bright'ning Orient beam" (II. 399) and the unfallen Eden's "Orient Pearl and sands of Gold" (IV. 238). Similarly, "shade," in Milton as in Spenser, ranges from the protection and refreshment afforded by Eden before the Fall (IV. 138-42) to the shelter Adam desires after it (IX. 1080-90), from the eternally decided Satanic shadow of death (I. 65) to the Vallombrosa of the well-known simile, a shady place whose final meaning is not yet determined.

The Fullness of Time

MILTON himself often tips the balance, creating a suspension, or profusion, of meaning, only to reprove it as a false surmise, and it is this movement which Fish describes as the exodus through "error" to a final end. Yet, almost as often as this sense of *telos*, or of *eschaton*, is reaffirmed, the desire, within the poem, for resolution or end appears as a form of temptation. Satan's admission, in Book IX of *Paradise Lost*— "only in destroying I find ease / To my relentless thoughts" (129-30)—and his declaration in *Paradise Regained*—"worst is my Port, / My harbor and my ultimate repose" (III. 209-10)—join the quest of the fallen angels for the oblivion and extinction of Lethe as movements in which the desire for a definitive ending is only a form of the desire for nonbeing, or certain "doom," like the fallen Adam's death-wish, his impatience with the divine "delay":

                                   why delays
His hand to execute what his Decree
Fix'd on this day? why do I overlive,
Why am I mockt with death, and length'n'd out
To deathless pain? How gladly would I meet
Mortality my sentence, and be Earth
Insensible, how glad would lay me down
As in my Mother's lap! There I should rest
And sleep secure; his dreadful voice no more
Would Thunder in my ears, no fear of worse
To mee and to my offspring would torment me
With cruel expectation.

                                        (x. 771-82)

Similarly, tipping the balance may be the sign of an already
completed fall. It is not Milton but the fallen Adam who introduces the punning connection of "O Eve, in evil hour thou
didst give ear / To that false Worm" (ix. 1067-68), the same
need for resolution which leads him to etymologize
"Woman" as "Woe to man" (xi. 632-33). Such verbal reduc-
tions are a kind of hermeneutic collapse, the counterpart of
the counsel to suicide, for they suggest a way out of the tension of uncertain meaning, a way of making a phenomenon
(Eve, woman) absolutely coincident with origin or result (evil
or woe). In Dante's *Paradiso*, Satan is the spirit who "fell un-
ripe" (xix. 48), because he was unable to wait, in patience, for
the final revelation, or "morning," of what was as yet only
dimly glimpsed. And in Michael's explanation to Adam in
Book xi of *Paradise Lost*, "temperance," the opposite of un-
ripeness, becomes the means of maturation, the condition of
life in the uncertain medium of time:

        So may'st thou live, till like ripe Fruit thou drop
        Into thy Mother's lap, or be with ease
        Gather'd, not harshly pluckt, for death mature.

                                        (xi. 535-37)

    The echoes of *Lycidas* in these lines make them a kind of
culmination of Miltonic meditations on time, on the relation

between waiting and fulfillment. The very open-endedness of *Paradise Lost*, in its closing books, makes it the model of so many later English novels which end "in prospect," a forerunner of what Roland Barthes calls "le texte pensif."[60] It is part of Adam's despair that his sin does not end with him, that it has a hamartiology, a bearing of the consequences from generation to generation. But deferral of the final end is also the promise of hope. And the ambiguous "twilight" in which Adam and Eve wander at the end of the poem is also potentially the threshold of vision, the first step in the process of revelation already figured in Eve's turning from her shadowy image in the pool.

The end of this wandering is explicitly promised and is imaged in the frequent glimpses of Apocalypse in the last two books.[61] This eschatology is underscored throughout by what H. R. MacCallum calls "loops in time," the Miltonic device of placing the end before the beginning, the pattern in which "we are first shown a moment of triumph, and then led back in time to a survey of the trials which preceded it."[62] The example he cites is that of the Exodus, Pharaoh's pursuit of the Israelites described in Book XII:

> the Sea
> Swallows him with his Host, but them lets pass
> As on dry land between two crystal walls,
> Aw'd by the rod of Moses so to stand
> Divided, till his rescu'd gain thir shore:
> . . . .
> Moses once more his potent Rod extends
> Over the Sea; the Sea his Rod obeys;
> On thir imbattl'd ranks the Waves return,
> And overwhelm thir War . . .
> (XII. 195-99, 211-14)

The effect of such "revolutions in time," observes MacCallum, is "to suggest that when history is seen from the viewpoint of eternity, it is no longer linear."[63] Adam before his descent into the vale, and veil, of history is granted a privileged vision of the promised End, of a rest beyond his wandering. This perspective from the end, however, remains a privileged vision and is no more the exclusive perspective of the fallen Adam than it is that of the poem. There persists, if we may revert once more to the Augustinian terms, an "evening" as well as a "morning" vision, the perspective of the creature as well as that of the Creator (Milton, perhaps, as well as God) and it is upon the poetic implications of this twilight zone that we may conclude.

The suspended period of waiting, or of patience in its root sense, is part of the discipline of the creaturely perspective. In Book VI of *Paradise Lost*, the emphasis in the three days of the War in Heaven falls upon the third, the resolution or ending by the Son of a battle which has reached a draw. Voltaire protested, in 1727, that a "visible Contradiction" governed that episode and asked how it could come to pass, "after such a positive Order, that the Battle hangs doubtful?" His question reflects a concern over the seeming powerlessness of the faithful angels which is still echoed in modern commentary.[64] The point would seem to be, however, not victory but faith: the angels do not share the eternal perspective, from which victory is assured, and their decisive action consists in the faithfulness of "standing" rather than in the battle's ultimate end.

This drama is enacted again when Christ, in *Paradise Regained*, affirms that "All things are best fulfill'd in their due time" (III. 182) and, tempted by Satan to cast himself down from the pinnacle and claim his divinity before the appointed time, instead stands and waits for a sign of God's will (IV. 561). Within Milton's brief epic, this act of "standing" is the culmination of a major theme, of Mary's constant "waiting" (II. 102), of Christ's own "hungering" in the "pathless Desert" (I. 296), and of the Disciples' uncertainty about the promised end, a fear which makes their waiting for the Son to return from the wilderness a foretaste of the waiting after the Ascension:

> Alas, from what high hope to what relapse
> Unlook'd for are we fall'n! Our eyes beheld
> Messiah certainly now come, so long

Expected of our Fathers; we have heard
His words, his wisdom full of grace and truth;
Now, now, for sure, deliverance is at hand,
The Kingdom shall to Israel be restor'd:
Thus we rejoic'd, but soon our joy is turn'd
Into perplexity and new amaze: .
For whither is he gone, what accident
Hath rapt him from us? will he now retire
After appearance, and again prolong
Our expectation?

(II. 30-42)

This "waiting" or "standing," in both epics, is not a static
suspension but a form of activity, like the dynamic suspension of the "self-balanc't" Earth or like the most seemingly
abstract of Miltonic Latinisms, terms which retain a residual
kinaesthesia, a sense of not-yet-completed movement.

   This throwing back of the emphasis on the interval of patience or trial rather than exclusively on its endpoint or result
has, finally, its analogue in the poetry itself. Stanley Fish's
analysis of *Paradise Lost* is a resolutely end-directed one, an
approach which culminates in his remarks on the "pseudo-
simile" as an indication of the poem's role as mere scaffolding, part of a discursive mode of knowing to be superseded,
and obliterated, by the immediacy of revelation. In the example he chooses, the comparison of Satan to the "leviathan" in
Book I, the simile is revealed to be a "pseudo-simile" as soon
as we realize that "what is offered as an analogy is perceived
finally as an identity."[65] Satan and the leviathan to which he is
compared are one: Satan is not only like the leviathan, he *is*
Leviathan. Once this identity is revealed, argues Fish,

   the scaffolding of the complete simile remains, but
   only as a means of marking out an area for the eye to
   move in. It is an artificial space, with no reference to
   the physical world of either the observer or of the
   characters in the plot. . . . Because each simile finds a
   kind of form within a system and not in its own
   internal coherence (although many of them have

that too), they reach out to one another and join
finally in an endless chain of interchangeable significances: Leviathan to Pharaoh to River Dragon to
Serpent to Giant to Locusts to bees to pygmies and
cranes to imbodied force to sedge to fallen leaves to
barbarian hordes and pagan Gods on the one side;
Moses, David, Orpheus, Josiah, etc. on the other.[66]

The "identity" of Satan and Leviathan is, of course, part of an
apocalyptic division of biblical imagery, the tendency of
metaphor to a radical congruence. But there is something in
poetry that will not join a lineup, and the tendency even of
this simile in Milton is not necessarily apocalyptic. The
Leviathan who is identical with Satan is, so to speak, a creature preempted by pure meaning, and Milton's deliberate inclusion of the leviathan among the creatures in Book VII
(412-16) suggests a natural neutrality not unlike that of the
serpent before his form is conscripted to a Satanic end. The
point of the simile would seem instead to be the crucial space
or interval between leviathan and Leviathan, between natural
phenomenon and final meaning, as between the "pendant
world" and its apocalyptic poles. Fish argues that the tendency of meaning in Milton's epic remains essentially the same:
"Correctly interpreted, the icons the visible world presents to
us will always have the same meaning no matter what formal
configurations surround them."[67] His interpretive principle
echoes Augustine's in the De doctrina, the assumption that
when potential interpretations conflict, those must be chosen
which lead to the already revealed "end." There always remains in poetry, however, the possibility of hermeneutic
leak. The early critics who both praised and blamed Milton
for his "digressions" suggest an important insight.[68] Miltonic
similes expand as never before the range of analogy beyond
an initial point of contact, but they also acquire a life of their
own; however interpretively integrated as "homologies,"
they sing too with a different music. The first extended simile
in Paradise Lost, the comparison of Satan to the leviathan
"haply slumb'ring on the Norway foam" (I. 203) is not only

the first feeling in the poem of a "grateful digression," of an expansion of locus or atmosphere beyond the single conflict of Heaven and Hell, but also the first of the poem's many shifts to creation, to a specifically human space.

James Whaler in his analysis of the Miltonic simile insists that Milton "does not digress in any simile for the sole purpose of drawing a diverting picture," even when that simile serves as a form of relief.[69] But the most memorable of the similes are a kind of dilation, a diversion which may wander farther and farther away from its source, or immediate context, before it is finally recalled by the authorial voice. Interestingly enough, virtually all of the similes classed by Whaler as "digressive" contain a shift to a human observer—to the trusting pilot (I. 204), the Tuscan artist (288), the belated peasant (783), the doubting plowman (IV. 983)—and in each the question of final meaning hangs in the balance.[70]

In the cluster of similes which ends Book I, the dilation of the picture of the bees, pygmies, and, finally, faery elves beyond the original context of the analogy—the comparison of number and size—means that the final recall to this context seems inevitably a kind of straightening, or restricting frame. The similes themselves, however, expand through the glimpse of the "fresh dews and flowers" (I. 771) visited by the bees in the Spring, the faraway prospect of a view "Beyond the Indian Mount" (781), and the midsummer night revels the peasant "sees, / Or dreams he sees" (783-84). Poetry here creates its own faerie, or twilight, zone. The mistaken pilot, the gazing Tuscan, and the uncertain plowman linger in our imaginations, long after the comparative "point" is made, as a virtually separable cast of characters, linked of course to the necessity of choosing, and yet allowing us almost to forget that all such allusions to the delight of creation must also be to a fallen one.[71] There is a fullness to the time of these similes which suggests that time's fullness is not simply its end, which opens up within the poem a kind of inner space, of worlds within worlds.

The movement towards conclusion or end is often present only as a kind of "cadence":

Nathless he so endur'd, till on the Beach
Of that inflamed Sea, he stood and call'd
His Legions, Angel Forms, who lay intrans't
Thick as Autumnal Leaves that strow the Brooks
In Vallombrosa, where th' Etrurian shades
High overarch't imbow'r; or scatter'd sedge
Afloat, when with fierce Winds Orion arm'd
Hath vext the Red-Sea Coast, whose waves o'erthrew
Busiris and his Memphian Chivalry,
While with perfidious hatred they pursu'd
The Sojourners of Goshen, who beheld
From the safe shore thir floating Carcasses
And broken Chariot Wheels . . .

(I. 299-311)

The sequence of tenses in this compound simile is instructive.[72] The first comparison is in the present tense of nature, the falling of the leaves as an annual event. The second is a compound ("hath vext") or transition, just as the "Red Sea" is syntactically a pivot, appearing first as mere geographical location and only retrospectively as a particular meaning. The third is in the simple past, part of an historical event with an established reference. The movement towards the specificity of the past tense provides an analogy to the movement towards the fixity of a particular meaning, the typology of this moment within the Exodus. But as a whole, it remains a movement, an interval in which the crucial focus becomes the process itself. The leaves may recall the fallen souls in Dante, and Vallombrosa suggest a more ominous kind of shady valley. Orion may gain in symbolic resonance from his biblical role as an instrument of judgment.[73] But they are also simply leaves and the name of a wind, just as the Red Sea retains some freedom from its purely typological meaning. The collapse of phenomenon and meaning would be Apocalypse, the end of this twilight space or "pendant world." But there still remains a meantime, and the point of coincidence is not yet.

The duality inherent in this mean-time helps, finally, to account both for the pivotal position of *Paradise Lost* within

English poetic history and for the polarization which has tended to characterize its reading. The space in which the end is paradoxically both "come" and "to come" already embodies a fundamental tension, "evening" as mere bridge or scaffolding, and "evening" as the space of creation dilated and enjoyed. But it has its poetic counterpart as well, in the dialectic of univalence and multivalence, of a single reading and a plurality of readings. The first would hasten the time of arrival, the revelation of final meaning, but it also involves the danger of a Satanic hastening, a reduction or foreclosing of possibility. The second may return the seeker to the realm of what the Disciples call "amaze" (PR ii. 38), the potential stagnancy, limbo, or endlessness of "wand'ring mazes lost," but it also allows for the dilation of meaning, the promise of something still to be. To the perversions of both, Milton opposes the difficult discipline of "standing," an action which is simultaneously a passion, possibilities held open rather than either reduced or fulfilled.

In Milton's epic, the movement towards "morning" is finally what separates evening as precursor from its shadow double, evening as perpetual retreat. But there is—in Book iv and elsewhere—a lingering which opens up a middle space, which resists the pressure of the great absolutes of End or meaning. Some Romantic readings of this Miltonic space fasten upon this element of Paradise Lost as its most attractive one. Coleridge sees in the suspensions of Book iv "Milton's sunny side as a man," the place in the poem where "the poet is predominant over the theologian."[74] Keats speaks of the conflict between the epic's high "Argument" and the "Elysian field of verse," and finds in its periodic reversion from the "ardours" to the "pleasures of Song" some of "the finest parts of the poem."[75] This last is clearly Keats reading Milton as an oblique way of reading himself; but his singling out of the softer imagination which put the "shading cool / Interposition" (PR iii. 221) of a suspended "vale" in Hell as well as in Heaven was a reading of a "second voice" in Milton as important for the course of subsequent criticism as the Satanism of the other Romantics.

The very development of this tendency points to a tension which Milton's poem leaves unresolved. The danger in the Miltonic "standing" is that the suspension may be collapsed on either side—to a simple unidirectional reading or to the dilation of the interval, or threshold, for its own sake. This element of "betweenness" in *Paradise Lost* may be one of the reasons why criticism of the poem has been so frequently divided, in a critical War in Heaven potentially endless as long as it proceeds by a taking of sides. A reading of Milton's poem is often shaped by what it opposes, and the reader who resists a resolutely end-directed reading may find himself turning to its opposite for relief. But *Paradise Lost* itself contains both directions, the sense of *telos* and of its final indeterminability, the dilation of the threshold and the threat of its possible "staying." The end of the poem is finally open-ended, not definitively either evening or morning, but both.

IV. Keats

> For Poesy alone can tell her dreams,
> With the fine spell of words alone can save
> Imagination from the sable charm
> And dumb enchantment.
>
> *The Fall of Hyperion*

Fairy Lands Forlorn

IN *The Burden of the Past and the English Poet*, W. Jackson Bate argues that we cannot arbitrarily separate the English Romantics from the century which preceded them, however striking the differences which make Romanticism a genuine literary epoch.[1] We may begin with this warning in turning to Keats, for the question of his relation to romance demands not only an historical preface but also one which includes the century he himself saw as a "schism"[2] in the history of poetry. "Romance" underwent a sea-change in the period between Spenser and the English Romantic poet who was most clearly his descendant, and a look at this history may provide the necessary counterpart to the view of Keats we have inherited from a more simply formal criticism, the kind of textual study to which his Great Odes so marvelously lend themselves and which ensured his continued popularity during a period when the other Romantics had fallen into eclipse.

Keats himself suggests the outlines of this history in his own allusions to earlier romance. His "Ode on Indolence" takes as its motto "They toil not, neither do they spin"—the invitation of Spenser's Phaedria to take no thought for the morrow—and the letter in which he explains the genesis of the Ode links it to the popular eighteenth-century imitation of Spenser, James Thomson's *Castle of Indolence*.[3] Both the Spenserian echo and the self-conscious reference to Thom-

son's poem suggest a context for the intervening progress of
romance and its ambivalences. In Book II of *The Faerie
Queene*, Phaedria's appeal is an invitation to swerve from the
onward movement of the quest, to withdraw from the world
of fruitless toil, and to imitate the careless ease of the lilies of
the field. Her appeal to "present pleasures" (vi. 17) echoes
Christ's words to men all too anxious about the morrow, but
it conceals a darker temptation. The "indolence" of her island
on the Idle Lake is closer to the crippling impotence of *accidia*
and the repose it offers is not a recreation but an end to all
movement, a permanent escape. Guyon resists this temptation to resign his responsibilities to a world of "care" and exposes Phaedria's appeal to Scripture as the fraud it is. But the
fact that, in the very next canto, he himself echoes her argument in his answer to Mammon's insistence upon getting and
spending (vii. 14-15) suggests that there is an ambivalence
within repose itself, that the alternative to the world of
Mammon may be at once a refusal to accept its anxious questing and the potential vortex of an enervating sloth.

Thomson's Spenserian imitation provides a crucial step-
ping-stone to Keats because it extends this dark temptation to
the pleasures of romance itself, and its refuge from the world
of Mammon. The charms offered by "Indolence," the poem's
"Archimage," are tinged with suggestions of romance, of
"gay Castles in the Clouds that pass, / For ever flushing round
a Summer-Sky" (I. vi. 3-4), and the "alas" of Thomson's
motto reveals that something larger is at stake, in the forsak-
ing of this realm, than a mere farewell to the individual sin of
sloth. Romance, like indolence, is simultaneously a refuge
from the waking world and a dangerous evasion, a form increasingly suspect in an enlightened age. Thomson is both a
Spenserian and a man of the Enlightenment, and the complexities of his farewell to the Castle's "Soul-dissolving"
charms (I. xxxix) reveal at once a desire to banish a potentially
seductive illusion and a melancholy sense of the impossibility
of recovering the "artful Phantoms" of its "Fairy-Land" (I.
xlv).

Thomson's poem illustrates a specifically historical schizo-

phrenia. As early as 1694, Joseph Addison could write that the
tales which pleased a "barb'rous age" could "charm an understanding age no more,"[4] and the view that the progress of enlightenment made their charms no longer palatable was
echoed countless times in a century which associated romance
increasingly with indolence and dream and opposed to all
three the poetic protestantism of a more active musing. Certainly there did persist a regret that the clue to this "faery
land" might be forever lost. The recovery of the "enchanted
ground" recalled by Thomson and others[5] was the common
concern of Percy, Hurd, and the Wartons. But this effort at
revival was accompanied in even the most minor magazine
poetry of the century by a sense that no real return was possible, that all that was left to an enlightened age was "A waking
sense of truth too plain, / That vainly sighs to dream again."[6]

Even the attempts to recapture this past betray a divided
mind. Thomas Warton defends his own "excursion into
Fairy-Land," however "monstrous and unnatural these com-
positions may appear to this age of reason and refinement,"
by arguing that they not only throw light on ancient customs
but "store the fancy with those sublime and alarming images,
which true poetry best delights to display." Yet this identification of romance with "true poetry" does not prevent him
from speaking of the "absurdities" of the romances or from
contrasting the "depths of Gothic ignorance and barbarity"
with the "new and more legitimate taste" established since
the Renaissance.[7] Mark Akenside chooses the "Pleasures of
the Imagination" over more mundane pursuits and scorns
"The busy steps, the jealous eye" of those who suspect the
"gay delusive spoils" of the Muse,[8] but he too asks that
"Fancy" in her "fairy cell" be tempered by that "Reason"
which calls the soul back to "Truth's severest test."[9] All these
pronouncements reflect a curiously double view of history.
Warton couches the progress of his *History of English Poetry*
from "rudeness to elegance" in the familiar metaphors of
darkness and light, yet he too seems haunted by the anxieties
of the epigone, a fear that reason's daylight has dispelled both
superstition's mist and imagination's golden haze, and ex-

presses a nostalgia for the age when "Reason suffered a few demons still to linger . . . under the guidance of poetry."[10]

This sense that the fortunes of romance were virtually synonymous with the fortunes of poetry itself emerges perhaps nowhere more vividly than in Hazlitt's famous description of the march of enlightenment:

> It cannot be concealed . . . that the progress of knowledge and refinement has a tendency to circumscribe the limits of the imagination, and to clip the wings of poetry. The province of the imagination is principally visionary, the unknown and undefined: the understanding restores things to their natural boundaries, and strips them of their fanciful pretensions. . . . It is the undefined and uncommon that gives birth and scope to the imagination; we can only fancy what we do not know. As in looking into the mazes of a tangled wood we fill them with what shapes we please, with ravenous beasts, with caverns vast, and drear enchantments, so in our ignorance of the world about us, we make gods or devils of the first object we see, and set no bounds to the wilful suggestions of our hopes and fears.[11]

That romance was a *chiaro-oscuro* border realm being crowded out by the empire of enlightenment links its attractions—and its dangers—to those of the secluded retreat, or enchanted ground, that countless eighteenth-century poems seek to rediscover. Each of the poems which invoke a power— "Contemplation," "Peace," "Solitude," "Fancy"—and ask to be led to that power's sequestered cell is in effect a brief romance, a quest for a respite from the waking world.[12] When the world of noisy care threatens to become as fatal to this retreat as the "rude Axe"[13] to the actual wooded haunt, the path the poet asks to be shown frequently tends to be synonymous with perception itself; his inability to find the enchanted bower or to remain for long within it brings not relief at the destruction of its "charm" but disappointment that "the fancy cannot cheat so well / As she is famed to do."

And yet, if exclusion from this bower prompts an "adieu" as full of regret as Thomson's farewell to his Castle, there is at the same time the nagging suspicion that the poet who seeks it may be guilty of the purely negative side of what Stevens was to call "evasion," a cowardly refusal of responsibility to the world of things as they are.

"Romance" was an ambivalent mode, then, because its charms were indistinguishable from its snares. Hazlitt's famous description of the Spenserian stanza—"dissolving the soul in pleasure, or holding it captive in the chains of suspense" and "lulling the senses into a deep oblivion of the jarring noises of the world, from which we have no wish to be ever recalled"[14]—had its counterpart in the attractions and dangers of romance itself, a dream from which there was potentially no awaking and a "suspension" from which there might be no exit. Geoffrey Hartman has described Milton's "L'Allegro" and "Il Penseroso" as crucial landmarks in the purification of romance, the mind as magus summoning its own moods and wandering, literally, at will.[15] But *Paradise Lost* delivers a harsher judgment on the dangers of wandering and the post-Miltonic poems which are closest to the form of the companion poems frequently internalize the anxieties of the epic's darker moral, the possibility of wandering past a point of no return. In a crucial passage of Burton's *Anatomy of Melancholy*, a signal text for Keats, the delights of the wandering imagination turn to terror when the way back is suddenly blocked:

> So delightsome these toys are at first, they could spend days and nights without sleep, even whole years alone in such contemplations, and fantastical meditations, which are like unto dreams, and they will hardly be drawn from them, or willingly interrupt, so pleasant their vain conceits are, that they hinder their ordinary tasks or employment; these fantastical and bewitching thoughts so insinuate, possess, overcome, distract, and detain them, they cannot, I say, go about their more necessary busi-

ness, stave off, or extricate themselves, but are ever musing, melancholizing, and carried along, as he (they say) that is led around about a heath with a Puck in the night, they run earnestly on in this labyrinth of anxious and solicitous melancholy meditations, and cannot well or willingly refrain, or easily leave off, winding and unwinding themselves, as so many clocks, and still pleasing their humours, *until at last the scene is turned upon a sudden*, by some bad object, and they being now habituated to such vain meditations and solitary places, can endure no company, can ruminate of nothing but harsh and distasteful subjects.

(Part. 1, Sect. 2, Memb. 2, Sub. 6; my italics)

This passage from the *Anatomy* is the one often simply cited as an example of the prose style known as the Senecan amble. But its theme, and the faintly Gothic suggestion of its sudden "turn," look forward to the ambulatory poetry of the century after Milton and its transformation of the Puckish delights of a fanciful wandering into the unsteady progress of a gloomy egotist among the tombs.

The ambivalences of romance and its delightful, and suspect, "error" suggest a context for the period we now call Romantic. In the course of one of his essays, John Stuart Mill pauses to consider the difference between two of his century's great figures, Jeremy Bentham and Samuel Taylor Coleridge, the man of enlightenment and the poet. The two are distinguished by what they led men to ask themselves with regard to any "ancient or received opinion."[16] Bentham, says Mill, would ask "Is it true?," Coleridge, "What is the meaning of it?" Bentham's question presupposes the possibility of an answer "yes" or "no," an axiom of logic which Aristotle termed the law of the excluded middle. Coleridge's question, on the other hand, suspends such direct answering in favor of an exploration, a dilation of the space between the logician's, or the pragmatist's, Either-Or. For Mill, this difference is a telling parable of the distance between the pragmatic and the poetical character; for the student of English Romanticism, it also provides an insight into the nature of this middle ground and its relation to the fine, if superstitious, fabling of the world of romance.

In his essay *Poetry Distinguished from other Writing*, Oliver Goldsmith singled out the history of the term "hanging" or "pendant" from Virgil to Milton as the epitome of the figurative or picture-making power of poetry, and his comments on the picturesque effect of the word "hung" in *Paradise Lost* anticipate Wordsworth's observation that this was Milton's most characteristic expression.[17] Could he have taken his history forward to the Romantics, he might have included Wordsworth's own version of the Miltonic "suspension." But he might also have explored the attractions of pendency in a context more sinister. Coleridge's own description of this "suspension" comes in his account of the division of labor between himself and Wordsworth in the *Lyrical Ballads*:

> It was agreed that my endeavours should be directed to persons and characters supernatural or at least romantic; yet so as to transfer from our outward nature a human interest and a semblance of truth sufficient to procure for these shadows of imagination that willing suspension of disbelief for the moment, which constitutes poetic faith.[18]

The familiarity of the passage obscures its menace; but the old ambivalence continues in the language of the description itself. The "willing suspension of disbelief" given to the "shadows of imagination" has as its undertone the Gothic danger of a *raptus* or rape by these shadows, and the passage weighs heavily on its all-important qualifier, that such suspension is only "for the moment."

Northrop Frye has called Romanticism a "sentimental" form of romance, that later re-creation of an earlier mode which Schiller explored in his famous essay.[19] One of the implications of this change is that re-creation involved distance as well as revival, that the historical schism, however lamented, also offered a form of protection. The odes of the ubiquitous Mrs. Robinson are all of a piece—a movement from fascination with the "haunted glade" to a hasty retreat when its charms appear to be darkening into necromancy and night,[20] a concern with "ground" which suggests, in countless other minor poems, a fear of transport of any kind. Keats inherits this eighteenth-century strain as well as the Spenserian-Miltonic one. In the final stanza of the "Ode to a Nightingale," it seems as if the speaker is involuntarily falling out of an enchanted space ("Forlorn! The very word is like a bell / To toll me back from thee to my sole self!"), but the previous stanza has already distanced the speaker from the nightingale even before it flies away, through a time scheme which journeys back through "ancient days" and the "sad heart of Ruth" to "fairy lands forlorn." It is difficult to avoid the conclusion that this historical distance enters the poem less as fact than as strategy—a means of distancing the speaker from an attraction, and a transport, which also means his death.

Keats's relation to romance shares, from the beginning, in this ambivalence. The verse epistle "To George Felton Mathew" begins with a version of the quintessential eighteenth-century theme, the desire to be led away from the sun of this world into some "flowery spot, sequestered, wild, romantic" (37), and the fear, in the epistle "To Charles Cowden Clarke," is that he comes too late to be admitted through the "enchanted portals" which separate this world from that of a more visionary company. Romance, even in the early Keats, however, is inseparable from anxiety, and there is even here the beginning of a sense that its attractions should be resisted in favor of the demands of the waking world. The verse epistle "To My Brother George" opens with the concern that he might not share the vision of knights and "ladies fair," but it soon moves forward to the wish that his "poetic lore" might be more than mere evasion. And it is this desire not to be caught in a "barren dream" that prompts his most famous farewell to romance, the sonnet "On Sitting Down to Read *King Lear* Once Again."

The siren form of "golden-tongued Romance" is opposed

both to the higher genres of tragedy and epic and to the
harsher world of waking reality, and Keats's poetry and
letters after *Endymion* signal his intention to move beyond
romance, in both directions.[21] So frequent are these pronouncements that critics have tended to see in Keats a
progression like that of "Sleep and Poetry" from the realm of
Flora and old Pan to the "nobler life" of the poems of 1819, an
application to his life and poetry of the images of progress
which abound in the *Letters*, from the speculations on the
march of enlightenment between Milton and Wordsworth to
the comparison of human life to a mansion of many apart-
ments.[22] The impression of such straightforward movement
in Keats's poetry, however, is deceptive. No purely developmental scheme will finally fit, just as the characteristic
fluidity or ambiguity of the verse makes any attempt to wrest
a coherent philosophy or definitive conclusion from Keats's
poetry inevitably doomed.[23] The farewell to romance remains an attempt to say farewell, and reading the progress of
Keats's career is no more linear a process than reading the
most complex of the individual poems.

Keats's statements are often difficult to conscript to the
scheme of a straightforward "progress" because they look
two ways at once.[24] One of the characteristics Keats shares
with Shakespeare is his dramatic showing forth of "attitudes"
which it would be as misleading to identify with Keats himself as it would be naive to speak of what Shakespeare "says."
Paul de Man has called the first *Hyperion* a poem more Shake-
spearean than Miltonic, and in this sense, Keats can be no
more identified with the position of Oceanus on the march of
progress than can Shakespeare with Ulysses' speech on degree.[25] Fixity of attitude defies everything Keats had to say on
the chameleon quality of the poetical character. The frozen
statuary of the fallen Titans in *Hyperion* is in one respect the
visible and outward form of their spiritual fixity, as if lack of
motion were a necessary consequence of any final taking of
position. Critics who attempt to identify single attitudes in
the most complex of Keats's poems often fix what is deliberately left uncertain and shifting.

Whatever else may ally Keats with the romance imagination, his complex diction and the interplay of literary allusions are part of its characteristic plenitude and frequently subvert the marshaling of meaning towards a single end. The dramatic center of *The Eve of St. Agnes* is the scene in which Porphyro watches Madeline awaken from her dream into the reality of the banquet he has set before her. Her awakening could be simply a poetic version of that transition from dream to reality which Keats outlined in the famous letter to Bailey: "The Imagination may be compared to Adam's dream—he awoke and found it truth."[26] But the echoes which surround this event make it difficult to determine whether this conclusion to Madeline's dream is a repetition in a finer or a grosser tone, whether it is a progress to fulfillment or a somewhat more complex fall. Porphyro re-creates the substance of her dream, but he is also subtly linked to Satan before the sleeping Eve and the villainous Iachimo before Shakespeare's Imogen.[27] Similarly, in the "Ode on Indolence," the attempt to wrest a definitive statement from the poem is impeded by the lack of clear subordination, or straightforward linear movement, in the syntax itself. Several of its critics have read it as a celebration of the *penseroso* mood, a deliberate embracing of the bower of indolence and its calm repose. This reading does account for the poem's motto—"They toil not, neither do they spin"—and for the speaker's firm refusal to be taken in by the "voice of busy common-sense" (40) and its designation of all apparent inactivity as unproductive. The poem itself, however, undercuts the simplicity of statement. The argument may be linear and the voice imperative ("Vanish, ye Phantoms, from my idle sprite / Into the clouds, and never more return!" 59-60), but the interplay of images qualifies even the speaker's final word. The "clouds" to which he banishes these "Phantoms" at the poem's end are the very clouds in whose lids still hang the "sweet tears of May" (46), and this echo of the earlier image reintroduces the fact of process and change into the attempt to exile it. The shades of Spenser's Phaedria and Thomson's Indolence still linger in this retreat. Though the speaker is one, the poem is not univocal and reading is a more circuitous process than simple linear movement towards conclusion.[28] The Odes are enduring because they are somehow at the heart of poetic diction, that plenitude of meaning which evades the Mammon world of stenolanguage and single referents. Ambiguity in Keats, however, is even more directly related to the question of romance's shadowy and evasive world. Keats is perhaps closest of all the English Romantics to a particularly Spenserian awareness of the doubleness of all things, but there is in this resemblance a significant difference. Through most of *The Faerie Queene*, the sense of doubleness is conveyed by a proliferation of dangerous lookalikes and "reading" is at least partly the activity of separating the counterfeit from the real, of uncovering the actual identity behind the seductive appearance. Keats borrows the romance motif of the revelation of a "lamia" from Burton, but in *Lamia* the elfin lady's real, or original, identity is left radically open to question. The contrary tendencies of the poem itself are finally not separable into a single conclusion about the poet's attitude or end. Lamia is compared both to the python killed by Apollo (II. 78-80) and to Eurydice (I. 248), and only critics who choose to privilege one of these allusions over the other can finally separate what the poem itself leaves in suspension.[29]

This complexity in a poem written as late as *Lamia* cannot but suggest that Keats's progress away from romance was far from a straightforward one. "Romance," as Keats inherited it, is no longer a strictly generic term and cannot, despite his own pronouncements, be so easily rejected. The romance embroidery of the earlier poems drops out, and Keats anticipates Yeats in the poetic enterprise of going naked. But chronology is no certain guide and the struggle continues in more subterranean forms. *Isabella* is a translation of "the gentleness of old romance" (387) into the "wormy circumstance" (385) of the Gothic, but it is not so much an "anti-romance" (as Jack Stillinger suggests)[30] as a variation of it, an indication that a form which tries to incorporate the pain of reality may become simply the *macabre*. In one sense, the attempt in Keats to awaken out of romance is analogous to his attempt to do without ritual trappings, like the superstitious stage-props of *melancholia* abandoned in the canceled stanza of the "Ode on Melancholy." Near the beginning of *The Fall of Hyperion*, there is a confused "heaping" of the vessels of the "Ode to Psyche" which may be as much the signal of a new direction as is the movement from the refuse of a Miltonic paradise. But Keats never fully gets rid of this baggage or of its ceremonial forms any more than he says a final farewell to the modes and superstitions of romance. Instead, he at once seeks freedom from the old forms and carries them forward as part of his assumption of the weight of tradition. Porphyro's "solution" to the transition between dream and reality is more efficacious than the antique ritual of the "legends old" (*Eve of St. Agnes*, 135), but it requires as elaborate a staging. And *The Fall of Hyperion* is an initiation ritual which, though ostensibly beyond the realm of romance, returns to its most elemental form—the healing of an ailing and impotent old king by a hero whose redemption is his "word."

None of these poems can be reduced to the linear frame of a "development" or the strict argumentative line of a particular thesis. The Keats we have often literally differs from himself, and it is difficult to reconcile the perspicacity of the Odes and the humanism of the *Letters* with the obsession of *Isabella* or the fetishism of "This Living Hand." Keats's is a poetry which yields some of its secrets to close reading, some to an exploration of related images, and still others to a more historical thematics. We shall therefore adopt the more characteristically romance technique of juxtaposition and association, exploring first the "negative capability" of wandering in the "Ode to a Nightingale" and *Endymion*, secondly the complex of images for this threshold state which connect *Endymion* with the impasse of the first *Hyperion*, and finally the darkening of this threshold and the drama of mutual trespass in *The Fall of Hyperion*, that fragment's second and final version.

Negative Capability and the Paradox of Questing

IN a famous essay, T. S. Eliot remarked that Keats was not typical of his age, chiefly because of that conception of the poetic character he called in a crucial letter "Negative Capability":

> I had not a dispute, but a disquisition with Dilke, on various subjects; several things dovetailed in my mind, & at once it struck me, what quality went to form a Man of Achievement especially in Literature & which Shakespeare posessed so enormously—I mean *Negative Capability*, that is when man is capable of being in uncertainties, Mysteries, doubts, without any irritable reaching after fact & reason—Coleridge, for instance, would let go by a fine isolated verisimilitude caught from the Penetralium of mystery, from being incapable of remaining content with half knowledge.[31]

What Thomas M. Greene calls "the mystery and melancholy of romance, which always accepts less than total knowledge"[32] has its Keatsian counterpart in this *chiaro-oscuro* state, where "doubt" retains its root sense of the ability to look two ways at once, of Janus as the threshold emblem of poetic surmise, and where the deferred revelation or end becomes at once the clear "identity" of naming and the desired objective, or object, itself. This description, in the letter of December 1817 to his brothers, complements another favorite theme of the *Letters*, Keats's preference for a wise passivity over an impatient questing, for the openness of "speculation" over the active pursuit of a predetermined object or end. His judgment on Coleridge is repeated in his description of his friend Dilke as "a Man who cannot feel he has a personal identity unless he has made up his Mind about every thing," who will "never come at a truth as long as he lives; because he is always trying at it." The converse means of strengthening one's intellect is rather "to make up one's mind about nothing—to let the mind be a thoroughfare for all thoughts,"[33] to enjoy that absence of identity which Keats associates with Men of Genius over Men of Power.

The paradox is that all such questing is self-defeating, that the very activity of pursuit itself defines and, in so doing, reduces the end it seeks, and the implication of Keats's most characteristic speculations is that the end sought by a more circuitous route may be less reduced simply because less certain:

> It has been an old Comparison for our urging on—the Bee hive—however it seems to me that we should rather be the flower than the Bee—for it is a false notion that more is gained by receiving than giving—no the receiver and the giver are equal in their benefits. . . . Now it is more noble to sit like Jove than to fly like Mercury—let us not therefore go hurrying about and collecting honey-bee like, buzzing here and there impatiently from a knowledge of what is to be arrived at: but let us open our leaves like a flower and be passive and receptive— budding patiently under the eye of Apollo and taking hints from every noble insect that favors us with a visit—sap will be given us for Meat and dew for drink.[34]

The suggestion here that an expectant emptiness is a precondition of all creation, that patience and passivity are more fruitful than an anxious concern for the morrow, has, for the poet, the implication that the Genius of Poetry "must work out its own salvation in a man," that it "cannot be matured by law & precept, but by sensation & watchfulness in itself."[35] Keats's letters strain on the paradox that effort cannot finally accelerate the "very gradual ripening of the intellectual powers,"[36] and the Great Odes of 1819, after months of agonizing, simply come. One of the "axioms" which Keats puts forward in a letter to his publisher is that "if Poetry comes not as naturally as the Leaves to a tree it had better not come at all"; and the opposite of such patience and openness is the willful and anxious fretting which informs the autoerotic and unnatural imagery of a poem such as the second sonnet "On Fame."[37]

We have characterized romance as a form which simultaneously projects the end it seeks and defers or wanders from a goal which would mean among other things the end of the quest itself. The paradox that questing may prevent the attainment of a desired end—or delimit it—is not, of course, new to romance. The Questing Beast of Malory (or Spenser's Blatant Beast) is in many ways a subtle parody of the quest itself, and Wolfram's *Parzival* openly contrasts the discontinuous and gratuitous operation of grace with the strict linear path of too active, or anxious, a concern with arrival.[38] In Keats, however, this characteristic feature of romance extends as well to the traditional form of the epiphanic Ode. It is not difficult to assimilate the trajectory of the Ode to the form of the romance quest; both depend on the separation of subject and object, and on the dialectic of absence and presence this separation begets. The "Ode to a Nightingale" provides, in this respect, perhaps the most striking instance of the way in which such questing projects, or prefigures, its own "end." The project of the Ode is literally the *projet* of the distance between the speaker and the nightingale to which he desires to find the "way" ("Away! away! For I will fly to thee . . ."). The entire Ode moves between these two poles, first towards and then away from the goal of desire. The song of the nightingale is pure prolepsis ("Singest of summer in full-throated ease") but the movement of the poem between the poles of its own creation is prefigurative in a darker sense. Prolepsis, like faith, is the evidence of things unseen. It maintains an open and unpredatory relation to a reality "to come." But the pursuit of the nightingale—the desire of the speaker to find a "way"—is closer to Keats's own description of the predatory or end-haunted consciousness, of the men who make their way with "the same unwandering eye from their purposes . . . as the Hawk."[39]

Northrop Frye and others have suggested that all quests for an elusive object end in some form of what Blake called the "Crystal Cabinet," that closing up of the object which is one of the most frequent romance analogues of a symbolic fixing.[40] In Keats's ode, this romance phenomenon takes the form of turning the nightingale into an "eternity symbol," a golden bird from which the speaker is by definition estranged. The location of the nightingale is at first indefinite ("some melodious plot / Of beechen green, and shadows numberless," 8-9), but when it is fixed into immortality and the speaker's quest for identity turns out to be inseparable from the quest for death, the latent polarities of the poem pull relentlessly apart, separating out into near and far, here and there, now and then, up and down. The *anastrophe* and *catastrophe* of the ode form enact the Icarus movement of failed flight. The illusion breaks up in two directions: the bird flies away and the poet falls out of vision. And yet, if there is separation here, it is at least partly the result of the speaker's own strict division of things into subject and object, mortal and immortal, and the poem sets in motion its own *Nemesis*, the final disjunction a simple consequence of such an absolute poetic logic.

This separation is all the more dramatic for the presence in the poem of a moment which resists such strict linear movement, the moment of virtual blindness in stanza v before the poet, as it were, "sees" the dialectical implications of his own imagery and the eye becomes the casement which separates him from his vision:

> I cannot see what flowers are at my feet,
>   Nor what soft incense hangs upon the boughs,
> But, in embalmèd darkness, guess each sweet
>   Wherewith the seasonable month endows
> The grass, the thicket, and the fruit-tree wild—
>   White hawthorn, and the pastoral eglantine;
>   Fast-fading violets covered up in leaves;
>   And mid-May's eldest child,
>   The coming musk-rose, full of dewy wine,
>   The murmurous haunt of flies on summer eves.

Suspended between absence and full revelation, arrested in the process of moving from *numen* to *nomen*, this middle or threshold state is the one Keats in a note on Milton called "the intense pleasure of not knowing," the state between the "burden of the mystery" and too complete a revelation.[41] The stanza is a space cleared between polarities, a scene whose "fast-fading violets" and "coming musk-rose" move in more than one direction and a poetic charm which unweaves in the very act of weaving, sounding the warning in words such as "embalmèd" even as it journeys inward through them. The simultaneous emptiness and fullness of stanzas I and II (the opiate "emptied" and the beaker "full of the warm South") is joined by the "plot" (8) which is at once place and project, the space presently filled by the bird's song and pure anticipation or conspiracy, like the "conspiring" of Sun and Season in the "Autumn Ode." In stanza v, the poet himself shares in the prolepsis of the nightingale's song, as "Singest of summer in full-throated ease" (10) is seconded by his own participation in "The murmurous haunt of flies on summer eves" (50).

This moment points to other aspects of the poem which resist the straightforward movement of the quest, and the fall away from it. In one of his notes on Milton, Keats spoke of the conflict in the epic poet between an "exquisite passion for what is properly, in the sense of ease and pleasure, poetical Luxury" and the great "Argument" of *Paradise Lost*.[42] The "Ode to a Nightingale" participates in the same opposition, a movement in which the linear pull of aspiration is attenuated by a contrary music. Reduced to its barest essentials, for example, stanza II of the Ode is the speaker's simple petition: "Oh, for a draught of vintage . . . / That I might drink, and leave the world unseen, / And with thee fade away into the forest dim—." The rest of the stanza, however, literally wanders from this strong sense of an end or objective and leads the mind in other directions:

> Oh, for a draught of vintage that hath been
>   Cooled a long age in the deep-delvèd earth,
> Tasting of Flora and the country green,
>   Dance, and Provençal song, and sunburnt mirth!
> Oh, for a beaker full of the warm South,
>   Full of the true, the blushful Hippocrene,

With beaded bubbles winking at the brim,
And purple-stainèd mouth,
That I might drink, and leave the world unseen,
And with thee fade away into the forest dim—

Repetition and elaboration in this stanza are not simply in ap-
position to the main syntactic line. They also gently oppose
it, opening as they do a space between the two ends of the
petition: the long train of modifiers even makes it momentarily uncertain whether the last "that" ("That I might drink") is
a movement forward to the completion of the sentence or yet
another expansion upon, or modifier of, that "draught." The
richly sensuous aspect of the verse carries the reader not to the
completion of the petition in the final lines but first to the
pause at "purple-stainèd mouth." The attention wanders
from the end to the attractive means, and ironically the very
stanza which states its absence from the nightingale picks up
echoes from the first stanza's description of it: "beechen
green" is echoed in "country green," "full-throated ease"
suggested in the phrase which leads from "Full" to "purple-
stainèd mouth," and "Singest of summer" echoed, and its
parts, as it were, redistributed, in the sound and heat of
"Provençal song, and sunburnt mirth." The form of the
petition—"leave the world unseen"—seems an ironic reduction after the sensuous fullness of the rest of the stanza, and
the impulse to quest is, in this sense at least, a failure to recognize the hidden affinity between the poet and the nightingale
which is already "there," an antiphony within the poem's
sound which connects by a different logic than the linear.

"Born for death" in the stanza which states the separation,
or "seeing," might be an emblem of this linearity, a *curriculum
vitae* with no saving digressions. "Quies" in this poem is
finally inseparable from "requiem," but the suggestion may
be as well that any such fixing of an end is death-like, or defined. What earlier critics of the poem called its "ironic coun-
terpoise" or "second voice" may also be an essential schizo-
phrenia of the self, wanting and not wanting to reach this
goal, and left, finally, in some realm in between:

Was it a vision, or a waking dream?
Fled is that music . . . Do I wake or sleep?

The wanderings of the "Nightingale Ode" allow us to
double back, chronologically, to the poem whose rejection of
a willful questing offers a much-needed clue to its digressive,
or wandering, structure. Keats himself spoke of his "Poetic
Romance," *Endymion*, as "a little Region to wander in,"[43] a
conception of the long poem which could not be further from
the express teleology of Miltonic epic, and many of its critics
have taken its ambulatory mode as an indication of its lack of
design or intention. Certainly the one immediately noticeable
feature of *Endymion* is the fact that it does not have any clearly
definable stanzas through which movement can be conveniently plotted, or staged. It is not, in appearance at least,
self-consciously "framed" like the "Ode to a Nightingale,"
but gives the impression instead of a movement which is
never entirely certain where it is tending, an uncertainty
which makes it the extreme Romantic example of the much-
vaunted Spenserian fluidity. The thread of the line is frequently the only clue to this labyrinth. And yet, in spite of
this apparent formlessness, the poem's windings do have a
characteristic direction perhaps more revealing than any
schematic plotting of its mythic realms,[44] and the structure is,
in a very different sense, intentional, related to the theme of
the fruitfulness of wandering, of the more circuitous route.

The end of Endymion's quest is the original of his vision,
the mysterious presence who calls him out of the community
of Latmos but withholds her identity. Endymion's dream of
his goddess in Book I is a repetition of Arthur's dream of
Gloriana in *The Faerie Queene*, and, once again, as in Spenser,
the interval between dream and fulfillment becomes implicitly the expanded space of the poem itself. Endymion
when we first meet him is compared to Ganymede (I. 170),
but this allusion to the translated favorite of Jove would seem
to be provided chiefly for contrast. Endymion is specifically
not simply "translated," though the end of his wanderings is
repeatedly promised, and this space between promise and end

becomes a crucial part of the education of the quester to the more negative capability of patience.

Harold Bloom remarks that "Endymion's fate is mostly a series of frustrations, and he ultimately achieves his quest only by abandoning it,"[45] but in another respect the "unlooked-for change" (IV. 992) of the ending is of a piece with the rest of the poem. The motto of the Cave of Quietude in Book IV—"Enter none / Who strive therefore—on the sudden it is won" (531-32)—might stand for the sense throughout that what is sought can be found only when it is given up. Endymion's description of his first dream of his goddess conveys the anxiety of his desire for possession (I. 653-54: "Madly did I kiss / The wooing arms which held me . . ."), but he falls, this time, as suddenly out of his dream into "stupid sleep," as if the consequence of too extreme a desire for presence were an inevitable consciousness of loss. When the goddess comes to him again in Book II, it is only when the quest for possession has been momentarily resigned, when the passive and receptive state of sleep has replaced a more willful snatching:

> "Where'er thou art,
> Methinks it now is at my will to start
> Into thine arms; to scare Aurora's train,
> And snatch thee from the morning . . .
>
> . . . .
>
> No, no, too eagerly my soul deceives
> Its powerless self. I know this cannot be.
> Oh, let me then by some sweet dreaming flee
> To her entrancements. Hither, sleep, awhile!
> Hither most gentle sleep! and soothing foil
> For some few hours the coming solitude."
>
> (II. 694-97, 701-6)

This paradox—that the object of his desire cannot be attained by direct pursuit—has its counterpart in the structure of a poem which defers the fulfillment of Endymion's dream and proceeds instead by a technique of indirection. In Book I of *The Faerie Queene*, Arthur reveals that the fulfillment of his dream of Gloriana is to come in the fullness of time—"As when iust time expired should appeare" (I. ix. 14. 4). The "just time" of the Spenserian original is the "unknown time" (II. 292) before the promise made to Endymion and constantly renewed throughout his "wandering in uncertain ways" (48) is to be answered, the journeying into "other regions" which must be accomplished before he can be taken from "every wasting sigh, from every pain," into the "gentle bosom" of his "love" (126-27). And this sense of the fullness of time is repeated in the episode of Glaucus, where the old man's period of waiting for the youth who is to end Circe's spell is informed with vaguely biblical echoings (III. 234: "Thou art the man!") of the yearning for "fulfillment." Both the episode of Venus and Adonis in Book II and the awakening of the prisoners of Circe in Book III defer even as they prefigure the apocalyptic end of Endymion's wanderings, and Endymion, like Spenser's Arthur, must assist in the fulfillment of other quests before he may complete his own. The "mighty consummation" of the reanimated lovers is filled with apocalyptic images of awakening and dawning, but Endymion himself remains within the twilight realm of "patience" (III. 906-16), still "wandering in the bands / Of love" (903-4).

Endymion, indeed, raises the question of whether all sense of "progress" in this kind of romance is simply an illusion. "Waiting" is, in this poem, a kind of marking time, or, to the extent that Endymion is the prisoner of an alien time-scheme, doing time, and his wandering the kind of incremental repetition that imparts a sense of déjà vu to so much of romance. Its nightmare strain is the deeply oppressive waiting of the Cave of Quietude, a kind of demonic counterpart of that moment of silence or "attente" in heaven just before the final movement of the Apocalypse,[46] a vigil which, in older romance, might be that sudden change in which the knight, on the verge of arrival at his goal, finds himself trapped in a tomb-like room. Escape from the Cave, in Endymion, is as inexplicable as entrance into it, and it is, like those moments in older romance, perhaps more powerful for being finally irreducible to meaning. But it provides, within the poem, the chilling shadow of a more fruitful waiting and anticipates the ordeal, in *The Fall of Hyperion*, of a darker vigil.

Temperance in Keats as in Spenser and Milton means partly the tempering of the apocalyptic impulse, and "patience" is the difficult discipline of learning how to move in time. In *Endymion*, time or temporizing seems at once a saving grace (I. 705-6: "Time, that agèd nurse, / Rocked me to patience") and a trial to be endured. The danger of impatience has its counterpart in the danger of falling into the "trancèd dullness" (II. 768) of melancholy, the analogue of Spenser's several versions of despair:

> Now indeed
> His senses had swooned off; he did not heed
> The sudden silence, or the whispers low,
> Or the old eyes dissolving at his woe,
> Or anxious calls, or close of trembling palms,
> Or maiden's sigh, that grief itself embalms;
> But in the self-same fixèd trance he kept,
> Like one who on the earth had never stepped.
> Aye, even as dead-still as a marble man,
> Frozen in that old tale Arabian.
>
> (I. 397-406)

And when the quest for complete possession fails, yet once again, in the repeated visitations of the goddess in Book II, the result is still another paralyzing "lethargy" (768-69).

"Patience" in this poem opens up a space between the extremes of possession and loss, turning the twilight zone of time between a first and second "coming" into a purgatorial journey which is as much a question of endurance as of active seeking. Keats does not so much consciously reactivate this biblical and romance tradition as he seems thoroughly to absorb its metaphors, in the gathering harvest of the sonnet "When I Have Fears" or in the "ripening" of the labors of Glaucus in Book III of *Endymion* (703-10). Learning how to move in time is, for Endymion, a more ominously purgatorial kind of ripening, the "ardent listlessness" (I. 825) of being at once led out into the realm of questing and yet still kept on the threshold of "prospect." Oxymoron is the trope of temperance, as of purgatory, and the two, in Keats, are virtually inseparable.

Endymion's "labours" are what finally win him the consummation of his own quest. The interval of deferral and delay which is the space of his wandering seems, however, to have another purpose as well. The myth of Cynthia and Endymion is a fable of heavenly condescension, of the "accommodation" of the divine to the human. Northrop Frye suggests that Endymion cannot approach his goddess directly for fear of sharing the fate of Actaeon; like Dante, he must take the long way round.[47] But the space opened up by this *lungo andare* also provides time for a change in the goddess herself, a softening of her dread virginity. The Ovidian stories of a failed questing depend on the linear logic of pursuit and flight: if the *animus* of the quest is at least partly the demon of possession, the motive for metamorphosis is the desire for self-preservation, or escape. Pan, the presiding deity of Keats's pastoral-romance, reveals in his duality the poem's hidden conflict, the tension between the perpetually forward, or displaced, movement of questing and the dilation of the present moment into a totality of presence, an *espacement* which simultaneously embowers. He is on the one hand the poem's emblem for a wholeness which obviates all need for questing, being, as his name suggests, everywhere at once. But the other Pan—the frustrated pursuer of "fair Syrinx" (I. 243)—is introduced as early as the opening hymn and initiates the Ovidian motif of pursuit and loss which is to continue in the interlude of Alpheus and Arethuse and in the journey of Endymion himself. Keats's image of a fruitful consummation in the great celebration of the reunited lovers in Book III is a Dance of the Seasons, a transformation of the linear procession of times into a round, and the sound-slip which transforms Dian the "Hunter" into the fair "Haunter" of Book II (302) reflects the poem's more general tendency to turn pursuit into "amidness," or presence. The true accommodation of divided realms can take place only when Cynthia

finally determines to be neither chaste nor chased. "Condescension" is the counterpart on the divine level of the tempering of Endymion's more possessive questing, and the gradual
conversion of the goddess finally turns the trajectory of pursuit and flight into a genuine encounter.

The poetic strategy of deferral and dilation allies *Endymion*
with the older romances where diversion and "error" allow
the poem to unfold. It also, however, distinguishes it from
the darker questing of the poem which has been repeatedly
recognized as its contemporary counterpart, Shelley's *Alastor*.[48] The Solitary of Shelley's poem reaches his end by a ruth-
less elimination, by a "career" (262) which is literally a race,
and his "impatient wandering" (300) is ultimately a quest for
death, the "shadowy lure" (294) to which he finally succumbs. Keats, in contrast, by making the capability required
of Endymion that of patience, opens up a space between the
beginning and the end of his solitary's quest which suggests
the hope that his ending will not be a solitary and solipsistic
death.

This aspect of the counterpoint with *Alastor* is subtle but
persistent. Alastor resists all diversion from his onward
course; and this headlong pursuit is suggested, in *Endymion*,
in a passage which looks forward in time to the anxious questing of the "Nightingale Ode":

> Increasing still in heart and pleasant sense,
> Upon his fairy journey on he hastes,
> So anxious for the end, he scarcely wastes
> One moment with his hand among the sweets.
> Onward he goes . . .
>
> (*Endymion* II. 351-55)

These very Shelleyan lines are soon followed by a passage on
the "consuming flame" of love, that state in which "half-
happy" is miserable (II. 365-75), and, once again, anxiety for
the end begets its polar opposite, loss. Significantly, and unlike the parts of *Alastor* it so closely echoes, Keats's passage
neither continues this headlong rush nor yields to the slowed
rhythm of despond, but brings its wanderer instead to a
"meantime" experience—the bower of Adonis—which if it

diverts him from the direct pursuit of his quest also saves him from the premature end of despair.

Such "diversion" in Keats's poem is not only a technique of error which defers the end of the journey, but also a kind of saving respite. Harold Bloom comments that "the mazes of romance, in *Endymion*, are so winding that they suggest the contrary to vision, a labyrinthine nature in which all quest must be forlorn. In this realm, nothing narrows to an intensity, and every passionate impulse widens out to a diffuseness, the fate of Endymion's own search for his goddess."[49] There is, however, in these Shelleyan echoes the suggestion of a fear of precisely such a narrowing. The center of the labyrinth is as likely to be the fixation of despair as it is to be the locus of vision, and decentering is the movement which keeps Keats's Solitary en route. Each of the intervening episodes of *Endymion* is literally an interlude which saves the seeker from the vortex of the self. Being led to the bower of Adonis saves Endymion from the "swart abysm" (II. 376) of self-reflection, and this diversion is repeated when the shepherd ponders the "blank amazements" of his own wanderings ("Now I have tasted her sweet soul to the core / All other depths are shallow . . .") and is distracted by the sight of the two streams (901-35).

This pattern is repeated too often to be accidental, or empty of meaning. At each stage, just as the wanderer is about to sink into the immobility of despair, some new refreshment, guide, or diversion saves him from paralysis and keeps both poem and pilgrim moving. A butterfly appears and the wanderer's limbs are "loosed" from "languor's sullen bands" (II. 66-67); the sight of "flowers, and wreaths" provides the visual refreshment which saves him from the blankness of "Desponding, o'er the marble floor's cold thrill" (338-50). This sense of recovery or di-version is reflected even in the turning of the syntax, where the linear movement towards a darker end is interrupted or qualified:

> And down some swart abysm he had gone,
> Had not a heavenly guide benignant led . . .
>
> (II. 376-77)

A cold leaden awe
These secrets struck into him, and unless
Dian had chased away that heaviness,
He might have died. But now, with cheerèd feel,
He onward kept . . .

(III. 136–40)

The solitary felt a hurried change
Working within him into something dreary—
Vexed like a morning eagle, lost and weary
And purblind amid foggy, midnight wolds.
But he revives at once, for who beholds
New sudden things, nor casts his mental slough?

(II. 633–38)

The opposite of this decentering movement is the menacing
solitude of a return to the center of the self:

There, when new wonders ceased to float before
And thoughts of self came on, how crude and sore
The journey homeward to habitual self!
A mad pursuing of the fog-born elf,
Whose flitting lantern, through rude nettle-briar,
Cheats us into a swamp, into a fire,
Into the bosom of a hated thing.

(II. 274–80)

The danger or potential impasse is the vortex of solipsism,
one of the new sirens of the wilderness once the familiar locus
of quest romance has been clearly "internalized,"[50] and the
skirting of this dark vortex is one of the ways in which
Keats's poem finally differs from Shelley's. The direct literary
reference here, however, is not to Shelley but to Milton, and
the simile which in Milton is an image of the dangers of wandering or deviation (the "delusive Light" which deceives the
"Night-wanderer" in *PL* IX. 634–42) becomes here, in contrast, an image of the removal of all saving diversions, the
profoundly melancholy experience of being tolled back to
one's sole self.

That the echo should be a Miltonic one, and specifically of a

Miltonic "wandering," provides a crucial insight into Keats's "Poetic Romance." In the first book of *Endymion*, after the close of the great hymn to Pan, the shepherds of Latmos disperse to their several pastimes. The scene is pastoral, the description leisurely, and the diction part of the expected sensuousness of Elizabethan romance. The situation itself, however, is Miltonic and bears inescapable echoes of another great congress and its aftermath, the dispersal of the fallen angels in Book II of *Paradise Lost*. The company of angels which in Milton's epic turn to "discourse" is echoed by the "sober ring" of aged shepherds around Endymion, discoursing upon the "fragile bar / That keeps us from our homes ethereal" (I. 360-61) and upon the nature of the world to come:

> Anon they wandered, by divine converse,
> Into Elysium, vying to rehearse
> Each one his own anticipated bliss.
>
> (371-73)

Their "wandering" is a direct echo of the wandering of the fallen angels in the passage which Keats turned to twice in his notes on *Paradise Lost*, once with the most important lines carefully scored:

> Others, more mild,
> Retreated in a silent valley, sing
> With notes angelical to many a harp
> Their own heroic deeds, and hapless fall
> By doom of battle, and complain that Fate
> Free Virtue should enthrall to Force or Chance.
> Their song was partial; but the harmony
> (What could it less when Spirits immortal sing?)
> Suspended Hell, and took with ravishment
> The thronging audience. In discourse more sweet
> (For Eloquence the Soul, Song charms the Sense)
> Others apart sat on a hill retired,
> In thoughts more elevate, and reasoned high
> Of Providence, Foreknowledge, Will, and Fate—
> Fixed fate, free will, foreknowledge absolute—
> And found no end, in wandering mazes lost.[51]

It is the difference within the echo, however, which is revealing. In Milton, such "wandering" is a wandering lost, its
most telling condemnation being that it leads nowhere. Like
the "evasions vain" of Adam after the Fall, it stands as a sign
of paradise lost. But in Keats, this wandering is, as it were,
rendered innocent, its end not a wandering lost but a pure
prolepsis, a vision of "anticipated bliss."

Endymion is filled with hints of this more dangerous wandering, but it is finally only the dark enemy to be banished,
like the contrary moods which shadow "L'Allegro" and "Il
Penseroso." It was while at work on the last book of his
"Romance" that Keats penned some of his most famous
speculations on the poetical character:

> O for a Life of Sensations rather than of Thoughts! It
> is "a Vision in the form of a Youth" a Shadow of real-
> ity to come—and this consideration has further con-
> vinced me for it has come as auxiliary to another
> favorite Speculation of mine, that we shall enjoy
> ourselves here after by having what we called hap-
> piness on Earth repeated in a finer tone and so re-
> peated—And yet such a fate can only befall those
> who delight in sensation rather than hunger as you
> do after Truth.[52]

Endymion is the closest Keats came to the poetic realization of
this speculation. Endymion's schooling in the discipline of patience is a more painful process than either pure "sensation"
or the transition from Adam's dream suggest, but his dream
is finally realized and his wandering, unlike that of Milton's
fallen angels, does reach an end. The suggestion in the description of the ripening "completions" of the realm of Pan (I.
259-60) and the passage which describes the wandering of a
lost "lamb" through "gloomy shades" (67) to the renewed
community of "the herds" (78) provide the pastoral equivalent of the final translation of Endymion, and in this respect
the ending is not, as many critics have protested, tacked on,
but has been implicit from the beginning.

The problem of progression towards a satisfying ending is

perhaps nowhere more clearly revealed than in the Miltonic and Shelleyan echoes of one of the poem's most insistent images for the romance's archetypal space—the veil of twilight or evening. As the temporal equivalent of the desire for temperance, a *tempe* between light and darkness when the sun is stayed "on the threshold of the west" (*Fall of Hyperion* II. 48), the image in *Endymion* recapitulates the dangers, and delights, of this "staying" in Keats's earlier romance poetry. One of his first Spenserian imitations, the fragment entitled "Calidore," opens with the image of evening as a desired suspension ("the beauty of a silent eve, / Which seemed full loth this happy world to leave, / The light dwelt o'er the scene so lingeringly"). The staying of this twilight, however, begins curiously to affect the movement of the poem itself; the verse keeps slowing down to quietude and is only fitfully awakened by a sound or "voice" (55, 99) which calls to something higher than mere reflection. The slowed rhythm is Keats's version of that Spenserian languor which Hazlitt described as holding the soul captive in the chains of suspense. But the voice which awakens from the potentially Narcissistic lingering has a closer, Miltonic, model—the reflection of Eve in the pool and her conversion by the warning voice. Eve's vision has its Romantic descendants in the twilight or suspended interval of self-reflection dwelt upon, or within, for its own sake. For the poets after Milton who share the apocalyptic frame of his images, evening is still a *mediatrix*, preparation for the brighter light of dawn; in Blake's "To the Evening Star," there is virtually no absence or night, a progress from evening to morning which is guided by a smooth transition or "apostolic succession" of lights. But for poets less certain of this progression, evening remains a more problematic threshold, its "staying" perhaps the only refuge from a darker abyss.[53]

The question of which way this twilight zone is tending is crucial for Keats because it is linked, as early as *Endymion*, to the problem of the transition from romance to reality, dream to truth. In Book IV of his "Romance," Keats makes a strange admission, that he has not only returned the translated Endymion of the myth to a space anterior to that happy ending but has in fact dilated, or prolonged, the threshold state which he describes in the revised preface as a form of sickness:

> Yes, moonlight Emperor! Felicity
> Has been thy meed for many thousand years,
> Yet often have I, on the brink of tears,
> Mourned as if yet thou wert a forester,
> Forgetting the old tale.
>
> (IV. 776-80)

Perhaps the reason Keats seems to want Endymion's wanderings not to proceed too quickly to their ending is that the "translation" of the "old tale" is now no longer possible except as a palpable design, while, at the same time, he fears the inevitability of the darker Shelleyan ending, the descent of this threshold into night.

In *Endymion* itself, there is an interplay of images of "twilight" both as preparation for the dawning of fulfillment and as mere prelude to the fall into darkness. So closely are the realm of dream and evening connected that waking to disappointment in this poem is inevitably accompanied by the decline of the momentarily suspended twilight into its darker successor, the disappearance of the dream goddess Cynthia, or the Moon.[54] The realm of delusive dream is linked with the more sinister aspect of twilight's "veil" as false surmise: the "specious heaven" Circe prepares for Glaucus in Book III is a "twilight bower" which, though it seems to be that of morning (418-19), in fact leads, when the entranced lover wakens to the truth of her identity, to the "dark lair of night" (560).

Once again, these images of decline seem deliberately to summon echoes of *Alastor*, where the Solitary's entry upon a "silent nook" over which the moon hangs "suspended" (*Alastor*, 647) recalls an earlier moment in which, like Milton's Eve, he gazes at his own image in a well (469-92). In the poem's final evening bower on the threshold of night ("a tranquil spot, that seemed to smile / Even in the lap of horror," 577-78), the Solitary's fate is so completely connected with the natural cycle that, as evening declines into darkness, he meets the end of his quest in death (645-62). Book IV of *Endymion* is filled with echoes of this Shelleyan ending, as Endymion, having identified with the natural cycle in his choice of the Indian Maid, repeatedly uses the image of evening as the inevitable emblem of his own decline.[55] The unexpected reversal of the actual ending is precisely that it pointedly turns from the Shelleyan abyss, as the compound female—dusky Indian Maid and Cynthia, goddess of the moon—brightens into dawn ("Her long black hair swelled ampler, in display / Full golden; in her eyes a brighter day / Dawned blue and full of love," 984-86). The sense in Book I that there can finally be no wandering lost in the realm of Pan is joined, in that image's temporal counterpart, by the transformation of the poem's twilight zone into a threshold on the verge of "day."

The Perilous Threshold: Spell and Counterspell

THE progress of *Endymion* is finally neither the Miltonic wandering lost nor the Shelleyan quest for an end which is death, but a journey in which the more circuitous route leads to a more fruitful ending. It is not, however, any less a form of wish-fulfillment. The darker echoes, both of Milton and of Shelley, persist, and its ending—the ascension or translation of Endymion—happens, significantly, offstage. The poetry after *Endymion* is so manifestly an attempt to leave it behind that criticism has frequently concurred in Keats's judgment of his first long poem by slighting it. There is within *Endymion*, however, a foretaste of problems which were to continue to haunt Keats's poetry,[56] and it is in the context of this continuity that the value of situating Keats within the history of romance most clearly emerges. The final translation of Endymion recapitulates the older romance typology in which the wilderness of wandering between the Egypt of a Mammon world and the Paradise of "identity" does finally lead to a higher realm.[57] This very movement, however, makes *Endymion* a consciously archaizing poem, part of a history no longer open in *The Fall of Hyperion*, where ascent to that

higher realm is effectively blocked, just as the gates of
Saturn's temple are "shut against the sunrise evermore" (I.
86). Blake among the Romantics still retains the typological
structure in which the middle realm of "Beulah" could lead
up to the Promised Land of "Eden" as well as down into the
Egypt of "Ulro." But for poets less certain of this upward
progression, this triadic scheme shrinks to a more fearful
symmetry.[58] The wilderness of wandering is traditionally at
once a passageway and a potential impasse, but it becomes
even more threatening when the upper, apocalyptic pole
drops out or becomes virtually indistinguishable from its
opposite.

Keats, most explicitly the poet of romance among the
Romantics, is in this sense truly the poet of transition, the
transmitter of symbols and traditions of whose origin he may
be unaware. He is not, as he frequently laments, a learned
poet in the tradition of Spenser and Milton, and he is a con-
spicuously unbiblical poet in an age when poets such as
Wordsworth or Shelley are Bible-soaked. But it may be that
his very absorption in the older poets, perhaps almost because
of his ignorance, makes him the Apollo of his own projected
Hyperion, a figure who divests himself of the trappings of an
older world at the same time as he conscripts the help of a
Mnemosyne, or memory-principle, to carry that world into
the future. Coleridge may be the most important of the English Romantics for the critical transformation and continuation of theological concepts; but it is John Keats who carries
forward even as he transforms and thoroughly internalizes, or
"in-feels," and Matthew Arnold's description of him as the
"merely sensuous man" is helpful if it enables us to see that he
did not so much recast or conceptualize these images as get
inside them.

It is for this reason that the clue to the progress of "romance" in Keats, between the successful translation of *Endymion* and the impasse of the first *Hyperion*, is often less at the
level of argument, or in his willed rejection of an outmoded
genre, than in the phenomenology of that genre's related images, the ambivalence of "twilight," shade, or wandering,

and the poetic state of "trance" or "sleep." The "staying" of evening in "Calidore" and the moments of trance as paralysis in *Endymion* are early turnings from the delights of virtuality celebrated in the *Letters*, and even in the early poetry the familiar Keatsian images for the lingering or the liminal turn into their nightmare opposites when all transition, or movement forward, is blocked. The crucial feature of "Sleep and Poetry" is that the poet does not sink into the passive state of sleep, but instead maintains a vigilance which turns the poem into a creative vigil, or "wake." The characteristic Keatsian stance is a poise or "listening" in which the transitional, "to come" dimension of the casement becomes an attitude, and it has its complement in the enclitic or "leaning" propensity of words in which we feel simultaneously the heaviness and the poise.[59] The emphasis seems always in Keats to be on the openness of the transition, on what is often the celebration of sheer directionality, like Thea in *The Fall* "Pointing somewhither" (I. 456) or like the "across" of "To Autumn" ("sometimes like a gleaner thou dost keep / Steady thy laden head across a brook"), a word which stays and goes at once.

The images which most clearly define the ambivalence of this threshold in Keats are those which carry with them the resonance of an ambivalence at the heart of romance itself, the dark doubles of its hopeful "foreshadowing" and of its delightful wandering or "error." Keats's description of the imagination as "a Shadow of reality to come" is virtually a translation of the older language of the "shadowy type" into the activity of the prefigurative imagination, and it retains that concept's authentically temporal dimension. But the proleptic "shadow" in Keats also carries forward a danger inherent in the older concept, the "shadow" of a paralyzing melancholy.[60] The delightful *clair-obscur* of "half-knowledge" and the "shadowy thought" of the "Ode to Psyche" have their darker counterpart in the "shade" of a late poem to Fanny Brawne ("Oh, for some sunny spell / To dissipate the shadows of this hell!"), the purely negative aspect of a threshold which separates the poet from the object of his desire. In the letter in which both Adam's dream and the prefigurative imagination appear, time is the medium in which the latent comes to light: "What the imagination seizes as Beauty must be truth—whether it existed before or not." But the possibility is also that this interval could be an abortive one, that the "shadow of reality to come" might remain, like the murdered Lorenzo of *Isabella*, a "shadow" dwelling forever "Upon the skirts of human-nature" (305-6), a cold disembodied spirit caught in its own limbo and reality-starved. A. B. Giamatti's contrasting of the peripheral voyeurism with the central vision of romance provides an insight into Spenser, where the jealous voyeur in an erotic triangle is also the poem's most notable specter,[61] but it provides as well a perspective on the "prefigurative" in Keats, the temporal counterpart of the eternal spectator reduced to the merely spectral. Keats's poems abound in Dantesque images of foretasting, of anticipation as a present fasting for an ultimate feast. "Foretaste" in Keats, however, is also potentially nothing but perpetual foreplay, starvation when the autumn's "granary" is full. "La Belle Dame Sans Merci" remains a hauntingly literary ballad because it is a tale not of consummation but of suspended desire, a poem in which the apocalyptic tendency of literature—what Paul de Man calls its temptation to fulfill itself in a single moment[62]—becomes instead a kind of shadowy impotence, an inability to fulfill itself at all.

The "shadow" which does not foreshadow has its counterpart in a wandering which leads nowhere at all. The transformation of the successful wandering of *Endymion* is nowhere more dramatic than in the poem which, in the crucial winter months of 1817-18, signals both a loss of direction and the darkening of the dilated threshold into a "Purgatory blind"—the "Verse Epistle to Reynolds." Of Milton's famous pair of poems, it is "L'Allegro" which begins with the banishing of "loathed Melancholy"; but in the numerous odes to Melancholy in the century after Milton, it is the *penseroso* mood itself which must be shielded from its more morbid counterpart, "Of Cerberus and blackest midnight born." Keats's "Epistle" is in form as much descended from Milton's pair as it is from the eighteenth-century loco-descriptive

poem, but it is in many ways an "Il Penseroso" gone wrong.
The poet is more the victim than the summoner of his moods
("Away ye horrid moods, / Moods of one's mind!" 105-6),
the ambulatory style of Milton's poems a strangely disjointed
verse, and "wandering" a more darkly purgatorial travail:

> Things cannot to the will
> Be settled, but they tease us out of thought.
> Or is it that imagination brought
> Beyond its proper bound, yet still confined,
> Lost in a sort of Purgatory blind,
> Cannot refer to any standard law
> Of either earth or heaven?
>
> (76-82)

The compulsive "dreamings" of this poem are the infernal
opposite of repetition in a finer tone, stated in the very images
of its conception, and the rejection here of both Wordsworthian "earth" and Miltonic "heaven"[63] is presented not as the
triumphant staking of a new poet's special ground but rather
as the discovery of unwilled confinement to the limbo between them.

Both the complaint against things which cannot "to the
will / Be settled" and the paralysis of an imprisoning shadow
echo as they invert the language of Negative Capability, and
the danger that liminality may be simply impotence seems
finally to haunt Keats's conception of the poetical character as
well. Negative Capability is one of the delights of the
threshold. But when, as in the late letters and poems to Fanny
Brawne, the state of patience and passivity threatens to become one of impotence and despair, the selfhood comes back
with a vengeance and all the accustomed imagery of the virtual is turned inside out:

> I cry your mercy, pity, love—aye love!
>   Merciful love that tantalizes not,
> One-thoughted, never-wandering, guileless love,
>   Unmasked, and being seen—without a blot!
> Oh, let me have thee whole—all, all, be mine!
>
> ("I cry your mercy, pity, love . . . ," 1-5)

The problem both of the threshold and of transition beyond it becomes more intense in Keats when waking into truth is not fulfillment but fall, not a movement, like Dante's, from the dream of a siren to the revelations of a *Paradiso*, but rather the awakening of a rude descent. *Lamia* and "La Belle Dame Sans Merci" chronicle an awakening into misery, or death, and raise the question of whether waking from a dream, however siren-like, is a good in itself; and Thea in the *Hyperion* fragments hesitates to waken Saturn if the only alternative to dream is a renewed consciousness of loss. The only "translation" in *The Eve of St. Agnes* is the uncertain one of the sonnet to Fanny Brawne. Keats's *Letters* are filled with a series of such counteractive pairs—"sensation" and image in the pool, prefers her unreal dream to its realization in Porphyro's presence, and the "painful change" of the transition ("There was a painful change, that nigh expelled / The blisses of her dream so pure and deep," 300-1) suggests that there may be something unavoidably lost in the exchange of old rituals for new. The wishful comparison of the imagination to Adam's dream is instead an ambivalence exquisitely dramatized as a virgin's dream ("No dream, alas!" 328), a moment of awakening which is simultaneously consummation and loss.

Moving from romance to reality, dream to truth, is partly a question, as early as *Endymion*, of smoothing or making more gradual the process of transition itself. "Gradual," in Keats as in Milton, always carries with it the buried metaphor of "steps," and both the "pleasure thermometer" ("gradations of happiness")[64] of *Endymion* and the conception of Heaven as a "repetition in a finer tone" are images of a graduated ascent, of a *translatio* in which there is no loss or fall. Keats even of necessity extends the Miltonic preoccupation with "degree"; if the end is simply night or loss, the only defense against discontinuity is to forestall it, to expand the intervening steps. The movement which in *Endymion* takes the form of a tension between questing and the expanding circumference of embowered moments has its verbal counterpart in what Newell F. Ford calls the "extensional" nature of Keats's images, a diction which both moves forward and dilates.[65] The spatializing imagination which in the earlier "Romance" can turn even a color into an environment ("So cool a purple," *Endymion* II. 444), reappears in *The Eve of St. Agnes* in the pure circumference or alive nothing of Madeline's "empty dress" (245) and "hollow lute" (289) and in the simultaneous reduction and intensification of the early sensuousness in which Porphyro ("purple") becomes a "throb."

This extension too, however, the graduating of the transition from threshold to fulfillment, has its nightmare aspect, a space in which not only the threshold but the movement of transition beyond it become a limbo, a potentially infinite multiplication of "degrees." Keats in *Endymion* is the poet of progress through zones, the stations or countries of the mind as romance landscape. But in *The Fall of Hyperion*, this movement becomes the perpetual transition of Moneta's face ("deathwards progressing / To no death," 260-61), and the Miltonic graduation, of premeditated "steps," becomes the involuntary "travail" of the poet himself through potentially endless or "innumerable degrees" (I. 91-92). Its "accommodation" is no longer, as in Milton, the divine descent which makes possible a gradual human ascent, but rather a drama in which the vision of a god "degraded" (322) is granted only after the poet's trial on the steps before Moneta's shrine.

This struggle has in Keats the aspect of a double bind, a state in which dilation of the liminal is no more desirable than progression towards an end or "fall." The tension inherent in romance is one which Keats both intensifies and transforms. The temporal paradox of the *nunc et nondum*, of the threshold space in which the end is both "come" and "to come," involves the possibility of a split which romance casts as two of its fundamental archetypes—the bower which threatens to provide a wholly present content or premature end and the wasteland of despair in which "not yet" darkens into "never" and "waiting" becomes the perpetual limbo of unsatisfied desire. In Keats, the split between the lapse into indolence, or despondency, and the impatience of too anxious a questing for end or fulfillment may finally be controlled only by the copresence of opposing tendencies, the reason, perhaps, why oxymoron is his characteristic trope. "Negative Capability" itself harbors a paradox, a yoking of passive and active which distinguishes and even saves it from the purely negative state of the sonnet to Fanny Brawne. Keats's *Letters* are filled with a series of such counteractive pairs—"sensation" and "thought," "mystery" and "knowledge," "indolence" and "effort"—where the latter is invoked to check the passivity of the former, and where oxymoron becomes the trope of spell and counterspell.

Keats knows perhaps best of all the English Romantics that there must be a Merlin for every Archimago, that the only satisfying counter to a paralyzing charm is not its breaking but a more powerful countercharm, and the hope in the poems after *Endymion* is that both "trance" and "spell" may somehow permit at once suspension and movement, that the poetic trance may be part of a transition, and that "spelling" may be both a way into enchantment and a way out of it, the "fine spell of words" (*Fall of Hyperion* I. 9) which might undo a darker charm. Just as the "Nightingale Ode" both spells and unspells, weaves and unweaves, at once, so the narrative of *The Eve of St. Agnes* both centers and unwinds, journeying progressively inward to the frozen center—the "steadfast spell" (287) or "midnight charm" (282) of Madeline's dream—and unwinding as the lovers glide "Down the wide stairs" (355), "into the wide hall" (361) and out "into the storm" (371). The conflict in Porphyro between the impulse to "gaze and worship" (80) from a distance and the desire to be sexually one with his "heaven" ("like a throbbing star / Seen mid the sapphire heaven's deep repose; / Into her dream he melted," 318-20) is also the problem for Keats of how to be both inside—the negative capable poet "filling" or animating bodies—and outside—directing the movement of the narrative—at the same time,[66] a perspective which would be finally beyond that of either solipsist or voyeur. In *The Eve of St. Agnes*, both wintry circumference and charmed center are frozen, and the "solution" seems to be in neither one world nor the other but in the whole poetic movement in between.

All of these—the danger of the liminal, the difficulty of a movement which does not imply a "fall," and the provision of both transition and saving counterspell—provide a frame for Keats's most dramatic late encounter with the ambivalence of romance, the "staying" or impasse of the first *Hyperion* and its recasting in the decisive contest of *The Fall*. In Book IV of *Endymion*, Keats virtually bids farewell to his "Romance" as a threshold to be crossed, mere preparation for a higher theme: "Thy lute-voiced brother will I sing ere long, / And thou shalt aid—hast thou not aided me?" (774-75). Northrop Frye comments that once Keats had explored the "garden of the moon" he was ready to move on to "the city of the sun," from *Endymion* to the projected *Hyperion*.[67] And Keats himself speaks in one letter of his intention to progress from his "moonlight emperor" to the sun-god Apollo, an imitation of the traditional Virgilian progression from the twilight zone of pastoral romance to the nobler realm of epic.[68] But Keats is not Blake, and the transition away from *Endymion* is by no means straightforward: *Hyperion* remains within the "morning twilight" (III. 33) in which Apollo still wanders before the fragment itself breaks off and the poem never reaches its projected dawn. If indeed "the fine spell of words alone can save / Imagination from the sable charm / And dumb enchantment" (*Fall* I. 9-11), we can only conclude from the disruption of the first *Hyperion* that "spell" as continuance, in this sense, falls prey to its more passive counterpart. The spell of twilight remains, like that of Tennyson's "Hesperides," an impediment to the epiphany of a sun-god. Though the poem is removed to a different register, Miltonic epic rather than Spenserian romance, the limbo of romance retains its hold. In one crucial sense, the prisoners of Circe are not yet liberated, and Apollo remains Endymion still.

Geoffrey Hartman suggests that one problem in this fragment is that movement from one realm to another happens too quickly, that Apollo is brought within moments from "forgetful, even indolent sensation" to "the flood stage of recollection," and that this "direct, precipitous transition from puberty to epiphany, from pastoral to apocalypse—

which aborts historical vision proper—puts all progress by
stages in doubt."[69] Endymion, Lemprière's "Sleeper,"[70]
moves through a realm in which the geography is uncertain
and transitions are often therefore accomplished by a melting
of image, or gradual brightening of lights. But this very liq-
uidity is what Keats seems to have wanted to get away from
in moving to the "more naked and grecian Manner" of *Hyperion*,[71] with the result that there is in this escape from the
gradual perhaps too iron a separation of realms, and transition
becomes either too abrupt or not possible at all. The movement from the Titans to Apollo in Book III of *Hyperion* is less
a transition than a self-conscious and awkward break, as if
Keats were simply uncertain how to move from one order to
the other.

The clue to this impasse may be partly in the nature of the
subject itself. Paul de Man finely remarks that we tend to con-
ceive of Apollo not as the antagonist of the Titans, but rather
as their liberator, like Endymion, the potential reanimator of
these frozen statues.[72] But this very reciprocity runs counter
to the myth's more insistently linear structure. The dramatic
given of *Hyperion* is the combination of classical and Christian
stories of a War in Heaven, a myth which debases some gods
while it exalts others, Saturn in the opening lines inevitably
recalling the fallen Satan at the beginning of *Paradise Lost*. To
both myths belongs the structure of a succession of powers, a
progress whose stages depend upon exclusion. Both are the
mythic analogues of the "march of mind" which Hazlitt describes as the progress from romance to enlightenment, a
paradigm which in the speech of Oceanus in Book II of *Hyperion* becomes a myth of successive displacement. Keats himself
wrote that he gave up *Hyperion* because it contained too many
Miltonic inversions,[73] but a more powerful reason might
have been the impasse of a transition built on a Fall. Instead of
the Miltonic, classical, or enlightenment myths of succession,
Keats seems to want a myth of translation, not the displacement of Saturn-Satan by Jupiter-God, or the sacrifice of romance to the march of intellect, but a figure who will carry
the "old stories" forward even as he bids them "adieu."

Oceanus envisions the progress to a "fresh perfection" (II.

212) as from darkness to light, but the fragment remains instead within a more veiled realm. The transitional or twilight, indeed, assumes within this first fragment its crucial historical dimension. Keats frequently sensed himself a late-comer in literary history, a poet singing at a time when "the sun of poesy is set" and the "count / Of mighty poets" already "made up" (*Endymion* II. 723-29), and even the celebration of the "patient" English Muse at the beginning of Book IV of *Endymion* is dampened by the thought of "poets gone." If, as Wallace Stevens once wrote, imagination is always "at the end of an era,"[74] the difficulty for the poet immersed in a particular time is to distinguish whether the twilight zone of the present imagining is the *Dämmerung* of former power or the "morning twilight" of a new Apollo. *Hyperion* sets out but fails to be this kind of transition, the transformation of the late into the early, of an ending into a beginning.[75]

The "Ode to Psyche," written in the same year as the two fragments, accomplishes this historical *translatio* not by the dismissal of figures or the replacement of darkness by light— as in the "Nativity Ode" it echoes—but rather through a refiguration, the rebirth of ritual as the ritual within. The fact that its re-presentation of the Apuleian myth collapses the long period of Psyche's purgatorial wanderings between the loss of Cupid and the lovers' reunion[76] suggests that its theme is the possibility of a successful translation, a progress poem with the pain of travail or loss left out. The traditional odic distance between "here" and "there," petitioner and power, dissolves by definition in what becomes a song of the "Psyche" to itself ("pardon that thy secrets should be sung / Even into thine own soft-conchèd ear," 3-4). The final "fane" is inseparable in sound as well as in sense from "feign," and all sense of the "profane" drops out because it is no longer possible to discern what, if anything, remains outside. The elision of boundaries in space (between inner and outer, heaven and earth) is extended to boundaries in time, and the distance of belatedness ("too late for antique vows! / Too, too late for the fond believing lyre," 36-37) is transformed into a projected presence, a meeting "in the midst."

The "Ode to Psyche" stands as the emblem of a translation

Hyperion fails to effect, a failure *The Fall of Hyperion* may be confronting in its presentation of the refuse of the Ode's paradisal bower (I. 25) and the instruments of its ritual ("Robes, golden tongs, censer and chafing-dish," 79) as a "mingled heap" (78). The poet of *The Fall* is also faced with mythic figures from the past, and his task is to move them into the present with no help but his own unmediated senses, a task which recalls the "Ode" and its exultant "I see, and sing, by my own eyes inspired." What is left out or elided in the "Ode to Psyche," however, becomes the second fragment's mode of being, its purgatorial foreground, and the exaltation of unmediated vision darkens into that dangerous interval when the poet must bear the giant forms "ponderous" upon his senses. Apollo in the first *Hyperion* is the pupil of Mnemosyne, the very un-Miltonic and un-Blakean Muse whose function is to bear the past across into the present, to forsake "old and sacred thrones" for the sake of "loveliness new born" (III. 77-79). In *The Fall*, the poet himself assumes this function by becoming, literally, the vehicle of transition, the "bearer" in a poetic *translatio* or purgatorial crossing. Dilation is experienced as a burden rather than as delight, and the contest of spell and counterspell becomes an encounter of poetry and "dumb enchantment" which turns the terrors of the liminal into Keats's version of the Romantic sublime.

Trial by Bearing

THE contest or trial which is the central drama of *The Fall of Hyperion* is introduced in the opening lines as the problem of expression, or voice:

> Fanatics have their dreams, wherewith they weave
> A paradise for a sect, the savage too
> From forth the loftiest fashion of his sleep
> Guesses at Heaven; pity these have not
> Traced upon vellum or wild Indian leaf
> The shadows of melodious utterance.
> But bare of laurel they live, dream, and die;
> For Poesy alone can tell her dreams,

> With the fine spell of words alone can save
> Imagination from the sable charm
> And dumb enchantment.

The first *Hyperion* begins with the evocation of silence—the air without a "stir," the "voiceless" stream and the Naiad pressing her "cold finger closer to her lips." This very silence is part of the "dumb enchantment" confronted in the second attempt, and the insertion of the *persona* of the poet into the scene suggests that the essential drama is to be not the War between Olympian and Titan but the movement of these stony figures by the only possible countercharm, the poet's revivifying word.

It is this dialectic of voice and stony silence which makes the second fragment an intensification both of the drama of mutual trespass concealed within the concept of "Negative Capability" and of the submerged contest of another of the Great Odes, the anxious questing or questioning of the "Ode on a Grecian Urn." Both the romance theme of trespass and the uneasy dialectic of this "Ode" provide an illuminating prelude to the quest of the poet-pilgrim of *The Fall*, but only if the "Ode" is perceived in its essential dramatic context. Criticism has focused on the problematic content or philosophy of the ode which ends "Beauty is truth, truth beauty," and an endless debate has been generated on the meaning of the poem as statement. But Kenneth Burke pioneered a reading in which the focus is, instead, on the confrontation, or *agon*, of speaker and object,[77] and it is this confrontation which leads most directly into the scene of *The Fall*.

We have characterized romance as a form which both projects an end and defers its arrival. The "end" of the "Ode on a Grecian Urn" is *ut pictura poesis*, the emulation of the urn's silent form:

> Heard melodies are sweet, but those unheard
>   Are sweeter; therefore, ye soft pipes, pl⸺
> Not to the sensual ear, but, more end
>   Pipe to the spirit ditties of no tone.

The genre of the ode is *ekphrasis*, the verbal reproduction of an *objet d'art*, and the poem comes full circle in imitation of the urn. But there is a contrary movement as well, a movement in which silence is not a goal but a potential threat, and the poet's task is to make this stony shape speak. The condition of sculpture is, in this sense, the "end" of poetry not as intention but as potential *nemesis*, the fixity which Hazlitt describes in his contrast of poetry and painting.[78] Keats's ode moves, as statement, towards the finality of the "Cold pastoral" as fixed object. But the language itself provides an elaboration of that fixity, an interpretation of "shape" by "legend," and *ekphrasis* becomes not just genre but contest. The urn itself ("Thou still unravished bride of quietness," 1) is suspended between two potential ravishers—the poet who desires to make this shape reveal its "tale," and "quietness," the fate to which it is betrothed but not yet finally joined.[79] The praise of the "Silvan historian, who canst thus express / A flowery tale more sweetly than our rhyme" (3-4) looks forward to the "unheard melodies" of the second stanza; but the active questioning of the first stanza already begins to violate that silence. The crescendo building to "What wild ecstasy?" (10) suggests the anxiousness of the poet's desire to rescue the urn from quietude, and though the poem's central stanzas privilege its "unheard melodies," the anxiety returns as the dark underside of stanza IV, the sense that the chasm which separates the poet from this enigmatic object and its "little town" is unbridgeable,[80] that no historical *transitio*, or bringing forward, may be possible.

This anxiety culminates in the "silent form" and "Cold pastoral" of the final stanza. The urn appears to have the last word, refusing to yield its secrets to the poet's obstinate questing. The ode ends with a paradox—a message so uncompromising in its finality that it has given birth to endless interpretation. If the statement is the oracle of which the whole poem is the viaticum,[81] the urn's singular pronouncement remains, like all oracles, ambiguous:

> O Attic shape! Fair attitude! With brede
> Of marble men and maidens overwrought,

> With forest branches and the trodden weed—
> Thou, silent form, dost tease us out of thought
> As doth eternity. Cold pastoral!
> When old age shall this generation waste,
> Thou shalt remain, in midst of other woe
> Than ours, a friend to man, to whom thou say'st,
> "Beauty is truth, truth beauty"—that is all
> Ye know on earth, and all ye need to know.

The process of the poet's earlier questioning is cut short or suspended. As a monument which does not yield its full story to the questioner, it becomes, as well, admonishment or proscription: thus far wilt thou go and no farther.

Ostensibly the victory is the urn's. And yet, if poetry here cannot reach the silence of *pictura*, it also takes full advantage of the gap between word and object. The very stanza which professes to surrender so much to the enigma of plastic form virtually riots in its own ambiguities, the fortuitous element of punning in language that creates its own interlace of sounds and meanings. Language—even language which strains to the condition of silence—retains its links with the impurities of the "sensual ear" and its "heard melodies" create here an echo chamber in the mind. The dead end of a single meaning is evaded as deftly as the fixity of the urn itself. The urn may be "cold," but in this stanza, "brede" warms to "breed" and generates the more animated sense of "overwrought," just as "Attic" provides a playful, or poetic, etymology for "attitude." The language seems almost to increase its antics in the first half of the stanza as a declaration of freedom from the proscription, or inscription, at the end, the "Cold pastoral" and its final commandment.

The dialectic of stone and voice behind the questioning of the "Ode" becomes in *The Fall of Hyperion* the poet's particular burden. Keats admired Milton's genius for "stationing or statuary,"[82] and the first *Hyperion* is in this respect a highly Miltonic poem. Its opening picture of Saturn sitting "quiet as a stone" (I. 4) is joined by the description of Thea and the aged king "postured motionless, / Like natural sculpture in cathedral cavern" (86-87) and, later, of the council of fallen

Titans as a "dismal cirque / Of Druid stones upon a forlorn moor" (II. 34-35). This sculptural positioning is part of what Geoffrey Hartman has called Keats's "picture envy," his fascination with "shaped and palpable gods."[83] But it is also, perhaps, one of the reasons why this fragment never gets moving. Saturn is not so much situated in the landscape as he is fixed in it, and the very language of the description ("Deep . . . / Far sunken . . . / Far . . .") manages to suggest at once a location and a fall. The fixity of the pictorial is part of the frozen limbo from which the fragment never completely emerges. Keats's image of a new awakening was of each man whispering results to his neighbor until "Humanity instead of being a wide heath of Furse and Briars with here and there a remote Oak or Pine, would become a grand democracy of Forest Trees!"[84] But in this fragment, voice rises in isolation and subsides, and even the speeches of the great Miltonic consult remain soliloquies. In order to move these stony forms, the poet of *The Fall of Hyperion* places himself in the scene. And the ancient quest motif of the young hero whose word is to restore the ailing *senex* and bring about a renewal of a dead landscape becomes the *agon* of the poet struggling to find his own voice.

The romance motif of reanimation has its counterpart in that dramatic capacity Keats, following Hazlitt, called "gusto," the absence of self distinguished from "the wordsworthian or egotistical sublime": "A Poet is the most unpoetical of any thing in existence; because he has no Identity—he is continually in for—and filling some other Body."[85] We are so accustomed to the Keatsian generosity of spirit—that "camelion" quality that "has as much delight in conceiving an Iago as an Imogen"—that we may fail to hear the overtones of menace in this dramatic "filling," a somewhat different aspect of the negative capability which informs the patience of *Endymion*. But slightly further on in the same letter, there is a passage which suggests that this absence of self has a more ominous side:

When I am in a room with People if I ever am free from speculating on creations of my own brain,

then not myself goes home to myself: but the
identity of every one in the room begins to to [*sic*]
press upon me that I am in a very little time an[ni]-
hilated. . . .

The letter is revealing when placed beside *The Fall of Hyperion*. The quest of the poet-persona is to animate the stony
forms, but the very bodies he seeks to fill threaten, in turn, to
annihilate him. In another letter written while he was at work
on the first *Hyperion*, Keats celebrates the ability of the mind
to wander at will, and alludes naturally to Milton's "Il Penseroso":

> I feel more and more every day, as my imagination
> strengthens, that I do not live in this world alone but
> in a thousand worlds—No sooner am I alone than
> shapes of epic greatness are stationed around me,
> and serve my Spirit the office [of] which is equiva-
> lent to a king's bodyguard—then "Tragedy, with
> scepter'd pall, comes sweeping by." According to
> my state of mind I am with Achilles shouting in the
> Trenches or with Theocritus in the Vales of Sicily.[86]

But the shapes of epic greatness which actually surround him
in *The Fall* are not so much protective as oppressive and the
free ranging of the *penseroso* mood is instead the possibility of
the suspension of all movement—the Gothic nightmare of
getting into a scene he cannot get out of.

If it is true, as is often remarked, that Keats swallowed
Spenser as completely as Blake did Milton, this may be partly
because "faerie" is of all literary landscapes the most shadowy
and uncategorizable. Dante and Milton are primarily poets of
clear boundaries and fixed places, so much so that the differences between them may be explained partly by a comparison
of cosmologies. But romance, while it intensifies one aspect
of place—its *numen* or mystery—also unfixes the boundaries
and clear dividing lines between places, creating, paradoxically, a heightened sense of the possibility of trespass. Keats's
concept of Negative Capability unfixes the boundaries of the
self, and, paradoxically, makes the possibility of trespass

more terrifying. Filling other bodies is part of a delightful *Einfühlung*, a wandering at will, but it also involves a trespass upon outer space which may invite, as part of a deadly compact, a violation in return.

In *The Fall*, the theme of trespass first takes its more traditional form, the poet's sense of "unworthiness" (I. 182) to be on holy ground—the *topos* of modesty which in Keats is frequently indistinguishable from a genuine sense of impotence—and is continued in the tortuous distinctions of the dialogue with Moneta and her reminders of a barely tolerated intrusion:

> Therefore, that happiness be somewhat shared,
> Such things as thou art are admitted oft
> Into like gardens thou didst pass erewhile,
> And suffered in these temples . . .
>
> (I. 177-80)

The subject of *Hyperion* is the War in Heaven just over, and the fragment itself never recovers from this fall, though it does arrest the fallen gods on this side of complete extinction. The whole effort of *The Fall of Hyperion*, in contrast, is an attempt to move back to the scenes which led to this event, now "enwombed" (I. 277) in the brain of Moneta. The poet desires to find himself before—in both senses—what he finds himself after, and this journey backward involves him in a succession of anterior scenes. The first step of the dream is literally a retrograde one, a pilgrim's regress from a Miltonic and Dantesque Eden into a Purgatory; the *katabasis* of the poet-persona, traditionally an inescapable part of the initiation ritual, is here a movement not only downward in space but backward in time. No longer the *observer ab extra* of the first *Hyperion*, the poet literally journeys back in order to bear the past forward, but the danger is that this very journey involves a trespass upon ancestral space, that he himself may be preempted by this past, as Apollo remained another Titan, or another Endymion. The Romantic sublime in this second fragment takes the form of a liminal contest: the poet who cannot recross a threshold may become one, the purely negative counterpart of the figure who is to be a "thoroughfare" for all thoughts; and the imagery of sickness, though defended before Moneta as a "sickness not ignoble" (I. 184), links the threshold state of *The Fall* once more to that of the revised *Endymion* preface, the "space of life between." Moneta herself is a threshold figure, a boundary between past and present, whose aspect, Janus-like, depends partly on her function. As "Moneta," she reflects the undertone suggestion of "doom" and admonition in the "eternal do`mèd monument" (71) she guards. As "Mnemosyne," she is the gateway from past to future, the authentic Muse of transition: Keats addresses her as "Shade of Memory" as soon as her veils are parted and he is admitted to the scenes hidden within the "dark secret chambers of her skull" (278).

This journey involves a dialectic of persona and poet not unlike that of Dante, the poet-pilgrim traveling to a destination which is at the same time the origin of the poem. In *The Fall of Hyperion*, as in the *Commedia*, the journey and the poem are finally inseparable because the subject is not only how the poem came to be written but how the poet himself was "born." The imagery is founded upon polarities— "parent" and "child," early and late, giant forms and "stunt bramble"—but the program of the fragment would seem to be to reverse these relationships, for the poet, finally, to father these ancestral forms as the children of his own brain. This initiation ritual involves a curious reversal, a "bearing" which moves at first not forward to birth, but rather, preposterous as it may appear, from "travail" back to conception, through the patient and purgatorial interval of labor necessary to give birth to his own "theme" (I. 46).

From early in the fragment, the sense of trespass inherent in this "travail" is linked to the problem of poetic "utterance" and to its potential termination:

> "Holy Power,"
> Cried I, approaching near the hornèd shrine,
> "What am I that should so be saved from death?
> What am I that another death come not
> To choke my utterance sacrilegious here?"
>
> (I. 136–40)

Dante's poem begins in a region of unlikeness and the poet who tries to ascend directly to vision falls instead into a place "dove 'l sol tace" (*Inf.* 1. 60). The ancient connection between light and sound, vision and voice, emerges again in the form of Keats's fragment. The trial moves first not forward to speech, to the "fine spell of words," but backwards to the "sable charm"—to the potential loss, or stifling, of voice—a return to infancy (*in-fans*) or speechlessness.

This movement suggests a rite of passage, as if the poet had to repeat the fall of the Titans into silence in order to in-feel, or invade, their space. But this particular negative capability involves as much risk as possibility. *Einfühlung* in Keats is a need as well as a capacity, and his preoccupation with the housing of the imagination continues a deep romance fear, that this Protean flexibility—the ability to assume identities at will—implies a more threatening absence of identity, its complete dissolution.[87] Keats's poetry is consistently preoccupied with the medium, with the particular body being filled or passed through: who but the poet of *Lamia* could give us, for better or for worse, the lines "the words she spake / Came, as through bubbling honey, for love's sake" (*Lamia* 1. 64-65)? This preoccupation reaches its culmination in *The Fall* where the mouth becomes the temple or "roofèd home" (1. 229) of the tongue and the desired vision takes place inside the "globèd brain" (245) of the prophetess. But this housing, or enclosing, is itself dangerous. If Ovidian metamorphosis—frequently in Keats the motive power of poetry—is often literally the transformation of self into scene, it is also the movement which romance modulates into the paralyzing spell, the moment when the house or bower of the imagination becomes a stifling enclosure, a medium which cannot be passed through.

Both the delight and the threat of in-feeling are expressed in Keats in the different shadings of words, such as "smothering," which suggest this housing or enclosure. In the early poem "I Stood Tip-Toe," the line "The soul is lost in pleasant smotherings" (132) is meant to be as purely a matter of pleasure as the declaration in "Sleep and Poetry" that "the imagi-

nation / Into most lovely labyrinths will be gone" (265-66).
But "smothering" elsewhere in Keats suggests the potential
threat of suffocation, just as the "labyrinth" raises the possibility of an endless wandering. In Book IX of *Paradise Lost*,
Milton's Satan undergoes a metamorphosis as a means to his
end, his entry into the "Labyrinth" of the sleeping serpent
(180-90). Milton carefully distinguishes medium from agent,
so carefully in the tortured phrasing of "nor nocent yet" (186)
as to suggest the danger of confounding means and end, a failure to perceive that the serpent's guilt is only by association,
or trope.[88] Keats's notes on this passage in Milton, however,
betray a horror at the possibility of being trapped within the
medium itself:

> Whose spirit does not ache at the smothering and
> confinement—the unwilling stillness—the "<u>waiting
> close</u>"? Whose head is not dizzy at the possible
> speculations of Satan in the serpent prison? No pas-
> sage of poetry ever can give a greater pain of suffoca-
> tion.[89]

"Close" in the Miltonic context is simply an indication of
proximity: Satan in his serpent body "waiting close th' approach of Morn" (*PL* IX. 191). But in Keats's reading, it conveys instead the "pain of suffocation," the danger of entering
a body from which, like the "serpent prison-house" of *Lamia*
(I. 203), there may be no egress.

The potential suffocation of not being able to proceed beyond a certain stage is frequently in Keats synonymous with a
threatened loss of voice, the nightmare anxiety which hides
behind the seemingly innocent muffling of Madeline in the
ritual of *The Eve of St. Agnes*:

> No uttered syllable, or woe betide!
> But to her heart, her heart was voluble,
> Paining with eloquence her balmy side,
> As though a tongueless nightingale should swell
> Her throat in vain, and die, heart-stifled, in her dell.
>   (203-7)

or manifests itself in the speechlessness of Lorenzo in *Isabella*,
which virtually prefigures the "ruddy tide" of his death:

> all day
> His heart beat awfully against his side;
> And to his heart he inwardly did pray
> For power to speak; but still the ruddy tide
> Stifled his voice . . .
>
> (41–45)

or informs, in the late "Ode to Fanny," the poet's own need
for an expressive outlet or "theme":

> Physician Nature, let my spirit blood!
>   Oh, ease my heart of verse and let me rest;
> Throw me upon thy tripod till the flood
>   Of stifling numbers ebbs from my full breast.
> A theme, a theme! Great Nature, give a theme . . .
>
> (1–5)

"Telling" in this last passage, however it might appear as
poetic exaggeration or pure *topos*, is clearly a kind of release,
an outlet in speech which rescues from the imminent threat of
"stifling." In the first *Hyperion*, in a passage directly reminis-
cent of the Miltonic Satan's metamorphosis into a serpent,
suffocation and the stifling of voice are part of a metamorphosis just barely escaped as Hyperion ends his address to the
fallen Titans:

> He spake, and ceased, the while a heavier threat
> Held struggle with his throat but came not forth;
> For as in theatres of crowded men
> Hubbub increases more they call out "Hush!",
> So at Hyperion's words the phantoms pale
> Bestirred themselves, thrice horrible and cold;
> And from the mirrored level where he stood
> A mist arose, as from a scummy marsh.
> At this, through all his bulk an agony
> Crept gradual, from the feet unto the crown,
> Like a lithe serpent vast and muscular

Making slow way, with head and neck convulsed
From over-strainèd might. Released, he fled
To the eastern gates . . .

(I. 251-64)

The threatened transformation here is in fact more Ovidian
than Miltonic—not metamorphosis as a means to an end, but
as victimization, and this passivity continues when, released
from this stasis, the Titan tries to bring on the dawn. Though
a "primeval God," he cannot force the "sacred seasons"
("Therefore the operations of the dawn / Stayed in their
birth," 294-95), and this failure is repeated in the failure of the
fragment itself to bring on a new dawn, the decisive advent of
its Apollo.

In *The Fall of Hyperion*, Keats's final attempt to move beyond this "staying," the threat of suffocation or smothering
becomes a disease, or dis-ease, which attacks the voice of the
poet himself. The limbo of speechlessness into which the Titans have fallen is suggested through the imagery of
sculptural immobility, of their fall as a kind of burial alive.
The fallen Saturn is a kind of giant Laocoön ("Still fixed he sat
beneath the sable trees, / Whose arms spread straggling in
wild serpent forms," I. 446-47) who speaks of being "swallowed up / And buried from all godlike exercise / Of influence
. . ." (412-14). And suffocation is the image Thea uses for
their present fallen state: "With such remorseless speed still
come new woes / That unbelief has not a space to breathe"
(366-67).

In *The Fall*, the implication is that the poet who trespasses
upon this scene may share this silent, or stony, immobility.
The danger is suggested as early as the "draught" which carries him from the Earthly Paradise of the opening scene to the
barer landscape of Moneta's shrine:

Upon the grass I struggled hard against
The domineering potion; but in vain—
The cloudy swoon came on, and down I sunk,
Like a Silenus on an antique vase.

(I. 53-56)

Suffocation and loss of voice are the first part of the poet's trial by ordeal, the dangerous interval which follows upon Moneta's challenge to mount the steps before the "gummed leaves be burnt" (I. 116) or "die" on the "marble" where he stands (108). The pilgrim who intrudes upon this shrine is almost stifled, in lines which at once recall Hyperion threatened with metamorphosis into serpent form ("through all his bulk an agony / Crept gradual . . .") and significantly conflate two powerful Dantesque scenes—the challenge of the Medusa who turns to stone and the image for the serpentine metamorphoses ("Thus up the shrinking paper, ere it burns, / A brown tint glides, not turning yet to black . . .")[90] of the Canto of the "Thieves":

> I heard, I looked: two senses both at once,
> So fine, so subtle, felt the tyranny
> Of that fierce threat and the hard task proposed.
> Prodigious seemed the toil; the leaves were yet
> Burning—when suddenly a palsied chill
> Struck from the pavèd level up my limbs,
> And was ascending quick to put cold grasp
> Upon those streams that pulse beside the throat.
> I shrieked; and the sharp anguish of my shriek
> Stung my own ears. I strove hard to escape
> The numbness, strove to gain the lowest step.
> Slow, heavy, deadly was my pace; the cold
> Grew stifling, suffocating, at the heart;
> And when I clasped my hands I felt them not.
> One minute before death, my iced foot touched
> The lowest stair; and as it touched, life seemed
> To pour in at the toes. I mounted up,
> As once fair Angels on a ladder flew
> From the green turf to Heaven.
>
> (I. 118-36)

The threat of immobilization is at once a threat from outside, delivered by Moneta, and a potential result of his own "staying," of the fixing of the senses upon an object which simultaneously involves the danger of being fixed by it, dwelling upon as a permanent dwelling in. Dante's contribution to the myth of the siren-Medusa was to reveal that her power derived from an initial movement of self-mystification or fixation.[91] Keats's version of this fixation and fixing is the interval in which he pauses to savor Moneta's warning upon his "senses" and is almost suffocated by a "chill" which threatens to reduce him to stone. The fixation in this passage is the logical culmination of what John Jones calls Keats's "aesthetic nominalism," the "glutting" of the senses upon a single object which connects the "one-pointed contemplation"[92] of the Odes to the fetishism of "This Living Hand" and the necrophilia of *Isabella*. Though the "Ode on Melancholy" banishes the clumsy machinery of a gothicized emotion, it does fix upon a single moment and single objects for the senses, a fixation which is at once a "glutting," a "feeding," and an "imprisoning":

> Then glut thy sorrow on a morning rose,
>   Or on the rainbow of the salt sand-wave,
>   Or on the wealth of globèd peonies;
> Or if thy mistress some rich anger shows,
>   Imprison her soft hand, and let her rave,
>   And feed deep, deep upon her peerless eyes.
>
> (15-20)

The visual gluttony of the "Ode on Melancholy" joins the "drowsy hour" of the "Indolence Ode" as a dwelling upon, or within, the embowered "Moment," and its dangers. Keats's admiring description of Milton's power of fixing— "he is 'sagacious of his Quarry,' he sees Beauty on the wing, pounces upon it, and gorges it to the producing his essential verse"[93]—is actually a description of the arch-Miltonic glutton, Death (*PL* x. 281), and in the crucial moment of fixation in *The Fall of Hyperion*, what might have been life to Milton is almost literally death to Keats. The Gothic terror of being imprisoned or fed upon—the extreme case of the romance enchantress *pasturando gli occhi* upon the paralyzed youth—is simply the gluttony and fixing of the "Ode on Melancholy" turned inside out: the poet yields momentarily to the tyranny of his senses and is almost "consumed."

The possibility of himself turning to cold stone on the

pavement before the shrine is in one sense the simple consequence of putting himself into the poem, of becoming one of
the shaped and palpable gods. In one of the versions of the
myth of Atlas cited in Lemprière's *Dictionary*, the Titan is
turned to stone when he is shown the head of the Medusa.[94]
The poet who survives the first trial by ascending the stairs
before the leaves are burnt wins, by this act, a second chance
or respite ("Thou hast dated on / Thy doom," I. 144-45) and
turns Moneta, at once Mnemosyne and potential Medusa,
into the Muse of his own singular "theme" (I. 46). As in the
Medusa episode in Dante which Keats carefully underscored,[95] this confrontation is a crucial passage, the conversion of a potential impasse into a possible transition, or way
through. The scene within *The Fall*, however, does not proceed to a *Paradiso*. Keats borrows from Dante the *scala* which
leads to Saturn's altar and the image of Jacob's ladder for his
miraculous ascent: "I mounted up, / As once fair Angels on a
ladder flew / From the green turf to Heaven." But the image
of Jacob's ladder which provides, in Dante, an ascent from the
sphere of Saturn as "Contemplation" to the heaven of the
fixed stars remains, in Keats's fragment, more within the
realm of Saturn as the astrological patron of a paralyzing
melancholia. Just as the first dream of the fragment awakened
only into a darker dream, so the pilgrim-poet emerges from
his first trial into another, that dangerous interval in which
the "shapes of epic greatness" become the oppressive forms
he must bear "ponderous" upon his senses. The growing
within the poet of a power to "see as a god sees" (I. 302-4)
suggests that of Dante's Glaucus in the opening vision of the
Paradiso, but it is also the more sinister visionary initiation of
the Glaucus of *Endymion* as he is paralyzed by Circe's spell.
Dante's "transhumanization" is, in Keats's poem, first the
threat of dehumanization, the burden of the shapes which
threaten to unrealize him:

> Long, long these two were postured motionless,
> Like sculpture builded-up upon the grave
> Of their own power. A long awful time
> I looked upon them: still they were the same;

The frozen God still bending to the earth,
And the sad Goddess weeping at his feet,
Moneta silent. Without stay or prop
But my own weak mortality, I bore
The load of this eternal quietude,
The unchanging gloom, and the three fixèd shapes
Ponderous upon my senses a whole moon.
For by my burning brain I measured sure
Her silver seasons shedded on the night,
And ever day by day methought I grew
More gaunt and ghostly. Oftentimes I prayed
Intense, that death would take me from the vale
And all its burthens. Gasping with despair
Of change, hour after hour I cursed myself—
Until Old Saturn raised his faded eyes,
And looked around and saw his kingdom gone . . .

                                              (I. 382-401)

This passage and its crucial "bearing" are an insertion into
the original version of the first *Hyperion*, as if this activity
were the second fragment's decisive drama and the price for
the poet of being privy to this scene were literally being able
to bear it, to be the Atlas, before he can be the Apollo, of his
chosen theme. Keats speaks in one letter of the creative revery
of a "voyage of conception," a phrase in which if "voyage"
suggests the activity of questing, "conception" retains its
more passive sense, of a truth more brought to birth than captured.[96] This kind of oxymoron reappears in the "patient
travail" (I. 91) of *The Fall of Hyperion*, a labor which is simultaneously active and passive. Keats cannot unperplex patience
and passivity from their common root in *patior*, and the quest
here, as in *Endymion*, is as much a passion as an action, something to be undergone.

The decisive trial of this fragment involves "bearing" in all
of Keats's characteristic senses—a poetic *translatio* or carrying
of these ancestral forms across into the present, the painful
interval in which the poet must endure the weight of his vision's "eternal quietude," and the creative passivity of
"travail" as a bringing to birth.[97] Even the language of the

fragment—"spherèd words" (I. 249), "globèd brain" (245)—
is ensphered and ponderous, and the doctrine traditionally
known as "accommodation" paradoxically becomes not a
mediating of the burden but a part of it. Moneta, like Milton's
Raphael, claims to "humanize" her sayings to the poet's ears
(II. 2), but the emphasis throughout falls instead upon dispro-
portion of size, the poet-pilgrim standing beside his "Shade of
Memory" like "a stunt bramble by a solemn pine" (I. 293).
The suggestion is that whatever "accommodation" is required will have to be on the side of the receiver, that part of
the threat of a "dumb enchantment" is the possibility of
something too large, perhaps, to be uttered, or withstood:

> As near as an immortal's spherèd words
> Could to a mother's soften, were these last.
> But yet I had a terror of her robes,
> And chiefly of the veils, that from her brow
> Hung pale, and curtained her in mysteries,
> That made my heart too small to hold its blood.
>
> (I. 249-54)

Moneta parts her veils, and admits the poet to his vision, but
he remains, despite her guidance, unlike Dante or Milton,
without certain guide, and faces the weight of this giant
world with nothing but his own unaided senses:

> In melancholy realms big tears are shed,
> More sorrow like to this, and such-like woe,
> Too huge for mortal tongue, or pen of scribe . . .
>
> (II. 7-9)

Even the sound carries the burden of the theme. The curse of
perpetual transition in Moneta's face is joined by the perpetual
transition of sound in "enwombed" / "tomb" / "doom" /
"domèd" / "moan" / "Moneta" / "moon"—a movement in
which it is impossible, finally, to unperplex sound from
sense.

   If the quest of the poet is the creation of the poem, the question at the end of the crucial interval of "bearing" in the dusk
vale is finally whether the persona of the poet grows up or

simply grows down by the time the fragment breaks off. That the poem in fact does not end may assimilate it to the curse of perpetual transition, the death-in-life of Moneta's face. The interval of "bearing" and the release which follows it may seem a negative victory; the fragment breaks off soon after this passage. The Dantesque geography instills an expectation of movement, of progression beyond this Purgatory to a higher realm. But the oxymorons here—unlike those which move Dante's pilgrim through the "solacing pain" of the *Purgatorio* (XXIII. 72)—are part of the stasis. If the fragment starts out to be a "progress of poesy," there is in this sense no "progress." The first and only completed canto ends with a reference to the "antichamber of this dream" (I. 465), and the last allusion to Dante, as the sun or Hyperion is "sloping to the threshold of the west" (II. 48), suggests that the pilgrim is still on some kind of threshold, still before a journey to be completed. The poem breaks off at an even earlier point in the narrative of the Titans than the first *Hyperion*.

The statues here never really wake up, any more than they do in *Hyperion*, and yet there is a sense in which, once the burden has been endured, the real "theme" of Keats's brief romance has been realized. Milton in *Paradise Regained* focuses on the period of trial, the patient travail of the Son, and when that trial has been undergone, the essential story has, in one respect, been told. Keats echoes Milton's shorter epic in *Endymion*, which ends not with the translated Latmian and his goddess, but with Peona still wandering "in wonderment" through the "gloomy wood" (IV. 1003). *The Fall of Hyperion*, in the form in which we have it, holds out no promise of a paradise regained, but the poet who sighs for removal from the "vale / And all its burthens" (I. 397-98) is finally removed to the upper region of "clear light" (II. 49), like Guyon emerging from his trial in the underworld. To rise beyond this sphere would perhaps, in Keats's terms, be an act of poetic bad faith or, like the ending of *Endymion*, a palpable design. "Translation" in this late fragment is finally not ascension, but a more purgatorial *translatio*, the process of "bearing" in and for itself.

The Fall of Hyperion is not Keats's final, or even definitive, version of the suspensions of the liminal. This too in Keats reaches no single conclusion. "Bearing" itself is relieved of its burden in the beautifully extended, and graduated, threshold of the "Autumn Ode," and its refusal either to mourn the songs of Spring or to quest anxiously for presence. But the anxieties of the late poems to Fanny and the obsession of "This Living Hand" are even darker versions of the purgatory of *The Fall*, of "consumption" and suspension become so close to truth as to be literally unbearable. The unfinished fragment, with its echoes of the impasse of the first *Hyperion* and of the earlier poetry's dream and spell, does, however, enable us to glimpse what in romance Keats appears to have transformed for good. Pater's famous "moments," Tennyson's extension of romance plenitude into phantasmagoria, and the Pre-Raphaelites' identification of poetry with the exclusions of the "embowered," all in their different ways seem to point back to Keats's mediation, or "translation," of romance tradition. And his preference for the virtual and endurance of transition with no prospect of anything beyond itself provide a bridge even beyond the English context, to the hesitations of Valéry's lyrics and the uneasy "betrothal" of Mallarmé's *Un Coup de dés*. The second chance or respite granted by Moneta ("Thou hast dated on / Thy doom") recalls the space of dilation in Spenser or Milton, but without its promised dawning, or theological ground. The threshold, though a darker one than that of *Endymion*, remains Keats's characteristic, and hard-won, poetic space, neither the Miltonic Paradise nor the Wordsworthian earthly one, but the difficult interval in between.

Epilogue

Cette perfection de ma certitude me gêne: tout est trop clair, la clarté montre le désir d'une évasion; tout est trop luisant, j'aimerais rentrer en mon Ombre incréée et antérieure. . . .

Mallarmé, *Igitur*

Je diffère le pur bonheur . . .

Valéry, *Eupalinos*

Inexplicable sister of the Minotaur, enigma and mask, although I am part of what is real, hear me and recognize me as part of the unreal. I am the truth but the truth of that imagination of life in which with unfamiliar motion and manner you guide me in those exchanges of speech in which your words are mine, mine yours.

Stevens, *The Necessary Angel*

"Inescapable Romance"—Mallarmé, Valéry, Stevens

"THE spirit of Chivalry," wrote Bishop Hurd in the first of his famous *Letters*, "was a fire which soon spent itself. But that of Romance, which was kindled at it, burnt long, and continued its light and heat even to the politer ages."[1] Just how far into the "politer ages" is finally an open question. Yeats proclaimed himself one of the "last romantics," but the more recent of modern critics follow Pater in extending the "romantic spirit" from a period concept into a more pervasive one, "an ever-present, an enduring principle, in the artistic temperament."[2] The progress of romance in the century and a half after Keats is a history almost too diffuse to follow. But the echoes of romance *données* in modern theories of linguistic errancy and narrative structure suggest that it provides, among other things, an emblem for the pre-apocalyptic, or threshold, nature of language itself.

The study of romance—its detours, postponements, and suspensions—not only illuminates the metaphors of much current speculation but provides it with an historical, and poetic, context. Modern linguistics teaches us that there is a distancing, or "différence," intrinsic to language, whether the play of differences be conceived as Saussure's "diacritics" or Jakobson's "binary opposition"; and the "error" of language is very much a part of recent preoccupation with the point of origin beyond its reach, Vaihinger's "summational fiction" or the structuralists' "zero degree."[3] Jacques Derrida's "différance," a neologism formed to convey both senses of the Latin *differre*, is virtually the reappearance, in the language of contemporary philosophy, of a romance formulation, the combination of spatial difference and temporal deferral which Ariosto exploited in his continuing "differire."[4] Derrida invokes the concept as part of a radical critique of "presence," of the metaphysical assumption of an ultimate Origin, Center, or End, and the various social and intellectual hierarchies it authorizes. And he applies it as well to the "detour of the sign," to language itself as "la présence différée," differentiated and deferred presence. But the term he chooses is a romance pun which extends—in another of its etymological branches—to a specifically narrative dilation.

Recent theories of narrative also invoke, though not always self-consciously, the strategies of deferral and *dilatio* employed by the romancers. For René Girard, the simultaneous expansion and revelation of error is part of the novel's dialectic of "mensonge romantique et vérité romanesque."[5] For Roland Barthes, the narrative locates its characteristic "plaisir" in the "opening" between beginning and end, subject and predicate, enigma and answer, an "espace dilatoire"—both dilated and dilatory space—in which straightforward movement towards the end is opposed by the delays, equivocations, and turnings of the "code herméneutique."[6] The suspensions which for Barthes become part of an erotics of the text recall not only the constant divagations of romance and its resistance to the demands of closure, but also the frustration in Ariosto of what Barthes calls the teleological form of vulgar readerly pleasure—the desire to penetrate the veil of meaning or to hasten the narrative's gradual striptease—by a continual postponement of revelation which leaves the reader suspended, or even erotically "hung up." The romance figure of Scheherazade is not, perhaps, accidentally the constantly reappearing enchantress of *Finnegans Wake*, that collection of "litterish fragments" in which literature itself emerges as an anti-epiphanic form, a warding off of the simultaneous revelation and catastrophe of the "bockalips."

The metaphor of the striptease or dance of veils is one of the privileged images of modern semiology for a process at once erotic and semiotic, the succession of representations as an infinite regression of veils. C. S. Peirce argues that the meaning of a representation can be nothing but another representation whose "clothing" is not "stripped" but only "changed for something more diaphanous."[7] But the "vale" of exile and the "veil" of language were assimilated long before even Blake's combination of the mysterious and lachrymose in the romance figure of Vala, and the figure of the veil and unveiling is one of the oldest of narrative—and semiotic—images, from the Book of Revelation to the series of romance enchantresses whose uncovering is related both to the discovery of meaning and to a sense of narrative ending. The modern figure is separated from the earlier one by the prospect of a perpetual regression, the impossibility of any final unveiling. But modern semiotics might still be best understood as part of the Romantic transformation of romance, the modulation of the revealed, or stripped, enchantress into a Lamia or Belle Dame figure whose unveiling is never unambiguous or complete.

The wealth of this modern speculation should not blind us to the fact that the association between the deviations of language and the "errors" of romance is a very old one indeed. In Rabelais' *Tiers Livre*—itself a "late" romance—the shape-shifting Panurge uses the multivalence of language for the same purpose as he uses continual digression, to evade the damning certainty of a one-to-one correspondence between sign and meaning, and the whole of his quest becomes paradoxically a form of evasion.[8] The gap between words and things is part of the Book's sorrow, the melancholy recognition that "Rien n'est, sinon Dieu, perfaict."[a] But this very absence of a certain referent also leaves a space for the fiction to unfold and makes Panurge's endless "on the contrary" into a declaration of freedom, for better or for worse.

Bishop Hurd did not elaborate on his assertion that the fortunes of romance were inseparably tied to the fortunes of poetry itself,[9] but the history of the debate over the "divagations" of poetic figure suggests that both involved the same kind of error. The opposition to Spenser's choice of the romance form was concurrent with suspicion of his linguistic mode, the devious ways of allegory and the "dark conceit" criticized by Jonson and others.[10] Puttenham, in his *Arte of English Poesie*, translated the trope of allegory as the figure of "Fals Semblant," the literary ancestor of Archimago from the *Roman de la rose*. Puttenham's choice seems to be guided simply by a sense of the disjunction between phenomenon and meaning, but this gap in the nature of poetic figure—and the potential within it for all kinds of "false seeming"—was what led in the century after Spenser to the attempt to purge all language of its duplicity, to make it the universal and transparent medium dreamed of by Descartes, Delgarno, Leibniz, and Wilkins.

An extreme nominalist like Berkeley might speak of language as the "curtain" hindering the advancement of science, and primitivist and rationalist alike ally troping and metaphor to tropical peoples and less advanced cultures.[11] But it is the religious poetry of the period after Spenser which most clearly provides the archetypes for the liminal status of language. For George Herbert, the divagations of poetic figure put poetry in the wilderness before the Promised Land, a problematic area in which the poet, like the Israelites who did

---

[a] "Nothing, except God, is perfect" (trans. mine)

not cross that threshold, might forever wander and find no final referent. In the two of his poems entitled "Jordan," images of poetry and its figural veil, "Curling with metaphors a plain intention," are associated with images of romance and the indolence of its "enchanted groves," with the suggestion that poetry, like the Law, remains within the shadowy realm of the figure, however much the poet might labor to chasten its excesses.

Behind the modern concepts of an infinite regression or perpetual transition lies a history whose best guides are finally the poets themselves. The anxiety of referentiality which haunts religious poets in the century of Herbert and Milton becomes even more acute as the possibility of an apocalyptic reference lessens. Dante distinguished Limbo from Purgatory, the place of perpetual suspension from the threshold of a genuine progress, but for the poets of the nineteenth century who echo his geography, the distinction is more difficult to make, and poetry itself frequently becomes a potential limbo, a medium which fails to mediate. Gérard de Nerval writes in the *Nuits d'octobre* of the "séraphin doré du Dante, qui répand un dernier éclair de poésie sur les cercles ténébreux dont la spirale immense se rétrécit toujours,"[b] consigning poetry to that fragile "lembo" of light which in Dante is poised before descent to the place "where no light shines."[12] *Les Fleurs du mal*, which Baudelaire described as "un livre saturnien, orgiaque et mélancolique,"[c] was originally entitled *Les Limbes*.[13] Coleridge speculated on a "figurative space" which would have "real Being and energy and the active power of figure."[14] But lingering in this figure is also, for him, a dilation too closely associated with romance and its more dangerous suspensions. If, in *Paradise Lost*, the temporal equivalent of the movement from "shadowy Types to Truth" is the vision of evening as a bridge to the greater light of day, Coleridge's anxious hope in his poems of this twilight zone is that Adam's description of the task of evening lights—to

[b] "Dante's golden seraph, who casts a last flash of poetry on the dark circles whose immense spiral forever contracts" (trans. mine)

[c] "a Saturnian book, orgiastic and melancholy" (trans. mine)

make Earth "apter to receive / Perfection from the Sun's more potent Ray" (*PL* IV. 672-73)—may apply as well to the enticing fables of romance, "Till Superstition with unconscious hand / Seat Reason on her Throne" ("The Destiny of Nations," 87-88). His intense consciousness of man's betweenness, as Geoffrey Hartman remarks, increases rather than chastens his apocalyptic passion,[15] but apocalypse is also an end from which he shrinks. The "crepuscular" state of the poem "Limbo" is the threshold before an end which is not fulfillment but destruction, night as *ne plus ultra*, the "mere horror of blank Nought-at-all." And Demogorgon—its reigning deity—is the traditional figure for the darker enchantments of romance, the god Boccaccio associates with the Medusa and the "Great Gorgon" upon which Spenser's Enchanter calls.[16]

Heidegger, in one of the essays on Hölderlin, speaks of the existential position of the poet as a *Zwischenbereich* between the "No-More of the gods that have fled and the Not-yet of the god that is coming."[17] In poetry from the Romantics forward, the poet himself approaches the condition of the wanderer between two worlds, a solitary doomed to an existence which is neither life nor death, the old poetry of heaven nor the impossible poetry of earth. The figure of the poet as vagabond or exile becomes virtually inseparable from the differentiated, exiled nature of poetic language. Jacques Derrida, in an essay on Edmond Jabès in *L'écriture et la différence*, conflates the historical situation of the "Wandering Jew" with the situation of the poet caught within the "error" of language, "le Désert de la Promesse."[18] In Baudelaire's "Le Cygne," the Virgilian melancholy ("Andromaque, je pense à vous!") is transformed both into the melancholy of the exiled poet, Hugo, and into the *parole exilée*, an anticipation of the Mallarméan transformation of "cygne" ("swan") to "signe" ("sign"). Paul de Man speaks both of the "persistent temptation of literature to fulfill itself in a single moment," and of "the confinement of literature within its own boundaries, its dependence on duration and repetition that Baudelaire experienced as a curse."[19] The melancholy of exile from the present or presence is the fact that they can only be "re-presented" in language, an activity which takes place in time. Augustine's model of temporality and of textuality was the form of the sentence, each syllable giving way in a successive, or syntagmatic, movement towards the "rest" at its end. Language, for Augustine, is a sign of man's distance, or difference, from God and his image of apocalypse is not surprisingly a textual one—the time, prophesied in Isaiah, when the heavens, like the Scriptures, will be "rolled together as a scroll."[20] The Augustinian notion of the *cognitio vespertina* or threshold state in which movement towards this end is "stayed" may seem a concept too heavy for modern poetry. But it is recapitulated, interestingly enough, by Hopkins in his description of the fall of Lucifer:

> This was the process of his own fall. For being required to adore God and enter into a covenant of justice with him he did so indeed, but, as a chorister who learns by use in the church itself the strength and beauty of his voice, he became aware in his very note of adoration of the riches of his nature; then when from that first note he should have gone on with the sacrificial service, prolonging the first note instead and ravished by his own sweetness and dazzled, the prophet says, by his own beauty, he was involved in spiritual sloth ("nolendo se adjuvare") and spiritual luxury and vainglory.[21]

This late revival of the Augustinian concept is not surprising in the poet turned Jesuit priest. What is surprising, however, is Hopkins' association of the Narcissism of Lucifer with his own conception of the nature of poetry: "Poetry is in fact speech only employed to carry the inscape of speech for the inscape's sake—and therefore the inscape must be dwelt on."[22] In the description of Lucifer, the act of "dwelling on his own beauty" is also "an instressing of his own inscape," an "incantation" which drew others in by its "enchantment" and "magic."[23] Lucifer's withdrawal from the "sacrificial service" is the opposite, for Hopkins, of a poetry which knows, and freely acknowledges, its own death.[24] But there may be, finally, no escape from inscape, and Narcissus is potentially the emblem of a self-referential and self-enclosed poetic form.

Hopkins' sense of the potential danger in all *carmina* is shared by religious poets from Herbert and Coleridge to T. S. Eliot. But the apocalyptic desire to precipitate "arrival," the impulse of the "self-consuming artefact," has its counter in the desire to delay or defer it, and in a poetry which dilates the intervening moment. Walter Pater, in the conclusion to *The Renaissance* (1873), subtly subsumes both the biblical imagery of the threshold or respite and the Miltonic "Limbo" of poets and philosophers in a highly self-conscious defense of *l'art pour l'art*:

> We are all *condamnés*, as Victor Hugo says: we are all under sentence of death but with a sort of indefinite reprieve—*les hommes sont tous condamnés à mort avec des sursis indéfinis*: we have an interval, and then our place knows us no more. Some spend this interval in listlessness, some in high passions, the wisest, at least among "the children of this world," in art and song. For our one chance lies in expanding that interval, in getting as many pulsations as possible into the given time. . . . Of this wisdom, the poetic passion, the desire of beauty, the love of art for art's sake, has most; for art comes to you professing frankly to give nothing but the highest quality to your moments as they pass, and simply for those moments' sake.

Pater's "moment" is an extension of Keats's: if apocalypse is destruction, the only hope for the artist lies in dilating the liminal space.

The contrary impulses of romance—its quest for, and simultaneous distancing of, an end or presence—continue in a poetry whose subject is at least partly the romance of language itself. Modern discussions of the deviant nature of poetic trope tend to recapitulate, or at least to recall, older ones.

The seventeenth-century dream of a transparent medium foundered on the inherent duplicity of words, their intractability to legislation.[25] But the goal of what Barthes calls "une écriture vraiment neutre"—a new humanism based on the abolition of linguistic "erring"—is perhaps even more attractive today.[26] We conclude, then, with three modern poets for whom the romance of poetry is an evasion of that end—Stéphane Mallarmé, Paul Valéry, and Wallace Stevens.

The desire to remain suspended on the threshold before arrival is the *projet* of one of Mallarmé's prose poems, "Le Nénuphar blanc." Rowing towards the site of his neighbor—"l'inconnue à saluer"[d]—the speaker is retarded in his progress towards that goal by a clump of weeds in the middle of the stream and reflects upon the pleasant "esclavage" of being at once bound to and separated from the unknown woman:

> Courbé dans la sportive attitude où me maintenait de la curiosité, comme sous le silence spacieux de ce que s'annonçait l'étrangère, je souris au commencement d'esclavage dégagé par une possibilité féminine: que ne signifiaient pas mal les courroies attachant le soulier du rameur au bois de l'embarcation, comme on ne fait qu'un avec l'instrument de ses sortilèges.[e][27]

The image of the straps connecting the rower's shoe to the wood of the boat is chosen to signify the poem's essential paradox, that that which separates also joins: "Séparés, on est ensemble." When the woman herself threatens to appear and thus to violate this suspension, the rower retreats, preferring the furtive threshold before revelation ("le furtif seuil où je

---

[d] "the unknown woman to be greeted"

[e] "Bent over in the sportive attitude in which curiosity held me, as if beneath the spacious silence of the stranger's announcing herself, I smiled at the beginning of enslavement brought about by a feminine possibility: a slavery adequately signified by the straps attaching the rower's shoe to the wood of the boat, as one is united with the instrument of one's enchantments."

règne") to a more precise sense of her appearance: "Si vague concept se suffit: et ne transgressera le délice empreint de généralité qui permet et ordonne d'exclure tous visages."[f] The moment of suspense on the water ("ce suspens sur l'eau où mon songe attarde l'indécise . . .")[g] is privileged over the possible crystallization of this "vierge absence" or "virgin absence" into a particular and determinate form. The rower departs, taking with him the symbol of the "nénuphar blanc,"[h] enclosing within its hollow whiteness "un rien, fait de songes intacts."[i]

The prose poem provides in little an enactment of what is elsewhere in Mallarmé a theory of the poetic figure: "Je dis: une fleur! et, hors de l'oubli où ma voix relègue aucun contour, en tant que quelque chose d'autre que les calices sus, musicalement se lève, idée même et suave, l'absente de tous bouquets."[j28] The end or "apparition" here deferred has its counterpart in the "objet" of the Parnassians, whose more direct expression destroys all sense of mystery: "*Nommer* un objet, c'est supprimer les trois quarts de la jouissance du poëme qui est faite de deviner peu à peu: le *suggérer*, voilà le rêve."[k29] Evocation is for Mallarmé poetry's necessary enigma, the enchantment he describes in "Magie":

Évoquer, dans une ombre exprès, l'objet tu, par des mots allusifs, jamais directs, se réduisant à du silence égal, comporte tentative proche de créer: vraisemblable dans la limite de l'idée uniquement mise en jeu par l'enchanteur de lettres jusqu'à ce que, certes, scintille, quelque illusion égale au regard. Le vers,

[f] "Such a vague concept is sufficient, and will not infringe on the delight marked by generality which permits and commands the exclusion of all faces."
[g] "this suspense on the water where my dream delays the hesitant lady"
[h] "white water-lily"   [i] "a nothing, made of intact dreams"
[j] "I say: a flower! and out of the forgetfulness where my voice relegates any contour, inasmuch as it is something other than known calyxes, musically arises, an idea itself and fragrant, the one absent from all bouquets."
[k] "*To name* an object is to eliminate three-quarters of the enjoyment of the poem, which comes from gradual divination: *to suggest* it, that is the ideal."

trait incantatoire! et, on ne déniera au cercle que per-
pétuellement ferme, ouvre la rime une similitude
avec les ronds, parmi l'herbe, de la fée ou du magi-
cien.[130]

Obscurity—the charge against which Mallarmé had constantly to defend both his theory and his poetry—is a species
of delay, the "labyrinthe illuminé par des fleurs"[m] through
which the reader must pass in his quest for meaning,[31] an activity in which progress by a direct route is retarded. Mallarmé's complaint, in "L'Art pour tous" or "Le Mystère dans
les lettres," that the public has forgotten how to read is countered by a poetics which—contrary to the usual assumption—necessarily involves the reader. The "labyrinthe" of
poetic diction dilates even further the space between words
and things, the écart which leaves room for error. The direct
route to meaning is retarded not by an absence of referents
but by their plenitude. The possibilities in the "noir roc" of
the "Tombeau de Verlaine"—the stone on the tomb, a cloud,
Verlaine himself—are part of a continual semantic play which
mocks the dull Polonius in each of us.[32] The "mal d'être
deux," experienced in "L'Après-Midi d'un Faune" initially as
a curse, is also part of the seminal ambiguity of poetic language. The pun—a characteristic Mallarméan device—
interrupts progress to a single referent as it crowds more than
one meaning into a single space. The poem entitled "Salut"
begins innocently enough with a kind of designation:

> Rien, cette écume, vierge vers
> A ne désigner que la coupe . . .[n]

[1] "To evoke, in a deliberate shadow, the silent object, by words that are
allusive, never direct, that reduce themselves to a like silence, involves an en-
deavor similar to creating: truth-seeming in the extremity of the idea
uniquely put into play by the sorcerer of letters until, most certainly, there
sparkles some illusion which is equal to the gaze. The poetic line, incantatory
stroke! and, one will not deny to the circle which rhyme perpetually closes,
and opens, a similarity with the rings, in the grass, of the fairy or magician."

[m] "labyrinth illuminated by flowers"

[n] "Nothing, this foam, virgin line of poetry, / but to designate only the
cup"

The statement seems purely linear: the verse designates the glass, the poet proposes a toast. But the fact that "vers" may also be heard as "verre" makes the first line into a pun and its designating function into a kind of tautology ("verre" pointing to "coupe"). And the fact that "la coupe" is potentially not only the physical object "cup" but the caesura or metrical "coupure" after "vierge vers" means that this "vers" also designates its own end. "Salut" is not only "toast" or "greetings," but "salvation"; "écume" the foam not only of champagne but of the sea; "coupe" both a nautical term and the poet's well of ink. In the midst of seeming to talk innocently about a single referent, the poem begins to expand upon itself.[33]

This suspension of, or before, a single designation is inherent in Mallarmé's conception of "Le Mystère dans les lettres":

> Les mots, d'eux-mêmes, s'exaltent à mainte facette reconnue la plus rare ou valant pour l'esprit, centre de suspens vibratoire; qui les perçoit indépendamment de la suite ordinaire, projetés, en parois de grotte, tant que dure leur mobilité ou principe, étant ce qui ne se dit pas du discours: prompts tous, avant extinction, à une réciprocité de feux distante ou présentée de biais comme contingence.[o][34]

The "suspens vibratoire," however, is only temporary; the ideal moment of poetic evocation can only be "fictitious or momentary,"[35] and this fact imports a crucial irony into Mallarmé's conception of this threshold space. The "erreur" of speech is contrasted several times by Mallarmé with the silence of nature;[36] the *durée* of suspended space, if a delight, is

[o] "The words, by themselves, rise up at many a facet recognized as the rarest or most significant for the mind, the center of vibratory suspense, which perceives them independently of the usual order, projected as on the walls of a cave, as long as their mobility or principle lasts, being that part of discourse which is not spoken: all of them ready, before they are extinguished, for an exchange of fires, distant or presented obliquely as contingency."

also a sign of impotence or failure. Nature is, as Paul de Man remarks, that from which we are forever separated—a realization which marks Mallarmé's own departure from the early, more naive poetics of "Pan." But it is also "La première en date, la nature,"[p] and as such it enjoys a certain priority.[37] The very threshold which is privileged in Mallarmé is put into question by the irony which gives to his most serious speculations the title of "Divagations," whether the end envisaged be silence, action in the world of history, or the supreme objective of "Le Livre." The image of the subway which he uses in "L'Action restreinte" for the age itself—"rampant sous la cité avant la gare toute-puissante du virginal palais central, qui couronne"[q][38]—was to become, for T. S. Eliot, the modern equivalent of Dante's Limbo. The threshold, as in romance, is a place at once of latency and of separation. Hamlet is "*le seigneur latent qui ne peut devenir*, juvénile ombre de tous."[r][39] His hesitation before the crucial moment of his action and death—"le suspens d'un acte inachevé"—is representative not only of the suspended nature of human existence but of artistic *espacement*, the interval for which the stage itself exists.[40]

Augustine invokes the movement of the sentence to urge arrival at its point of revelation, or ending. But in the crucial drama of *Un Coup de dés*, the completion of the "sentence"—"Un coup de dés jamais n'abolira le hasard"[s]—is also a form of "doom," and the suspended threshold of art itself becomes part of a saving strategy of delay.[41] Apocalypse here is an end whose fulfillment is simultaneously a disaster, the swallowing of all that is differentiated and separated into a Baudelairean "Abîme," "*la neutralité identique du gouffre*" (p. 473).[t] But the intervening space between beginning and end is a kind of romance in which troping or turning is a means of defense, and

[p] "the first in time, nature"

[q] "creeping beneath the city before the all-powerful station of the virginal central palace, which crowns"

[r] "*the latent prince who cannot become*, youthful shadow of us all"

[s] "A throw of the dice never will abolish chance."

[t] "the identical neutrality of the abyss"

the italicized text inaugurated by "COMME SI" (p. 466) the
"As if" of fiction as a form of divagation or dilation. The
turning begins graphically with the transformation of the
shapeless chaos of the sea into a visual representation of a sail-
boat leaning across the first full page ("la coque / d'un bâti-
ment / penché de l'un ou l'autre bord").[u] The end to which
the whole sentence tends is a shipwreck, but the "naufrage
. . . direct" (pp. 462-63), a premature giving in to this end
("jouer . . . la partie / au nom des flots"),[v] is rejected in favor
of a crucial hesitation ("*rythmique suspens du sinistre*," p. 473)[w]
which sets up a kind of *interregnum*, suspended, like the extended series of intervening clauses, before that end. The suspension begins as the interval between the decision to throw
the dice and the action itself ("LE MAÎTRE . . . / hésite . . . /
ancestralement à n'ouvrir pas la main," pp. 462-64),[x] a hesitation which produces an interval of time parallel to the suggested separation in space ("cadavre par le bras écarté du secret qu'il détient").[y] And it continues in a period referred to
ironically as "Fiançailles" (p. 464). There is, from the beginning, no illusion about the consummation towards which this
period of "betrothal" tends: the veil of the Temple whose
rending is traditionally the promise of Apocalypse or Revelation becomes, in Mallarmé's version, the "voile d'illusion"
whose fate is destruction. The entire italicized section in the
mode of a fictional "As if" occurs between the penultimate
and final word of the sentence, an interval Mallarmé, in "Le
Démon de l'analogie," calls a "suspension fatidique."[z] But it
does defer that destruction to the future tense ("chancellera /
s'affalera," p. 464) and the respite creates its own space of
time in which the fiction remains still suspended over the
abyss ("*voltige autour du gouffre / sans le joncher / ni fuir . . .*").[aa]

---

[u] "the hull / of a vessel / leaning to one or the other side"
[v] "to play . . . the game / in the name of the waves"
[w] "rhythmic suspension of the sinister" (also "of the left hand")
[x] "The Master . . . / hesitates . . . / ancestrally not to open the hand"
[y] "corpse kept apart by the arm from the secret it holds"
[z] "fateful suspension"
[aa] "hovers around the abyss / without strewing it / or fleeing . . ."

Though the "plume" finally falls with the conclusion of the sentence on "LE HASARD" (p. 473), something survives in the final, though hesitating and uncertain, "Constellation" of the final page. Modern poetry is rarely so exacting an exploration of this fictional suspension and its inevitable tragedy. "Rythmique suspens," however, remains the mode of any poetry which reflects upon itself, and romance continues unabated in the lyric which evades even as it envisages an end or center. Roland Barthes speaks in *S/Z* of the necessary fragmentation of the sentence, the temporal progression in which the "terre promise" at the end of syllabic enumeration can never be present.[42] Valéry's "Les Pas" is a beautiful and brief romance which enacts this fragmentation,[43] a temporal progression of syllabic and metric feet which distances the goal towards which it tends:

> Tes pas, enfants de mon silence,
> Saintement, lentement placés,
> Vers le lit de ma vigilance
> Procèdent muets et glacés.
>
> Personne pure, ombre divine,
> Qu'ils sont doux, tes pas retenus!
> Dieux! . . . tous les dons que je devine
> Viennent à moi sur ces pieds nus!
>
> Si, de tes lèvres avancées,
> Tu prépares pour l'apaiser,
> À l'habitant de mes pensées
> La nourriture d'un baiser,
>
> Ne hâte pas cet acte tendre,
> Douceur d'être et de n'être pas,
> Car j'ai vécu de vous attendre,
> Et mon coeur n'était que vos pas.[bb]

[bb] "Your footsteps, children of my silence, / With gradual and saintly pace / Towards the bed of my watchfulness, / Muted and frozen, approach . // Pure one, divine shadow, / How gentle are your cautious steps! / Gods! . . . all the gifts that I can guess / Come to me on those naked feet! // If, with your lips

The suspensions and inversions of the verse itself delay or circumvent both fixed point and fixed meaning, making the movement of poetry into a kind of Zeno's paradox. The kiss is its *telos*, but it is also its erotic origin ("enfants de mon silence"); source and end are the same place, and the poem turns upon itself ("Tes pas . . . vos pas") though it preserves the appearance of linearity. We are both before and after the point of origin or end: the final stanza shifts inexplicably from anticipation to the past tense ("j'ai vécu . . ."). The rhyming of "vos pas" with "n'être pas" suggests the simultaneous presence of direction and the negation of it, a contrary movement which parallels the appeal for delay ("Ne hâte pas cet acte tendre, / Douceur d'être et de n'être pas"). The "Douceur d'être et de n'être pas" conveys by a kind of foreshortening, in the double meaning of "pas," a state which is at once being and not-being, and the process of "step" which cannot be named as such before the action is completed. The entire poem is an *écart* or opening between beginning and end which enacts the suspension the speaker requests: the predicate of the subject introduced in the first line is held over until the fourth ("Tes pas . . . / Procèdent . . ."), interrupting the straightforward, or processional, movement. The object of "preparation" in the third stanza ("Tu prépares . . . / La nourriture d'un baiser") is postponed until its final line. Verbs and prepositions suggest directionality ("Procéder," "venir," "préparer," "vers") but it is an orientation suspended in favor of expectancy or "attente." The presence described as "divine" shifts subtly through rhyme to the act of divination, the interval of the not-yet-present ("tous les dons que je devine"), the state of expectancy which also reabsorbs the alliterative series building from "doux" to "Dieux!" "Le lit" is placed by the meter of the line in which it appears less as the definitive goal of movement than as part of the attitude of "attente" ("le lit de ma vigilance"). The *quies* to

advancing, / You are preparing to appease / The inhabitants of my thoughts / With the sustenance of a kiss, // Do not hasten the tender act, / Bliss of being and not being, / For I have lived on waiting for you, / And my heart was only your footsteps."

which the movement tends ("Tu prépares pour l'apaiser . . .")
is postponed for the sake of the movement itself, which is also
a form of "nourriture."

"Les Pas" suggests the romance of a language which distances an envisaged end in order to remain present to itself, as
movement or "marche pure," and this privileging of the
virtual—a state where intense expectation is not as yet be-
trayed by appearance or event—is characteristic of Valéry's
major poems, within and beyond *Charmes*.[44] "Magie" is for
Valéry, as for Keats, awakening to find a dream true, but the
movement or transition beyond the threshold state of "enchantment" is not always so smooth.[45] Valéry's own description of the writing of "Le Cimetière marin" begins with his
preference for "une puissance de transformation toujours en
acte"[cc] over the "chose *finie*" or completed poem, but it also
evokes the sadness of the shadow between conception and
act.[46] The moment of pregnancy or latency Valéry describes
in "Matin" is simultaneously "la promesse, et la vanité de la
promesse."[dd][47] When the construction of Thebes is completed, in *Amphion*, the Muses, no longer interested, depart.
The theme of "attente" or "attention" in *Monsieur Teste* is inseparable from the notion of "la douleur," the painful consciousness of an essential lack. And in "L'Abeille," the
speaker who desires the consummation of "un prompt tour-
ment: / Un mal vif et bien terminé"[ee] reminds us that the "patience" of the verse which keeps within the realm of the
"supplice dormant" is also a variant of *patior*.[48]

This "patience," however, remains representative not only
of *Charmes*, of the incantatory nature of a poetry which suspends the conventional sense of words, but of Valéry's sustained conception of the need for poetry and its "error" in a
universe obsessed with "ends":

L'univers pratique se réduit à un ensemble de *buts*.
Tel but atteint, la parole expire. Cet univers exclut

[cc] "a power of transformation always in action"
[dd] "the promise, and the vanity of the promise" (trans. mine)
[ee] "an instant pang: / A vivid and a clear-cut pain"

l'ambiguïté, l'élimine; il commande que l'on pro-
cède par les plus courts chemins, et il étouffe au plus
tôt les harmoniques de chaque événement qui s'y
produit à l'esprit.[ff49]

In contrast to the directionality of prose, poetry thrives on
ambiguity, on resonance and repetition, on a thickening of
the medium rather than the "shortest way." The linear tendency of words, "leur propriété de se consommer en un sens
défini et certain,"[gg50] is precisely what it seeks to evade. The
"Nécessité de la Poésie" consists, finally, for Valéry, in this
evasion: in a world consumed with hurry and increasingly
rapid means of communication, it deliberately perplexes and
retards.[51]

Valéry's conception of the necessity of this evasion brings
us finally to the figure of Wallace Stevens. We close with Stevens not simply because he is among the most recent dis-
coverers of "inescapable romance" ("An Ordinary Evening
in New Haven"), but because, unlike Mallarmé or Valéry
whose work, though it revives the ancient pun on *carmina*, is
less grounded in a native romance tradition, he provides a
retrospect on the meaning of romance for English poetry
since Spenser. In one of the *Letters on Chivalry and Romance*,
Bishop Hurd remarks that modern men are "doubly dis-
gusted" to find, in the romances, "a representation of things
unlike to what they have observed in real life and *beyond* what
it was ever possible should have existed."[52] Stevens' project
two centuries later is still the domestication of the imagination, an activity which, as he remarks in one essay, involves
cleansing it of the "romantic."[53] His own poem entitled
"Re-Statement of Romance" is part of a continuing reductive
quest,[54] the search for a "neutral centre" ("Landscape with
Boat") freed of all the "rotted names" ("The Man with the

[ff] "The practical universe is reduced to a collection of *aims*. An aim being
reached, the word expires. That universe excludes ambiguity, eliminates it; it
demands that one should proceed by the shortest way, and it stifles as soon as
possible the harmonics of each event that occurs in the mind."

[gg] "their capacity for being consummated in a defined and particular
meaning"

Blue Guitar," xxxii), the accretions of the errant imagination
and its exploded fancies, and for the "poem of pure reality,
untouched / By trope or deviation" ("An Ordinary Evening
in New Haven," ix). The mode in which this reduction is
practiced in poem after poem seems to make him part of the
anti-romance of the plain style or *écriture neutre*, the poetic
counterpart of the quester of "Landscape with Boat":

> he rejected, he denied, to arrive
> At the neutral centre, the ominous element,
> The single-colored, colorless, primitive.

This technique of rejection is partly Wordsworthian or
Keatsian in intent: "the great poems of heaven and hell have
been written and the great poem of the earth remains to be
written."[55] Stevens knows with Keats that "The greatest
poverty is not to live / In a physical world, to feel that one's
desire / Is too difficult to tell from despair" ("Esthétique du
Mal," xv). And the "necessary angel" of his essays is the one
whose task it is to enable men to "see the earth again, /
Cleared of its stiff and stubborn, man-locked set" ("Angel
Surrounded by Paysans"), to clear away the veil of successive
mediations and to provide an "Evening without Angels."

Reduction to this center, however, is not always in Stevens
a source of pleasure or a matter of choice. The "he" of "The
Latest Freed Man," having divested himself of all the rotted
names, describes the exhilaration of being "At the centre of
reality," seeing everything as "more real." But what in this
poem is experienced as exhilaration is in others a form of poverty. "Esthétique du Mal" becomes another in the long line of
post-Spenserian poems which lament the progress of enlightenment and its destruction of many "blue phenomena"
even as it celebrates the emergence of a "physical world":

> Phantoms, what have you left? What underground?
> What place in which to be is not enough
> To be? You go, poor phantoms, without place
> Like silver in the sheathing of the sight,
> As the eye closes . . . How cold the vacancy

When the phantoms are gone and the shaken realist
First sees reality.

(VIII)

The destitution of a man for whom the moon can no longer
be a "round effendi" (IX) is a poverty like that of the moment
of "pain and ugliness" in Keats's *Lamia*, when nothing "is left
but comic ugliness / Or a lustred nothingness" ("Esthétique,"
IX). And the reduction of the "paradise of meaning" to the
Mammon world of "one meaning alone"—"the sky divested
of its fountains"—raises the call for "Another chant, an incantation," music that "buffets the shapes of its possible halcyon /
Against the haggardie."

   This ambivalence, the search for the neutral center or "veritable ding an sich" beneath the "last distortion of romance"
("The Comedian as the Letter C," I) and the realization that
this reduction will, finally, not suffice, is what makes Stevens'
"Notes Toward a Supreme Fiction" the supreme poem it is.
It begins in the search for the "first idea," the "muddy centre"
which existed "before we breathed." But if it is to this reduction that the poem is driven by "the celestial ennui of apart-
ments," there is equally "an ennui of the first idea," an
awareness that it is not possible for men to remain within the
"final no." If, as in the title of another poem, "Reality is an
Activity of the Most August Imagination," the autumnal vision is not the "veritable season" ("Examination of the Hero
in a Time of War," XVI), and "disillusion" is finally only "the
last illusion" ("An Ordinary Evening in New Haven," V).
Reduction in poetry to the "single-colored, colorless" center
is not finally possible because figuration itself is part of the
"inescapable romance." The poet of "Someone Puts a
Pineapple Together" seeks a way through the "pale arron-
dissements," a reduction to "The angel at the centre of this
rind," "the irreducible x / At the bottom of imagined artifice." But the "angel" itself remains the irreducible figure.
Even the reduction to the "first idea" in "Notes" ends in an
"imagined thing." The ephebe is to learn that "Phoebus is
dead," to "clean the sun" of all its images. But the sun which

must "bear no name" is simultaneously, and beautifully, called "gold flourisher," a kenning which reimports figuration in one of its most elemental forms.

Stevens is by no means unaware of the sorrows of being exiled from a single center or abiding presence:

> It would be enough
> If we were ever, just once, at the middle, fixed
> In This Beautiful World of Ours and not as now,
>
> Helplessly at the edge, enough to be
> Complete, because at the middle, if only in sense,
> And in that enormous sense, merely enjoy.
>
> ("The Ultimate Poem is Abstract")

Stevens' poems of this exile recapitulate the romance tradition of its melancholy, the perpetual sense of being on the periphery, debarred. And yet he also shares this tradition's wariness of the center: the frozen solipsist of "This Solitude of Cataracts" is a fixity, a "bronze man" breathing "his bronzen breath at the azury centre of time." In "Prologues to What Is Possible," the journey to the "point of central arrival" is described in images of fire and weightlessness like those which accompany Dante's ascent of his Mountain of Vision. But when we reach the goal of the quest, at the end of the first section, and hear the lines

> As at a point of central arrival, an instant moment,
>   much or little,
> Removed from any shore, from any man or woman,
>   and needing none . . .

it is difficult not to hear echoes of the "expunge all people" of "Sailing after Lunch" or the solipsistic "third world without knowledge, / In which no one peers" of "Esthétique du Mal" (xii). What saves this poem from this more dangerous center, however, is the corresponding outward, or less directed, movement of its second section, the fact that the journey to the center, here, is not a final end but only a "prologue" to the "possible," a pure projection.

Stevens' wariness of apocalypse or center is partly a peculiarly American preoccupation—the wariness which causes Emily Dickinson to pause before the moment of Revelation in "Our journey had advanced" or to seek in another poem to keep "Eternity / From presenting—Here—"("Crisis is a Hair"). But the constant *andirivieni* of a poetry which incessantly qualifies even as it approaches a satisfying center or place of rest allies Stevens finally with Spenser, the other English poet who knew that "Death is the mother of beauty" ("Sunday Morning").[56] If T. S. Eliot inherits the purgatorial typology of romance, Stevens inherits its preference for the *clair-obscur*, however much he may proclaim that all distance from the center is a "tragic chiaroscuro" ("Notes"). The poet is, by definition, an eccentric whose vision is always slightly off center, making the visible a little hard to see ("The Creations of Sound"). Spenser begins the second Book of *The Faerie Queene* with a defense of "Faerie," the latent world of the not-yet-discovered on the threshold of the actual. Stevens' "Faerie" is the shadowy "spirit's universe" of the poem "Description without Place," an "affair / Of the possible; seemings that are to be, / Seemings that it is possible may be."

It is this preference for, or interposition of, the "possible" which imports a contradiction into the quest for the "neutral centre" or for a poetry exactly coincident with "Things as they are" ("The Man with the Blue Guitar"). In "The Noble Rider and the Sound of Words," one of the essays in *The Necessary Angel*, Stevens writes:

> There is, in fact, a world of poetry indistinguishable from the world in which we live, or, I ought to say, no doubt, from the world in which we shall come to live, since what makes the poet the potent figure that he is, or was, or ought to be, is that he creates the world to which we turn incessantly and without knowing it and that he gives to life the supreme fictions without which we are unable to conceive of it.[57]

The shift from "the world in which we live" to "the world in which we shall come to live" is unobtrusive and as characteristically Stevensian a feint as the equivocation ("Invisible or visible or both") in "Notes" ("It Must Be Abstract," vi). But the temporal disjunction is crucial. The imagination's locus is finally not the "veritable ding an sich" which Crispin confronts when freed from the "last distortion of romance," but something closer to that pregnant virtuality Keats called a "shadow of reality to come," the promise of "the possibilities of things."[58]

This necessary disjunction or gap applies, finally, even to the Supreme Fiction of the "Major Man." If he is the figure whose "solitaria / Are the meditations of a central mind" ("Certain Phenomena of Sound," xi), it is a centrality "eccentric" in relation to the present circumference of vision, "not too closely the double of our lives, / Intenser than any actual life could be" ("Description without Place," vi). The hermitage at this center is not the fixed and frozen point of solipsistic withdrawal because it is a sphere which is, in the words of "The Sail of Ulysses," the "centre of the self" but of "the self / Of the future" (iv). The "major men" of "Paisant Chronicle" are finally

> characters beyond
> Reality, composed thereof. They are
> The fictive man created out of men.
> They are men but artificial men. They are
> Nothing in which it is not possible
> To believe . . .

In a tradition in which, as Yeats complained, romance and the Mammon of relevance were very early at odds, this eccentricity necessarily involves Stevens in one of the romance tradition's characteristic anxieties, from the potential limbo of Spenser's "Faerie" to the darker aspect of Keats's "shadow of reality to come."[59] The poet who cannot sing of "things as they are" is potentially the creator of nothing but a barren "abstraction," however much he might deny that "abstraction is a vice" ("A Thought Revolved"). For the poet of "Notes Toward a Supreme Fiction," the two qualifications of the Fiction—"It Must Change" and "It Must be Abstract"— are flanked by the perversions of each pole. The perversion of

"It Must be Abstract" is "abstraction" in the sense of mere "evasion" ("The poet evades us / As in a senseless element"). The other side of "It Must Change" is the endless round of the cycle of nature, the reason, finally, why the "muddy centre" of the "first idea" will not suffice. Each of these extremes leads to the same dead end, a fact which may explain why the song of mere being in "It Must Change" ends on the same note as the description of the human abstract, the statue of General Du Puy. Both share the essential stoniness of a "granite monotony," the one part "Of an earth in which the first leaf is the tale of leaves" and the sparrow a "bird / Of stone, that never changes," the other "Of a suspension, a permanence so rigid / That it made the General a bit absurd," where "Nothing had happened because nothing had changed."

For Stevens, the alternative to the radical sameness of these extremes is the "pendant," or "dependent," relation of that section of "Notes" which comes between the two:

> Two things of opposite natures seem to depend
> On one another, as a man depends
> On a woman, day on night, the imagined
>
> On the real. This is the origin of change.
> Winter and spring, cold copulars, embrace
> And forth the particulars of rapture come.
>
> Music falls on the silence like a sense,
> A passion that we feel, not understand.
> Morning and afternoon are clasped together
>
> And North and South are an intrinsic couple
> And sun and rain a plural, like two lovers
> That walk away as one in the greenest body.

This fruitful dependency is Stevens' *Concordia*, a Creation or "mundo" made possible by a tempering of both kinds of possession, the violence from without and the violence from within. It is neither a collapse of subject and object into oneness, nor their estrangement: the "Supreme Fiction" remains both "a part" and "apart." It is, rather, part of the ongoing

...rioso (Milan: Mondadori, 1964). Unless otherwise specified, all translations ...e taken from Allan Gilbert, trans., *Orlando Furioso*, 2 vols. (New York: ...F. Vanni, 1954). References are to canto, stanza, and line.

2. D. S. Carne-Ross, "The One and the Many: A Reading of *Orlando* ...rioso, Cantos 1 and 8," *Arion*, 5 (Summer 1966), 195-234.

3. See Ramat, *La critica ariostesca dal secolo xvi ad oggi* (Florence: La Nuova ...lia, 1954); A. Cioranescu, *L'Arioste en France*, 2 vols. (Paris: Les Presses ...odernes, 1938-39); and the opening chapter of Herbert Frenzel, *Ariost und* ... *romantische Dichtung* (Cologne: Böhlau-Verlag, 1962).

4. The passage is quoted as it appears in the Naples (1725) edition, ...26-27.

5. *Lettres*, ed. Monmerqué (Paris: Hachette, 1862), iv, 409.

6. Cioranescu, ii, 10, cites among others the observations of Roland Des-...arests, *Epistolae* (Paris, 1655), p. 262; Pierre de Deimier, *Académie de l'art* ...étique (Paris: Jean de Bordeaulx, 1610), p. 541; and F. Langlois, *Le Tombeau* ...s romans (Paris: C. Mollot, 1626), pp. 12-13.

7. A revealing example of the difficulty caused by the poem's hybrid na-...re is provided in French classicist René Rapin's *Reflexions sur l'éloquence, la* ...étique, l'histoire et la philosophie (Paris: Fr. Mignet, 1684). The *Furioso* shares ...his condemnation of the romances, which "s'égarent sans cesse" (p. 126); ...ut the poem's inclusion of so much romance material is an enigma, since ...L'Arioste a je ne sçay quoy de poëme epique plus que les autres" (p. 140).

8. See, for example, Francesco Patrizi's *Parere, in difesa dell'Ariosto* included ...his *Apologia del S. Torquato Tasso* (Mantua, 1585), pp. 175ff.

9. Pigna, *I romanzi* (Venice, 1554), pp. 18-19.

10. See, for example, Galileo's famous preference for Ariosto over Tasso ...*etter to Rinuccini*, May 19, 1640), and Bernardo Tasso's remark that if Aris-...otle had read Ariosto, he would have modified his conception of the epic ...*etter to Varchi*, 1559).

11. *Cinque canti* v. 26. The edition used in all references to these cantos, ...irst published as an appendix to the Aldine edition of the *Furioso* in 1545, is ...Ariosto's *Opere minori*, ed. Cesare Segre (Milan: Ricciardi, 1954).

12. In Oratio Toscanella's "Allegorie dei nomi proprii," in his *Bellezze del* ...*urioso* (Venice, 1574), for example, "Atlante" is "Amore," who tricks lov-...rs under various guises and imprisons them. See Harington's 1591 transla-...ion, p. 412, and, for a stimulating modern view of the "palazzo" and the ...rrant nature of "fantasia," A. Momigliano's *Saggio su L'Orlando furioso* ...1925; rpt. Bari, 1959), p. 2.

13. *Gerusalemme liberata* (1575) i. 1. 7-8, announces Goffredo's uniting of ...his "compagni erranti" under the Christian banner.

14. See Durling, *The Figure of the Poet in Renaissance Epic* (Cambridge, Mass.: Harvard Univ. Press, 1965), p. 161, and the illuminating remarks on the Orlando-nature and Astolfo-nature of the narrator in Peter V. Marinelli, "Redemptive Laughter: Comedy in the Italian Romances," *Genre*, 9, No. 4 (Winter 1976-77), 525.

process Stevens calls "taming the monster of the incredible,"[60] an activity which does not divest itself of romance and its ghostlier demarcations, but moves instead towards a concord of opposites, "the imagined and the real, thought / And the truth, / Dichtung und Wahrheit" ("The Man with the Blue Guitar," xxiii), a dependency which makes these "Notes," dedicated to Henry Church, into Stevens' Legend of Friendship. And it is finally what makes this strain in Stevens, so different from either Mallarmé or Valéry, still part of the metamorphoses of a romance still open-ended.

Notes

INTRODUCTION

1. See W. P. Ker, *Epic and Romance: Essays on M*
(London: Macmillan, 1908); Eugène Vinaver, *Th*
York: Oxford Univ. Press, 1971); Erich Auerbach,
tion of Reality in Western Literature, trans. Willard Tr
Univ. Press, 1953), pp. 123–42; Northrop Frye's dis
Anatomy of Criticism (1957; rpt. New York: Atheneu
cently, in *The Secular Scripture: A Study of the Str*
bridge, Mass.: Harvard Univ. Press, 1976). Other s
studies include Rosemond Tuve's *Allegorical Imager*
and Their Posterity (Princeton: Princeton Univ. Pre
Beer's *Romance* (London: Methuen, 1970); Christop
and Realism, ed. Samuel Hynes (Princeton: Princet
John Stevens' *Medieval Romance* (New York: Nort
Ryding's *Structure in Medieval Narrative* (The Hagu
Paul Zumthor's *Essai de poétique médiévale* (Paris: Edi

2. As in, for example, Frank Kermode's *Sense of a*
ford Univ. Press, 1966); Barbara H. Smith's *Poetic C*
Poems End (Chicago: Univ. of Chicago Press, 1968
David H. Richter's *Fable's End: Completeness and Clo*
(Chicago: Univ. of Chicago Press, 1974).

3. "Magical Narratives: Romance as Genre," *New*
1 (Autumn 1975), 161.

4. "Magical Narratives," p. 142.

5. *Mimesis*, p. 136.

6. See Roland Barthes, *S/Z: Essai* (Paris: Editions d
and the first chapter of Helen Vendler's *On Extended*
Longer Poems (Cambridge, Mass.: Harvard Univ. Pres

7. *The Secular Scripture*, p. 15.

8. See his essay entitled "La Différance," reprin
philosophie (Paris: Editions de Minuit, 1972), pp. 1–29.

9. *Anatomy of Criticism*, p. 186.

I. ARIOSTO

1. The text used in this and all subsequent references
it appears in Cesare Segre, ed., *Tutte le opere di Ludovi*

15. *The Descent from Heaven: A Study in Epic Continuity* (New Haven: Yale Univ. Press, 1963), p. 16.

16. The symbolic density of the *Innamorato* (1495) might be illustrated by the underwater Crystal Palace and the description of the Fata Morgana as a Fortuna figure (II. ix. 1-17), a description with all the allegorical detail of an illustration out of Cartari's *Imagini*. Harington (1591), p. 405, explains that the *Furioso*'s relative lack of "Allegorie" prompts his allegorical supplements. For a stimulating interpretation of the *Furioso*'s "anti-allegorical" strategies, see Daniel Javitch, "Rescuing Ovid from the Allegorizers," *Comparative Literature*, 30 (1978), 97-107. The edition used in all references to Boiardo is A. Scaglione, ed., *Orlando Innamorato, Amorum Libri*, 2 vols. (Turin: UTET, 1963). References are to Book, canto, stanza, and line. All translations from Boiardo are mine.

17. Boiardo is far from the naive, straight-faced romancer the usual contrast with Ariosto paints him as—as the tongue-in-cheek references to Angelica's virginity (II. xix. 50) and his irreverent description of Brandimarte and Fiordelisa (I. xix. 61) attest—but he fails to develop the implications of such "errors" as the labyrinth of Theseus and Ariadne (II. viii. 15-16) beyond their fixed locations.

18. These lines echo Petrarch's *Rime* IV. 5-6, on Christ "vegnendo in terra a'lluminar le carte / Ch'avean molt'anni già celato il vero." The connection between the veils of *figura* and of romance enchantress is further suggested by the *Cinquecento* allegorization of Logistilla's book as the Old Testament interpreted through the New, and by Ariosto's use of another textual metaphor for Astolfo's infatuation with Alcina: "ogni pensiero, ogni mio bel disegno / In lei finia, né passava oltre il segno" (VI. 47. 7-8).

19. See, for example, the *exordia* to cantos VI, IX, XV, XVIII, and XXIV of the *Morgante* (1483).

20. The cantos just before Boiardo breaks off move towards the siege of Paris, but leave this for the sequel to effect. There is a similar suspension of the story of Fiordespina's "vain love" for Bradamante, a problem Ariosto solves by providing a twin brother.

21. See II. x. 22ff; II. iv. 74ff.

22. See, for example, XVIII. 8. 1, and the endings of cantos IV, VI, X, XI, XIII, XVII, XXIX, XXXVIII, and XL. Ariosto specifically uses "differire" in relation to the two fairies in XV. 74. 7.

23. One counterpart to such tapestries in the *Furioso* is the series of paintings of future history in the Castle of Tristan (XXXIII. 1ff).

24. The most spectacular of these revelations is the discovery, in canto XXIX, that the mad knight briefly encountered by Angelica and Medoro as early as canto XIX is Orlando. The intervening cantos suspend this meeting in order to fill in the story of how Orlando went mad.

25. See, for example, the *Morgante* II. 36ff; IV. 102; X. 117; XII. 66; and the *Innamorato* I. xvii. 36. 8.

26. One of the reasons why the *Cinque canti* do not finally belong in the

Furioso is that the latter does come to an end. The renewed war with enchantment in these cantos and the doubling effect of events such as Astolfo's falling once again into illusion suggest the very cyclical repetition which the *Furioso* terminates.

27. Orlando's awakening out of his madness (xxxix. 60. 3) echoes both the awakening of Silenus in Virgil's sixth *Eclogue* (24) and the curing of the madness of Hercules in Seneca's *Hercules furens* (1063-81: "Solvite tantis animum monstris . . ."), the play which Pigna and other *Cinquecento* readers saw as a possible antecedent of the *Furioso*.

28. *Descent from Heaven*, p. 120.

29. Rodomonte's assault on Paris (xvi. 23. 1-2; xvii. 11) is described with similes from the slaughter wrought by Turnus within the Trojan gates (*Aen.* ix. 730) and the entrance of Pyrrhus into Priam's palace (*Aen.* ii. 469-75), while the arrival of Rinaldo with the British troops (xvi. 28) recalls Aeneas' return with aid from Evander in *Aeneid* x. Astolfo's exploits include the story of the Orco, who combines both Homer's Cyclops and the Polyphemus of the highly "Odyssean" *Aeneid* iii.

30. See, for example, his treatment of the Virgilian episode of Nisus and Euryalus in canto xviii. 165ff, and the liberal scattering of allusions to Dido and Aeneas through the *Furioso*.

31. Cacus is the son of Vulcan, and Caligorante's net is said to be the one used by Vulcan to ensnare Venus and Mars (*Od.* viii. 272ff).

32. Canto iii. 50. 1 echoes *Metamorphoses* xv. 750-51 as well as more generally Anchises' prophecies in *Aeneid* vi.

33. The important account of Dido's love and death in *Aeneid* iv, for example, is reduced to a mere four lines in *Metamorphoses* xiv. 78-81, while the Sibyl's reminder that Aeneas has no time to linger (*Aen.* vi. 33-41) is reversed (*Met.* xiv. 116ff), as the descent into Hades is deferred while the Sibyl tells Aeneas the long story of her involvement with Apollo.

34. The famous Renaissance addition of a thirteenth book to the *Aeneid* by Maffeo Vegio is different again, but the distinct verbal similarities in the episode of Aeneas' apotheosis (*Met.* xiv. 580ff and Vegio, 593-630) suggest that Vegio saw a precedent in Ovid.

35. This is very suggestively stated by Carne-Ross, "The One and the Many," pp. 215-28.

36. Servius thought that the "arma" of the *Aeneid*'s opening referred to the *Iliad*, and the "virumque" to the *Odyssey*. Minturno's discussion of the "Odissea, alla quale è più simile, che alla Iliada il Romanzo," in the *Arte poetica*, usefully suggests the commonplace Renaissance view, while Viktor Pöschl's *Art of Vergil*, trans. Gerda Seligson (Ann Arbor: Univ. of Michigan Press, 1962), pp. 25ff, provides a brilliant modern interpretation of the two elements in the *Aeneid*.

37. See *Purg.* xviii. 133-38, where the Trojans left behind in Sicily and the Israelites who fell behind in the wilderness are used together as types of *accidia*.

38. The passage, as it appears in the Naples (1725) edition, p. 29, may be translated as follows: "It is not doubted that Aeneas came to Italy . . . nor that Patroclus was killed by Hector and Hector by Achilles. . . . On the other hand, the writer of romances, without having any regard for truth, feigns that which never was: since, although neither writing nor report ever bore witness to the love or the madness of Orlando, Boiardo feigns him 'in love' and Ariosto 'mad.' "

39. The passage is cited as it appears in Bortolo ·Tommaso Sozzi, ed., *Opere di Torquato Tasso*, 2 vols. (Turin: UTET, 1955-56), I, 657-58.

40. XXXIII. 108ff. See also Virgil, *Aen.* III. 227ff; Valerius Flaccus, *Argonautica* IV. 428ff; Dante, *Inf.* XIII. 10-15.

41. The literary antecedents of this vision of earth include the dream of Scipio in Cicero's *De re publica* VI. 16, Lucian's *True Story*, and Dante's *Paradiso* XXII.

42. The suggestion that "Helen" and "Ilium" survived only because taken up by the poets may also be found in Horace's *Odes* IV. 9, a passage Ariosto, imitator of the Horatian *Satires*, would undoubtedly have known well.

43. The illustration for canto XXXV in the revised 1634 edition of Harington's translation, for example, shows Astolfo with St. John in the foreground, but includes other episodes of the canto in the background.

44. The phrase is borrowed from Frank Kermode's stimulating study of the problem of closure in *The Sense of an Ending* (London: Oxford Univ. Press, 1966).

45. "Or l'alta fantasia, ch'un sentier solo / non vuol ch'i' segua ognor . . ." (XIV. 65. 1-2) is an *apologia* for the *Furioso*'s digressive refusal to follow a "single path," whereas the phrase occurs in the *Purgatorio*'s canto on the limits of imagination (XVII. 125) and just before the failure of poetry in the final vision of the *Paradiso* (XXXIII. 142).

46. G. Maruffi notes the difference between the tripartite Dantesque version and Ariosto's in his *La Divina Commedia considerata quale fonte dell'Orlando Furioso e della Gerusalemme Liberata* (Naples, 1903), p. 9, and cites (p. 7) Landino's interpretation of the Dantesque canto, which Ariosto would almost certainly have known.

47. Dante's version of the Ulysses story, in *Inferno* XXVI and in the Siren's claim that she did stop him with her song (*Purg.* XIX. 22) is a rewriting of the traditional account derived from Homer (though Dante did not know the Homeric texts). Ariosto clearly echoes the Dantesque canto of Ulysses in the description of the flight of Olimpia (IX. 43), where the rhyme "acque" and "come a Dio piacque" recalls the "acque" and "com'altrui piacque" of *Inferno* XXVI. 139, 141.

48. In, for example, Greene, *Descent from Heaven*, pp. 132ff; Durling, *The Figure of the Poet*, pp. 129, 250-53; Marinelli, "Redemptive Laughter," pp. 516-26; and A. Bartlett Giamatti, *The Earthly Paradise and the Renaissance Epic* (Princeton: Princeton Univ. Press, 1966), pp. 137-64.

49. For a masterful interpretation of Ariosto's rejection, here, of the Dan-

tesque mode of signifying, see David Quint, "Astolfo's Voyage to the Moon," *Yale Italian Studies*, 1, No. 4 (Fall 1977), 398-408.

50. Augustine, *Confessions* IV. x: "ecce sic peragitur et sermo noster per signa sonantia. non enim erit totus sermo, si unum verbum non decedat, cum sonuerit partes suas, ut succedat aliud."

51. See his *Rhetoric of Religion: Studies in Logology* (1961; rpt. Berkeley: Univ. of California Press, 1970).

52. For structuralist uses of the model of the sentence, see the essays of Claude Bremond, Tzvetan Todorov, A.-J. Greimas, and Roland Barthes in *Communications*, 8 (1966). Ariosto's constant "differire" as a strategy of narrative deferral is suggestively close to Jacques Derrida's concept in "La Différance," in his *Marges de la philosophie* (Paris: Editions de Minuit, 1972), pp. 1-29. On Ariosto and fictionality, see Eugenio Donato, "The Shape of Fiction: Notes Towards a Possible Classification of Narrative Discourses," *MLN*, 86 (1971), 818-19, and Giamatti, "Headlong Horses, Headless Horsemen: An Essay on the Chivalric Epics of Pulci, Boiardo, and Ariosto," in G. Rimanelli and K. J. Atchity, eds., *Italian Literature* (New Haven: Yale Univ. Press, 1976), pp. 299-300.

II. SPENSER

1. *The Faerie Queene* I. Pro. 1. 5. The text used in all references to Spenser's poetry is *Spenser: Poetical Works*, ed. J. C. Smith and E. de Selincourt (1912; rpt. London: Oxford Univ. Press, 1965). Reference is to Book, canto, stanza, and line.

2. See Frank Kermode, *The Sense of an Ending*, p. 78, and H. G. Lotspeich, *Classical Mythology in the Poetry of Edmund Spenser* (Princeton: Princeton Univ. Press, 1932), p. 32.

3. *Descent from Heaven*, p. 327.

4. For a survey of views, see Alice F. Blitch, "The Mutability Cantos 'In Meet Order Ranged,' " *English Language Notes*, 7, No. 3 (March 1970), 179-86. S. P. Zitner, in his edition of *The Mutabilitie Cantos* (London: Nelson, 1968), stresses the hopefulness of the vision of last things, while Greene, p. 323, points to the distance from the "hearsay Sabbath." See also Harry Berger, Jr., "The *Mutabilitie Cantos*: Archaism and Evolution in Retrospect," in Harry Berger, Jr., ed., *Spenser: A Collection of Critical Essays* (Englewood Cliffs: Prentice-Hall, 1968), pp. 146-76; Sherman Hawkins, "Mutabilitie and the Cycle of the Months," in *Form and Convention in the Poetry of Edmund Spenser*, ed. W. Nelson (New York: Columbia Univ. Press, 1961), pp. 76-102; Lewis J. Owen, "Mutable in eternity: Spenser's despair and the multiple forms of Mutabilitie," *The Journal of Medieval and Renaissance Studies*, 2, No. 1 (Spring 1972), 49-68; and Judith H. Anderson, *The Growth of a Personal Voice: "Piers Plowman" and "The Faerie Queene"* (New Haven: Yale Univ. Press, 1976), pp. 201-2.

5. Ficino uses *dilatio* in his translation of Plotinus' Fifth *Ennead*, for the dilation of form within the body. See also his translation of *Enneads* 6: 7. 2, 3;

De immortalitate animorum I. iii; v. x; and *De vita coelitus comparanda*, ch. I. For a discussion of Spenser's Neo-Platonic use, see Brents Stirling, "The Concluding Stanzas of *Mutabilitie*," *Studies in Philology*, 30 (1933), 193-204; Rosalie Colie, *Paradoxia Epidemica: The Renaissance Tradition of Paradox* (Princeton: Princeton Univ. Press, 1966), pp. 345-46; and John Erskine Hankins, *Source and Meaning in Spenser's Allegory* (Oxford: Clarendon Press, 1971), p. 291.

6. *De consolatione*, Book III, metrum 2, 34-38, as translated in F. N. Robinson, ed., *The Works of Geoffrey Chaucer*, 2nd ed. (Cambridge, Mass.: Riverside Press, 1957), p. 343. The original Boethian passage reads: "Repetunt proprios quaeque recursus / Redituque suo singula gaudent / Nec manet ulli traditus ordo / Nisi quod fini iunxerit ortum / Stabilemque sui fecerit orbem."

7. Origen, in the *Homily on Joshua*, for example, writes: "Rahab, which means breadth, *dilatio*, increases and goes forth, until her name extends over the whole limits of the earth." For the use of the Latin term in connection with Rahab, see Jean Daniélou, *From Shadows to Reality: Studies in the Biblical Typology of the Fathers*, trans. Dom Wulstan Hibberd (London: Burns and Oates, 1960), pp. 250ff.

8. *Patrologia Latina* CCX. 137.

9. See his sermon on Joshua VI in the Parker Society edition of *The Works of John Jewel, Bishop of Salisbury*, ed. Rev. John Ayre (Cambridge: Cambridge Univ. Press, 1847), II, 970. This interpretation in Patristic writing is outlined in Daniélou, pp. 229ff.

10. Holy Sonnet #179. The theme of the Church as mistress or harlot is anticipated in Donne's Satire III.

11. For the combination and confusion of meanings from the Latin roots, see the *Oxford English Dictionary* (*OED*) s.v. "dilate," "defer," and "differ."

12. See, for example, Sir Walter Scott's comments in his review of Robert Southey's edition of *Pilgrim's Progress*, in the *Quarterly Review*, 43 (September 1830), 486-87.

13. Tasso, *Prose diverse*, ed. Cesare Guasti (Florence, 1875), I, 44-45.

14. *De consolatione*, Book IV, prosa 6, as translated in Chaucer, *Works*, p. 368. The original is as follows: "Sicut enim artifex faciendae rei formam mente praecipiens mouet operis effectum, et quod simpliciter praesentarieque prospexerat, per temporales ordines ducit, ita deus prouidentia quidem singulariter stabiliterque facienda disponit, fato uero haec ipsa quae disposuit multipliciter ac temporaliter administrat."

15. Book IV, metrum 6, 40-43.

16. The text here is *Gerusalemme liberata*, ed. A. M. Carini (Milan: Feltrinelli, 1961), I. i. 5-8. The Edward Fairfax translation (1600) used here renders "Ridusse" as "reduced" rather than the sense of "ridurre" as "ricondurre."

17. See the preface to his translation of Rapin's *Reflections on Aristotle's Treatise of Poesie* (1674), in A. Zimansky, ed., *The Critical Works of Thomas Rymer* (New Haven: Yale Univ. Press, 1956), p. 5.

18. *ST*, II-II, qu. 35, a. 3, ad 1.

19. For the history of the relation between *accidia* and the noonday demon

of Ps. 91:6 (Vulgate 90:6), see Siegfried Wenzel, *The Sin of Sloth: "Acedia" in Medieval Thought and Literature* (Chapel Hill: Univ. of North Carolina Press, 1960), pp. 6ff; Roger Caillois, "Les démons de midi," *Revue de l'Histoire des Religions*, 115 (1937), 142-73, and 116 (1937), 54-83, 143-86; and Rudolph Arbesmann, "The 'Daemonium Meridianum' and Greek and Latin Patristic Exegesis," *Traditio*, 14 (1958), 17-31.

20. Ernst Robert Curtius, *European Literature and the Latin Middle Ages*, trans. Willard Trask (1953; rpt. New York: Harper and Row, 1963), pp. 490-93, and Eugène Vinaver's chapter entitled "The Poetry of Interlace," in *The Rise of Romance*, provide excellent introductions to this narrative style.

21. "Symbolic parody" is Northrop Frye's term in "The Structure of Imagery in *The Faerie Queene*," in his *Fables of Identity* (New York: Harcourt, Brace & World, 1963), p. 79. On Arthur and Orgoglio, see James Nohrnberg, *The Analogy of "The Faerie Queene"* (Princeton: Princeton Univ. Press, 1976), p. 50.

22. See, respectively, Thomas Warton, *Observations on "The Faerie Queene" of Spenser*, 2 vols. (1754; rpt. London, 1807), I, 158, and George Puttenham, *The Arte of English Poesie* (1589 ed.), III. xxii, s.v. *Pleonasmus*.

23. I borrow the phrase from the suggestive discussion of this episode in Donald Cheney, *Spenser's Images of Nature* (New Haven: Yale Univ. Press, 1966), pp. 27ff.

24. IV. xv. For an intriguing interpretation of the relation of these concepts to narrative form, see Kenneth Burke, *The Rhetoric of Religion*, pp. 226ff.

25. See the introduction to his edition of the *Poems of Spenser* (1902), in *The Cutting of an Agate* (New York: Macmillan, 1912), pp. 234ff.

26. See, for example, Hazlitt's "On Chaucer and Spenser," *Lectures on the English Poets*, 2nd ed. (London: Taylor and Hessey, 1819), p. 80.

27. On the relationship between externalization as a form of "reading" and the process of daemonization, see Ludwig Binswanger, *Being-in-the-World*, trans. Jacob Needleman (New York: Harper & Row, 1967), pp. 298-99. On Fradubio as a number of texts—Virgil's Polydorus, Dante's Piero delle Vigne, Ariosto's Astolfo—transformed into a "living emblem," see Isabel G. MacCaffrey, *Spenser's Allegory* (Princeton: Princeton Univ. Press, 1976), p. 157.

28. James Nohrnberg's analysis of the seminal importance of this episode, in *The Analogy of "The Faerie Queene,"* pp. 135ff, is very helpful here.

29. Implication as "the law of infolding" is discussed by Arthur Koestler in "Literature & the Law of Diminishing Returns," *Encounter*, 34 (May 1970), 44. For the relation of narrative *entrelacement* to Spenser's design, see Rosemond Tuve, *Allegorical Imagery* (Princeton: Princeton Univ. Press, 1966), pp. 459-70. I am indebted to Thomas M. Greene for suggesting the relation of this narrative principle to Nicholas of Cusa's concepts of *complicatio* and *explicatio*, on which see Ernst Cassirer, *The Individual and the Cosmos in Renaissance Philosophy*, trans. Mario Domandi (Philadelphia: Univ. of Pennsylvania Press, 1963), pp. 43ff.

30. Letter to Bailey, October 8, 1817, in Hyder Rollins, ed., *The Letters of John Keats 1814-1821*, 2 vols. (Cambridge, Mass.: Harvard Univ. Press, 1958), I, 170.

31. See Edwin Greenlaw et al., eds., *The Works of Edmund Spenser: A Variorum Edition*, 11 vols. (Baltimore: The Johns Hopkins Press, 1932-57), I, 180.

32. Chaucer, *Parlement of Foules*, 176-82, which in turn echoes Boccaccio's *Teseida* VII. 51-56.

33. I am indebted here to the discussion of these "pairs" in A. Bartlett Giamatti, *Play of Double Senses: Spenser's "Faerie Queene"* (Englewood Cliffs: Prentice-Hall, 1975), p. 107.

34. *Quarterly Review*, 43 (September 1830), 486.

35. See also *Orlando furioso* XV. 14-15, and the linking of Astolfo's horn to Joshua 6 in Simon Fornari's *Spositione sopra l'Orlando furioso* (Florence, 1549).

36. See Bennett, *The Evolution of "The Faerie Queene"* (Chicago: Univ. of Chicago Press, 1942), ch. 9; Frye, *Fables*, pp. 77-78; Hankins, *Source and Meaning*, pp. 99ff; and Nohrnberg, *Analogy*, pp. 178ff.

37. John Jewel cites both passages for the biblical prophecies of the "erring" of the Church in his own time, in his *Apology, or Answer, in Defence of the Church of England*, IV. xiii, in *Works*, III, 80.

38. *Aen.* I. 723-56, and, behind it, *Od.* VIII-IX.

39. See Greene, *Descent*, p. 332.

40. On these relations, see A.S.P. Woodhouse, "Nature and Grace in *The Faerie Queene*," *ELH*, 16 (1949), 194-228; A. C. Hamilton, *The Structure of Allegory in "The Faerie Queene"* (Oxford: Clarendon Press, 1961), pp. 90ff; and Frye, *Fables*, p. 79.

41. Letter VIII, *Letters on Chivalry and Romance*, 2nd ed. (London, 1762), p. 66.

42. Wallace Stevens, "An Ordinary Evening in New Haven," sect. v; W. B. Yeats, "The Magi."

43. This is suggestively argued in Harry Berger, Jr., "The Discarding of Malbecco: Conspicuous Allusion and Cultural Exhaustion in *The Faerie Queene* III. ix-x," *Studies in Philology*, 66, No. 2 (April 1969), 135-54.

44. See James Carscallen, "The Goodly Frame of Temperance: The Metaphor of Cosmos in *The Faerie Queene*, Book II," *University of Toronto Quarterly*, 37, No. 2 (January 1968), 137.

45. See, respectively, A. Bartlett Giamatti, "Spenser: From Magic to Miracle," in *Four Essays on Romance*, ed. Herschel Baker (Cambridge, Mass.: Harvard Univ. Press, 1971), p. 18, and Greene, *Descent*, p. 112.

46. Lewis, *The Allegory of Love* (1936; rpt. New York: Oxford Univ. Press, 1958), p. 313; Frye, *Anatomy of Criticism* (1957; rpt. New York: Atheneum, 1966), p. 195.

47. For an analysis of such syntactical ambiguities, see Paul J. Alpers, *The Poetry of "The Faerie Queene"* (Princeton: Princeton Univ. Press, 1967), pp. 82ff. Kathleen Williams, in *Spenser's World of Glass* (Berkeley: Univ. of California Press, 1966), p. 8, argues that after Book I the alignment of characters with Day and Night lessens.

48. *Anatomy of Criticism*, p. 58.

49. William Patten, in *A Calender of Scripture* (London, 1576), s.v. "Elizabeth," derives her name from Hebrew *Eli-sheba*, and expounds upon the meaning of the queen's name as the "seventh of God." For the interpretation of "Elizabeth" as *domini requies*, see A. C. Hamilton, "Our new poet: Spenser, 'well of English undefyld,' " in *A Theatre for Spenserians*, ed. J. Kennedy and J. Reither (Toronto: Univ. of Toronto Press, 1973), p. 110, and Nohrnberg, *Analogy*, p. 83n.

50. See Michael Murrin, *The Veil of Allegory* (Chicago: Univ. of Chicago Press, 1969), p. 16.

51. A useful survey of the concept is provided in Katharine Gilbert and Helmut Kuhn, *A History of Esthetics* (New York: Macmillan, 1939), pp. 165ff.

52. Giamatti, "Spenser: From Magic to Miracle," pp. 17-31.

53. Natalis Comes, in his article on Daedalus in the *Mythologiae* (Venice, 1581), VII. xvi, is generally sympathetic to the "artifex ingeniosus," as is Charles Estienne in his entry in the *Dictionarium* (1512; Oxford, 1670), p. 322. However, the original notes to Drayton's *Heroical Epistle* of Rosamond to King Henry, in *Works*, ed. J. W. Hebel (Oxford: Blackwell, 1961), II, 138-39, includes the statement that the name of "Dedalus" is "suspected" because it is nothing "else but, Ingenious, or Artificiall," and the seventeenth-century mythographer Alexander Ross, in the *Mel Heliconium* (1642), associates the architect of the labyrinth with its deviousness.

54. The use of "shade" and "shadow" in *The Faerie Queene* reflects its ambiguity within Patristic commentary, where "shadow" can be variously "figura," "refrigium consolationis" (Rabanus Maurus, *Patrologia Latina* CXII. 1085), "protectio divina," "oblivio, vel peccata," and "torpor mentis" (S. Eucherius, *Pat. Lat.* L. 741). Of *compendia* of the image and its scriptural bases, one of the most fertile sources is Gregory the Great's *Moralia in Job*, XXXIII. 5.

55. *Positions* (1581), p. 269, quoted in Giamatti, *Play*, p. 6.

56. "Nor anie little moniment to see, / By which the trauailer, that fares that way, / This once was she, may warned be to say" (5-7).

57. *The Allegorical Temper* (1957; rpt. New Haven: Archon Books, 1967), p. 113.

58. *The Allegory of Love*, p. 353.

59. Deuteronomy, or the *deutero-nomos*, places the Israelites, already many years settled in the Promised Land, back into the wilderness on the threshold before that crossing, literally making them, once again, an audience of displaced persons, still en route.

60. For these parallels, see William Nelson, *The Poetry of Edmund Spenser* (New York: Columbia Univ. Press, 1963), pp. 163ff, and Nohrnberg, *Analogy*, p. 163.

61. This is not necessarily the implication in the breaking off of the tale at "Til on a day," but it is suggestively interpreted as such in Giamatti, *Play*, pp. 49-52.

62. See Marie de France's *Lanval* and the interpretation of St. Paul's vi-

sionary *raptus* to the "third heaven" at the end of Augustine's *De genesi ad litteram*.

63. Maleger has been variously interpreted as the state of sin, in Woodhouse, "Nature and Grace," p. 221, and Hamilton, *Allegory*, pp. 102-3; and as the "body of death" in Carscallen, "The Goodly Frame of Temperance," p. 149. For the relation of his description to the humor of melancholy, see Erwin Panofsky's description of its characteristics in *Dürer's "Melencolia I"* (Leipzig, 1923).

64. See the masterful reading of this episode in Nohrnberg, *Analogy*, pp. 317-23.

65. The concept of σπεῦδε βραδέως or *festina lente* is developed through Aulus Gellius, *Noctes Atticae*, x. xi; Macrobius, *Saturnalia* vi. viii, and the discussion of Augustus' motto in Suetonius, *De vita Caesarum* ii. xxv. 4, and termed the "royal" proverb by Erasmus in the *Adagia*. See Edgar Wind, *Pagan Mysteries in the Renaissance*, rev. ed. (Harmondsworth: Penguin, 1967), pp. 97ff. The possible connection between temperance and *tempus* is discussed by Leo Spitzer in his *Classical and Christian Ideas of World Harmony*, ed. Anna Granville Hatcher (Baltimore: The Johns Hopkins Press, 1963), pp. 81-82.

66. Angus Fletcher, *The Prophetic Moment: An Essay on Spenser* (Chicago: Univ. of Chicago Press, 1971), p. 50.

67. See Carscallen, "The Goodly Frame of Temperance," p. 145.

68. Harry Berger, Jr., in *The Allegorical Temper*, p. 66, lists the several implications in Acrasia's name through associations with *krasis* and *kratos*.

69. *Gerusalemme liberata* xiv. 62ff, the garden built on the "dead" or "standing" lake.

70. See Frederick Goldin's *The Mirror of Narcissus in the Courtly Love Lyric* (Ithaca: Cornell Univ. Press, 1967).

71. The "perspectivism" of romance and metaphor are provocatively allied in Harold Bloom, *A Map of Misreading* (New York: Oxford Univ. Press, 1975), pp. 106-22.

72. The openness of Spenser's poem at such junctures makes it an interesting instance of what Roland Barthes, in *S/Z: Essai* (Paris: Editions du Seuil, 1970), pp. 222-23, calls "le texte pensif": "plein de sens . . . il semble toujours garder en réserve un dernier sens, qu'il n'exprime pas, mais dont il tient la place libre et signifiante. . . . *A quoi pensez-vous?* a-t-on envie de demander . . . au texte classique. . . . le texte ne répond pas, donnant au sens sa dernière clôture: la suspension."

73. This is not specifically suggested in Spenser's text, but it is interesting that the girdle should function as a fetish object when Collins later makes use of it in his "Ode on the Poetical Character."

74. On the Hermaphrodite, see Marie Delcourt, *Hermaphrodite: Myths and Rites of the Bisexual Figure in Classical Antiquity*, trans. J. Nicholson (London: Studio Books, 1961); Nelson, *Poetry*, pp. 236ff; Nohrnberg, *Analogy*, pp. 604-7; and A. R. Cirillo, "The Fair Hermaphrodite: Love-Union in the Poetry of Donne and Spenser," *Studies in English Literature*, 9 (1969), 81-95.

75. "Preposterous" is the English term used by Puttenham in his *Arte of English Poesie* III. xii for the trope of *histeron proteron*.

76. For this combination of male and female in Britomart, see Giamatti, "Spenser: From Magic to Miracle," p. 27; Lotspeich, *Classical Mythology*, p. 43; and Williams, *Spenser's World of Glass*, p. 91.

77. Alpers, *The Poetry of "The Faerie Queene,"* pp. 197ff.

78. This is the term used to characterize Book v in Fletcher, *The Prophetic Moment*, pp. 146ff.

79. For readers interested in numerology in Spenser, there is even the possibility that he is deliberately following the canto numbers of the *Furioso*, where the prophecy to Bradamante, like the prophecy to Britomart in *FQ* III. iii, is placed in the third canto.

80. "Notes Toward a Supreme Fiction," sect. IV of "It Must Change."

81. Peter de la Primaudaye, *The French Academie* (London, 1618), p. 74.

82. *The Kindly Flame* (Princeton: Princeton Univ. Press, 1964), p. 17.

83. "The Spenserian Dynamics," *Studies in English Literature*, 8, No. 1 (Winter 1968), 10.

84. Joanne Field Holland, "The Cantos of Mutabilitie and the Form of *The Faerie Queene*," *ELH*, 35, No. 1 (March 1968), 29.

85. See Giamatti, *Play*, pp. 118-33 ("Poets and Proteus") and "Proteus Unbound: Some Versions of the Sea God in the Renaissance," in *The Disciplines of Criticism*, ed. Peter Demetz, Thomas M. Greene, and Lowry Nelson, Jr. (New Haven: Yale Univ. Press, 1968), pp. 437-75.

86. *Allegory: The Theory of a Symbolic Mode* (Ithaca: Cornell Univ. Press, 1964), pp. 49-67.

87. Harry Berger, Jr., "A Secret Discipline: *The Faerie Queene*, Book VI," in Nelson, ed., *Form and Convention in the Poetry of Spenser*, p. 37.

88. *The Poetry of "The Faerie Queene,"* p. 389.

89. The delaying of names is typical of romance. Chrétien de Troyes, for example, keeps the reader waiting until line 3575 of the *Conte del graal* for the name "Perceval" and until line 3676 of *Roman de la charrette* for the name "Lancelot." On the importance of naming in romance, see Leo Spitzer, "Linguistic Perspectivism in the *Don Quijote*," in *Linguistics and Literary History* (Princeton: Princeton Univ. Press, 1948), pp. 41-86.

90. Berger, "Spenserian Dynamics," pp. 4-5.

91. The possibly negative perspective, or at least the ambiguity, in Shakespeare's presentation of the Fable in *Coriolanus* was, of course, exploited by Brecht in his rewriting of the play, a version which provoked a counter-interpretation in Grass's *Die Plebejer proben den Aufstand*.

92. T. K. Dunseath, *Spenser's Allegory of Justice in Book V of "The Faerie Queene"* (Princeton: Princeton Univ. Press, 1968); Jane Aptekar, *Icons of Justice* (New York: Columbia Univ. Press, 1969).

93. For the parallel, see Dunseath, pp. 47ff.

94. *Spenser's Courteous Pastoral* (Oxford: Clarendon Press, 1972), p. 19. I am indebted in what follows to Harry Berger, Jr.'s fine discussion of the "reflective" nature of Book VI in "A Secret Discipline," pp. 35-75.

95. One of the fullest discussions of the figure of the circle or ring in Book VI is provided in Nohrnberg, *Analogy*, pp. 659-64.

96. MacCaffrey, in *Spenser's Allegory*, p. 420, discusses the question of Spenser's authorship of the mottos.

97. The simplicity of Book VI is remarked by MacCaffrey, *Allegory*, p. 405, and by Williams, *Spenser's World of Glass*, p. 190.

98. See Lewis, *The Allegory of Love*; Tuve, *Allegorical Imagery*, esp. pp. 389ff; and Fletcher, *The Prophetic Moment*, pp. 11-23, 45-53.

99. A useful compendium of its complementary and conflicting meanings is provided in Eugenio Garin, *Italian Humanism: Philosophy and Civic Life in the Renaissance*, trans. Peter Munz (Oxford: Blackwell, 1965), pp. 117-22.

100. See, in this regard, Durling's chapter on Spenser in his *Figure of the Poet*.

101. The link between the "hermeneutic" and the figure of Hermes derives, of course, from the function of the latter as the message-bearer of the gods. On the resonances of Hermes surrounding the episode of Colin Clout's piping and generally in Spenser, see Nohrnberg, *Analogy*, pp. 729-30, and Geoffrey Hartman, "The Interpreter: A Self-Analysis," in *The Fate of Reading and Other Essays* (Chicago: Univ. of Chicago Press, 1975), pp. 13-15.

102. Kathleen Williams, in "Vision and Rhetoric: The Poet's Voice in *The Faerie Queene*," *ELH*, 36 (1969), 144, stresses the limitation, while Paul Alpers, in "Narration in *The Faerie Queene*," *ELH*, 44 (1977), 33, stresses the "gesture of human connection."

103. On the tradition of the "eloquent" Hercules, a combination of Hercules and Orpheus, see Jean MacIntyre, "Spenser's Herculean Heroes," *Humanities Association of Canada Bulletin*, 17 (1966), 5-12; and Thomas H. Cain, "Spenser and the Renaissance Orpheus," *University of Toronto Quarterly*, 41, No. 1 (Autumn 1971), 39-40.

104. See the praise of Spenser as "Bryttane Orpheus" by "R. S." in the Commendatory Verses published with *The Faerie Queene*; Comes' description of Orpheus in the *Mythologiae* (Venice, 1568), VII. xiv; and, on Orpheus' triumph over time, Boccaccio in the *Genealogia deorum* v. xii.

105. Lecture III, in *Coleridge's Miscellaneous Criticism*, ed. T. M. Raysor (Cambridge, Mass.: Harvard Univ. Press, 1936), p. 36.

106. Sir Walter Raleigh, *The History of the World in Five Books* (London, 1614), II. vi. 7.

107. Anderson, *The Growth of a Personal Voice*, p. 201.

III. MILTON

1. All references to Milton's poetry are to the *Complete Poems and Major Prose*, ed. Merritt Y. Hughes (New York: Odyssey Press, 1957).

2. Aquinas, *ST* Ia. 63. 6: "Sic igitur instans primum in angelis intelligitur respondere operationi mentis angelicae, qua se *in se ipsam convertit per vespertinam cognitionem*; quia in primo die commemoratur vespere, sed non mane.

Et haec quidem operatio in omnibus bona fuit. Sed ab hac operatione quidam *per matutinam cognitionem ad laudem Verbi sunt conversi*; quidam vero *in se ipsis remanentes facti sunt nox, per superbiam intumescentes*, ut Augustinus dicit . . ." (my italics). See also Augustine, *De genesi ad litteram* IV. 22, Aquinas, *ST* I. 58; LXIII. 6 ad 4, and the illuminating interpretation of this tradition in John Freccero, "Dante and the Neutral Angels," *Romanic Review*, 51, No. 1 (February 1960), 3-14.

3. D. C. Allen applied the tradition of *cognitio vespertina* to Book IV. 449-75, in a short note on "Milton's Eve and the Evening Angels," *MLN*, 75 (December 1960), 108-9; the suggestion has been incorporated into the subsequent editions of Douglas Bush and Fowler and Carey, along with the customary reference to *Met*. III. 402-36. On the turn towards otherness, see Charles Monroe Coffin, "Creation and the Self in *Paradise Lost*," *ELH*, 29, No. 1 (March 1962), 1-18.

4. See, for example, Millicent Bell's "The Fallacy of the Fall in *Paradise Lost*," *PMLA*, 68, No. 4 (September 1953), 863-83; Cleanth Brooks, "Eve's Awakening," in *Essays in Honor of Walter Clyde Curry* (Nashville: Vanderbilt Univ. Press, 1954), pp. 281-98; William G. Madsen, *From Shadowy Types to Truth* (New Haven: Yale Univ. Press, 1968), pp. 104ff.

5. On the six ages of man and the relation of the tradition to *Paradise Lost*, see H. R. MacCallum, "Milton and Sacred History: Books XI and XII of *Paradise Lost*," in Millar MacLure and F. W. Watt, eds., *Essays in English Literature from the Renaissance to the Victorian Age Presented to A.S.P. Woodhouse* (Toronto: Univ. of Toronto Press, 1964), pp. 150ff.

6. The *crepusculum* which can be the "twilight" preceding either night or day is described as the consciousness of the creation in itself in Augustine, *De genesi ad litteram* XXII. 39; XXVIII. 45; and, as follows, in XXXII. 50: "Vidit etiam se in se, id est distante, quod factum est, ab eo, qui fecit. . . . *facta est et vespera, quia necessaria erat et ista cognitio, qua distingueretur a creatore creatura aliter in se ipsa cognita quam in illo*" (my italics). The "evening" and "even-ing" pun was detected in *Samson Agonistes*, line 1692, by L. S. Cox, "The 'Ev'ning Dragon' in *Samson Agonistes*: A Reappraisal," *MLN*, 76 (1961), 577-84.

7. Du Bartas, The Fourth Day of the First Week, 251-52. The notes in Alastair Fowler and John Carey's edition of *The Poems of John Milton* (New York: Longman Group, 1968) on the themes of "equinox" and "balance" in Book IV are invaluable in this regard.

8. Richard Bentley's comment in his edition of *Paradise Lost* (1732) is quoted in William Empson, *Some Versions of Pastoral* (1935; rpt. Harmondsworth: Penguin, 1966), p. 129.

9. In "An Essay on Milton," *The Burning Oracle* (London: Oxford Univ. Press, 1939), pp. 101-2.

10. *De genesi ad litteram* IV. 22, 39; XXX. 47. See also Aquinas, *ST*, Ia. 58. 6 and 7, and the *Glossa ordinaria* on Gen. 1:5.

11. *De libero arbitrio* II. 16. 43, trans. Dom Mark Pontifex, *The Problem of Free Choice*, Ancient Christian Writers, No. 22 (Westminster, Md.: Newman Press, 1955).

12. See, for example, Augustine's commentary on Psalm 19 (Vulgate 18) in the *Enarrationes in Psalmos*, and the imagery of *figurae* as stars in Gregory the Great, *Moralia in Job*, I. preface. 13.

13. See Origen, *Homilies on Exodus*, VII. 7-8, and Samuel Mather, *The Figures or Types of the Old Testament*, 2nd ed. (London, 1705), p. 9.

14. Mather, *Figures or Types*, pp. 449, 431.

15. This is, of course, only one part of the drama of *Paradise Regained*, but it is suggested particularly in the references in the poem to the kingship of David (as in, for example, II. 432ff). Barbara K. Lewalski provides an informative survey of such "figures" in *Milton's Brief Epic* (Providence: Brown Univ. Press, 1966), esp. pp. 164ff.

16. On the necessity of this discontinuity, see Gregory, *Moralia*, on Job 39:5, in Book XXX. 66, and Madsen, *Shadowy Types*, pp. 107ff.

17. Justinus, "The First Apology," in Alexander Roberts and James Donaldson, eds., *The Ante-Nicene Fathers*, 24 vols. (Grand Rapids: Eerdmans, 1969), I, 165-81.

18. Clement, "Exhortation to the Heathen," in *Ante-Nicene Fathers*, II, 178.

19. See, for example, the analyses of the myths of Bellerophon and Aesculapius in Alexander Ross's *Mel Heliconium*.

20. *Descent*, p. 400.

21. "On Shakspeare and Milton" (1818), in his *Lectures on the English Poets*, p. 115.

22. *Shadowy Types*, p. 179.

23. The importance of this interval is the starting point of the argument of Leslie Brisman's *Milton's Poetry of Choice and its Romantic Heirs* (Ithaca: Cornell Univ. Press, 1973).

24. See *Tetrachordon*, in *Complete Prose Works of John Milton*, ed. Don M. Wolfe et al. (New Haven: Yale Univ. Press, 1953-), II, 678-79, and Stanley Fish, *Surprised by Sin: The Reader in "Paradise Lost"* (1967; rpt. Berkeley: Univ. of California Press, 1971), pp. 21-22.

25. *The Reason of Church Government*, Book II, in *Complete Prose*, I, 820.

26. See *Surprised by Sin*, p. 313, and his *Self-Consuming Artefacts: The Experience of Seventeenth-Century Literature* (Berkeley: Univ. of California Press, 1972).

27. See his *Studies in Milton* (London: Chatto & Windus, 1951), pp. 8-52, and *The English Epic and its Background* (London: Chatto & Windus, 1954), pp. 430-47, 528-31.

28. F. R. Leavis, "Milton's Verse," was originally published as an article in *Scrutiny* in 1933 and appeared in *Revaluation* in 1933. See also Jackson Cope, *The Metaphoric Structure of "Paradise Lost"* (Baltimore: The Johns Hopkins Press, 1962), pp. 77ff.

29. "Adam on the Grass with Balsamum," in his *Beyond Formalism: Literary Essays 1958-1970* (New Haven: Yale Univ. Press, 1970), p. 138.

30. Richardson, *Explanatory Notes and Remarks on Milton's Paradise Lost* (1734), p. 484, inherits the tradition of commentary on the six ages of man.

See Augustine, *Contra Faustinum*, v, and Mather, *Figures or Types*, p. 66. Georgia B. Christopher, "The Verbal Gate to Paradise: Adam's 'Literary Experience' in Book x of *Paradise Lost*," *PMLA*, 90, No. 1 (January 1975), 69-77, approaches the relation of gradual and apocalyptic somewhat differently, through the countering of the predominantly prefigurative conception of the Old Testament in the Reformation theologians' insistence that all times are equal before the Word.

31. On the development of the more technical forms of meditation, see Louis Martz, *The Poetry of Meditation*, rev. ed. (New Haven: Yale Univ. Press, 1962), pp. 13ff.

32. Joseph H. Summers very suggestively discusses this problem in *The Muse's Method* (London: Chatto & Windus, 1962), pp. 149ff.

33. A.J.A. Waldock, *Paradise Lost and its Critics* (Cambridge: Cambridge Univ. Press, 1947), p. 61.

34. See Augustine, *De trinitate* x, together with Bonaventure, *Itinerarium mentis in Deum*, sect. iii, and Martz, *Poetry of Meditation*, p. 36.

35. *An Essay Towards a Real Character and a Philosophical Language* (1668), pp. 17-18.

36. See Webster's *Academiarum Examen* (London, 1654), pp. 29-30, and the discussion of these theories in Fish, *Surprised*, pp. 115ff.

37. See D. C. Allen, "Some Theories of the Growth and Origin of Language in Milton's Age," *Philological Quarterly*, 28, No. 1 (January 1949), 5-16, and H. R. MacCallum, "Milton and Figurative Interpretation of the Bible," *University of Toronto Quarterly*, 31, No. 4 (July 1962), 397-415.

38. *De doctrina christiana*, Book i, ch. 2, in *Complete Prose*, vi, 133-34.

39. See *PR* iv. 343-44, and *The Reason of Church Government*, Book ii, in *Complete Prose*, i, 811.

40. *The Reason of Church Government*, Book ii, in *Complete Prose*, i, 817-18, 830.

41. *The Earthly Paradise*, pp. 298ff.

42. See the informative glosses on *anakuklesis* or the change in the course of the sun supposed to accompany entry into a new World Cycle, and its relation to the "staying" of the sun in Josh. 10:12-14, in Fowler and Carey, *Poems of Milton*, p. 780n.

43. See Fowler and Carey, p. 760n.

44. See Gen. 3:8, Eph. 4:26, and Fowler and Carey, p. 930n.

45. The deliberate temporal vagueness of the close, where the "Ev'ning Mist" (xii. 629) is posited only in a simile, is striking in a poem which maintains such an otherwise precise time-scheme. See Katherine Hanley, C.S.J., "Morning or Evening? The Conclusion of *Paradise Lost*," *English Record*, 22, No. 1 (Fall 1971), 57-61.

46. *Milton's Epic Voice: The Narrator in "Paradise Lost"* (Cambridge, Mass.: Harvard Univ. Press, 1963), pp. 150ff.

47. *PR* ii. 246. There, the romance analogues of the wilderness are suggested in the temptations of Book ii and particularly in the echoes of Armida's banquet in Tasso (*PR* ii. 337ff).

69. "The Miltonic Simile," p. 1060.

70. For a particularly suggestive account of the middle space opened up by these similes, see Geoffrey Hartman, "Milton's Counterplot," in *Beyond Formalism*, 113-23.

71. Ferry, *Milton's Epic Voice*, pp. 80ff, suggests this delight in her remarks on the fortunate fall which is not the theological one but the one into the variety of the natural world.

72. I am indebted here to the remarks on verb tenses in Ferry, *Milton's Epic Voice*, p. 81.

73. See Job 9:9 and Amos 5:8.

74. Lecture x (1818), in *Coleridge's Miscellaneous Criticism*, ed. T. M. Raysor, p. 164.

75. See the opening of Keats's notes on *Paradise Lost*, reprinted in H. Buxton Forman, ed., *The Complete Works of John Keats*, 5 vols. (Glasgow, 1901), III, 256.

IV. KEATS

1. *The Burden of the Past and the English Poet* (New York: Norton, 1970), p. 33.

2. "Sleep and Poetry," 181, in the passage in which Keats attacks the Augustan poets ruled by "one Boileau" (206). The edition used for this and all subsequent references to Keats's poetry is Miriam Allott, ed., *The Poems of John Keats* (London: Longman Group, 1970).

3. See Thomson, *The Castle of Indolence: An Allegorical Poem Written in Imitation of Spenser*, 2nd ed. (London, 1748), and Keats's journal-letter to the George Keatses, February-May 1819, in Hyder Rollins, ed., *The Letters of John Keats 1814-1821*, II, 78. All subsequent references are to these editions.

4. *Account of the Greatest English Poets* (1694), 17-31, quoted in Arthur Johnston, *Enchanted Ground: The Study of Medieval Romance in the Eighteenth Century* (London: Athlone Press, 1964), p. 6.

5. See, for example, Thomson's *Summer* (1744), 1573-75; Richard Steele, *Tatler*, 254; Bishop Hurd, *Letters on Chivalry and Romance* (1762); and Bishop Thomas Percy's *Reliques of Ancient English Poetry* (1765).

6. John Bidlake, "Ode Written near a Solitary Chapel," in his *Poems* (1793). See also Southey's "To Contemplation" and its regret for the passing of Fancy's "visions gay" (67), and William Cowper's *The Task* (1785), where he dismisses the "Airy dreams" of the past as the poets' imposing "a gay delirium for a truth," but "still must envy them an age / That favor'd such a dream, in days like these / Impossible" (IV. 526-32).

7. *Observations on "The Faerie Queene,"* 2nd ed., 4 vols. (1762), III, 267-68, and I, i, quoted in René Wellek, *The Rise of English Literary History* (Chapel Hill: Univ. of North Carolina Press, 1941), p. 170. Similarly, James Beattie remarks in the final paragraph of "On Fable and Romance," *Dissertations Moral and Critical* (London, 1783), that the "usefulness of Romance-writing"

48. *The Burning Oracle*, p. 97. For Janus used to indicate a textu[al] tion, see the opening of Book II of Whitney's *Choice of Emblemes* (15

49. Christopher Ricks, *Milton's Grand Style* (Oxford: Clarendo 1963), p. 96.

50. Pearce's note on these lines (1733) is quoted in Empson, *Some of Pastoral*, p. 133.

51. See Ricks, *Style*, pp. 81ff.

52. See Empson, *Pastoral*, p. 131.

53. William Forde, in *The True Spirit of Milton's Versification* (18[3] ranges the verse into logical units "so that the reader may attend sol[e] sense and the harmonious order of the words, without feeling an[y] rassment from the contrariety between the linear division, and the of the language." On *occupatio*, see Abraham Fraunce, *The Arcadian* (1588) and Henry Peacham, *The Garden of Eloquence* (1577).

54. This is suggestively analyzed by Fish in "Interpreting the V[a] *Critical Inquiry*, 2, No. 3 (Spring 1976), 474-78, an essay which sig[n] differs from the more resolution-directed thesis of his *Surprised by S[in]*

55. Here I would differ with the interpretation suggested for this tion in the charting of the simile by James Whaler, "The Miltonic *PMLA*, 46, No. 4 (December 1931), 1054.

56. Ricks, *Style*, pp. 98-99.

57. See Joseph Anthony Wittreich, Jr., ed., *The Romantics o[n]* (Cleveland: Case Western Reserve Univ. Press, 1970), p. 129.

58. I would agree, here, with J. B. Broadbent, *Some Graver Subj[ect]* don: Chatto & Windus, 1960), pp. 184-85, who emphasizes the po[sitive] phrase. Giamatti, in *The Earthly Paradise*, pp. 308-9, emphasizes r[the] ways in which the balance is tipped towards the more sinister roma[nce] text.

59. Summers, in *The Muse's Method*, p. 28, brilliantly characte[rizes] style.

60. *S/Z*, pp. 222-23. The endings of Dickens' *Little Dorrit* and *Gre[at Expec-]* *tations* are only two Victorian examples of the influence of the close o[f Paradise] *Lost*.

61. For a full-length treatment of this dimension of the poem, se[e] Ryken, *The Apocalyptic Vision in "Paradise Lost"* (Ithaca: Cornell Uni[v. Press,] 1970).

62. "Milton and Sacred History," p. 166.

63. "Milton and Sacred History," p. 167.

64. In, for example, John Peter's *Critique of Paradise Lost* (New Y[ork: Co-] lumbia Univ. Press, 1960), p. 78.

65. *Surprised by Sin*, p. 310.

66. *Surprised*, p. 313.

67. *Surprised*, p. 316.

68. Zachary Pearce, in *A Review of the Text of Paradise Lost* (1[7] Jonathan Richardson, in *Explanatory Notes* (1734), both comment on "wandering" in this respect, and Joseph Trapp, in his *Lectures [on Poetry]* (1715), finds such digressions indefensible.

is not to be estimated by his lengthy treatment of it, since "Romances are a dangerous recreation"; and Clara Reeve, though she defends the romances in the introduction to *The Progress of Romance* (1785) as "equally entitled to our attention and respect, as any works of Genius and literature," still cautions against their indiscriminate availability to "young persons."

8. "On Lyric Poetry," 91-100.

9. "Hymn to Science," 38-42.

10. See Thomas Warton, *History of English Poetry*, 3 vols. (1774-81), preface to I, and III, 496.

11. "On Poetry in General," *Lectures on the English Poets*, p. 18.

12. See, among others, Southey's "To Contemplation," Akenside's "To Sleep," "To the Muse," and "To the Evening Star," Mason's "Ode to Melancholy," in Dodsley's *Collection*, VI (1775), and Collins' "Ode to Simplicity." I am indebted to the discussion of this "sacred precinct" by Martin Price in "The Sublime Poem: Pictures and Powers," *Yale Review*, 58 (Winter 1969), 194-213.

13. The phrase is from "Il Penseroso" (136-38), but the threat to these woods—both the disappearing pastoral woods of an increasingly commercial England and the enchanting "selva" of romance—remains a constant one in a line of poets from Marvell to John Clare.

14. "On Chaucer and Spenser," *Lectures on the English Poets*, p. 85.

15. "False Themes and Gentle Minds," *Beyond Formalism*, p. 287.

16. "Coleridge," in M. Cohen, ed., *The Philosophy of John Stuart Mill* (New York: Random House, 1961), p. 58.

17. On Wordsworth, see Joseph Wittreich, Jr., ed., *The Romantics on Milton*, p. 129.

18. Chapter XIV, *Biographia Literaria*, ed. George Watson (London: Dent, 1965), pp. 168-69.

19. *Anatomy of Criticism*, p. 35.

20. See especially her "Ode to the Muse" and "Ode to Melancholy."

21. "In drear-nighted December" and the sonnet to Spenser, for example, both suggest a turn from the idealizings of *Endymion* to a more wintry vision. The "Lines on Seeing a Lock of Milton's Hair" and the letter in which he dedicates himself to a more rigorous program of "study and thought" (To John Taylor, April 24, 1818, in *Letters*, I, 271) chart his movement away from the Spenserian mode of pastoral romance to the Miltonic epic design of the projected *Hyperion*. His preference for the realism of Smollett over the romance coloring of Scott, as later for the human tales of Chaucer over the marvels of Ariosto (in, respectively, the letters to his brothers of January 5, 1818, in *Letters*, I, 200, and to Taylor of November 17, 1819, in *Letters*, II, 234) represents a virtual reversal of his earlier stance. In a letter to Bailey on January 23, 1818, a single question conveys his sense of the uselessness of romance: "*Why should Woman suffer?* . . . These things are, and he who feels how incompetent the most skyey knight errantry is to heal this bruised fairness is like a sensitive leaf on the hot hand of thought" (*Letters*, I, 209).

22. Letter to J. H. Reynolds, May 3, 1818, in *Letters*, I, 280–81.

23. The developmental frame is, in my view, a weakness in the approach of Jack Stillinger in "Keats and Romance: The 'Reality' of *Isabella*," *The Hoodwinking of Madeline and Other Essays on Keats's Poems* (Chicago: Univ. of Illinois Press, 1971), pp. 31ff, and Morris Dickstein, *Keats and His Poetry: A Study in Development* (Chicago: Univ. of Chicago Press, 1971), pp. 131ff, though the latter modifies Stillinger's "anti-romance" thesis and suggests that Keats's attempt to leave romance behind remained an attempt. Similarly, the endless debates over the ending of *The Eve of St. Agnes*, over the question of "consummation" in "La Belle Dame Sans Merci," and over the final tendency of *Lamia* seem to be the inevitable result of a poetry which looks so many ways at once.

24. See, for example, the simultaneous farewell to the old oak forests of romance and the lament for their passing in "Robin Hood."

25. Paul de Man, ed., *John Keats: Selected Poetry* (New York: Signet, 1966), p. xxv.

26. November 22, 1817, in *Letters*, I, 185.

27. The multiplicity of these allusions is suggestively interpreted by Stillinger in the famous essay "The Hoodwinking of Madeline: Skepticism in *The Eve of St. Agnes*," in *Hoodwinking*, pp. 67ff.

28. It is for this reason that I have difficulty with the more straightforward interpretations of the "mind" of the "Ode" in Harold Bloom, *The Visionary Company*, rev. ed. (Ithaca: Cornell Univ. Press, 1971), pp. 420-21, and Charles I. Patterson, *The Daemonic in the Poetry of Keats* (Urbana: Univ. of Illinois Press, 1970), pp. 158-65.

29. Paul de Man, for example, in his introduction to *Keats: Selected Poetry*, p. xxxiii, stresses the victory of the philosopher over the "serpent," while Northrop Frye, in the essay on Keats in his *Study of English Romanticism* (New York: Random House, 1968), p. 154, emphasizes the aborting of a possible passage of this "Eurydice" to the human world.

30. "Keats and Romance," *Hoodwinking*, p. 37.

31. Letter to George and Thomas Keats, December 1817, in *Letters*, I, 193-94. T. S. Eliot's essay "Keats" appeared in *The Use of Poetry* (Cambridge, Mass.: Harvard Univ. Press, 1933).

32. *Descent*, p. 112.

33. Letter to George and Georgiana Keats, September, 1819, in *Letters*, II, 213.

34. To Reynolds, February 19, 1818, in *Letters*, I, 232.

35. To J. A. Hessey, October 8, 1818, in *Letters*, I, 374.

36. To George and Thomas Keats, January 23, 1818, in *Letters*, I, 214.

37. "How fevered is the man who cannot look. . . ." See Keats's letter to John Taylor of February 27, 1818, in *Letters*, I, 238, and the sensitive analysis of this poem in Dickstein, *Keats*, pp. 16-18.

38. This aspect of the quest in *Parzival* is explored in Hermann J. Weigand, *Wolfram's "Parzival"* (Ithaca: Cornell Univ. Press, 1969), p. 137.

39. Journal-letter to George and Georgiana Keats, February-May 1819, in *Letters*, II, 79.

40. See Frye, *English Romanticism*, p. 140, and the analysis of the nightingale as "eternity symbol" in David Perkins, *The Quest for Permanence* (Cambridge, Mass.: Harvard Univ. Press, 1959), p. 245.

41. See Keats's note on *PL* I. 710-30 in H. Buxton Forman, ed., *Complete Works*, III, 260, and his letter to Reynolds of May 3, 1818, in *Letters*, I, 281.

42. Forman, III, 256.

43. Letter to Bailey, October 8, 1817, in *Letters*, I, 170.

44. As in, for example, Northrop Frye's analysis of *Endymion* in *English Romanticism*, though this approach does enable us to "see" the form of Endymion's journey.

45. *The Visionary Company*, p. 371.

46. Rev. 8:1, a puzzle to interpreters, but generally glossed as a tarrying, suspension, or "rapture" before the end.

47. *English Romanticism*, p. 134.

48. See, for example, Leonard Brown, "The Genesis, Growth, and Meaning of *Endymion*," *Studies in Philology*, 30 (1933), 618-53; Bloom, *The Visionary Company*, p. 367; Stillinger, *Hoodwinking*, pp. 23ff. The edition used in all references to Shelley is Thomas Hutchinson's 1905 edition of *Shelley: Poetical Works*, 2nd ed. rev. by G. M. Matthews (Oxford: Oxford Univ. Press, 1970).

49. "The Internalization of Quest Romance," in his *Ringers in the Tower* (Chicago: Univ. of Chicago Press, 1971), p. 34.

50. See Bloom, "Internalization," p. 16, and the persuasive discussion of Keats's fear of the abyss of the self in Paul de Man's introduction to *Keats: Selected Poetry*.

51. *PL* II. 546-61. The passage is reproduced as it appears with Keats's underlining in Forman, III, 261.

52. Letter to Bailey, November 22, 1817, in *Letters*, I, 185.

53. Post-Miltonic Evening poems frequently echo the description of Twilight in *PL* IV. 598-609, but with less of Adam's assurance of the return of dawn. See, for example, Mason's "On Melancholy," John Bidlake's "Ode to Evening," night's halting of an indolent evening "fancy" in Cowper's *The Task* (IV. 302-7) and, despite his faith's apocalyptic metaphors, Isaac Watts's "Hope in Darkness" and "Forsaken, yet Hoping" in Book I of the *Horae lyricae*. For a masterful study of Collins' relation to the Miltonic "evening," see Paul Sherwin, *Precious Bane: Collins and the Miltonic Legacy* (Austin: Univ. of Texas Press, 1977), esp. pp. 102ff. On the "apostolic succession" of lights in Blake's "To the Evening Star," see Geoffrey Hartman, "Blake and the Progress of Poesy," *Beyond Formalism*, pp. 199-200.

54. See *Endymion* I. 680-703, II. 140-98, and the opposite movement from "gentle moon" to dawn in III. 72-119.

55. *Endymion* IV. 427-41, 927-35.

56. Keats's imagination, for example, never stops playing upon the

Spenserian romance scene of Arthur's dream of Gloriana, and the problem of what dream wakens into is a constant theme, from the banquet of Porphyro in *The Eve of St. Agnes* to the rude awakenings of "La Belle Dame Sans Merci" and *Lamia*, from *Hyperion* III, where an awakened Apollo beholds before him the goddess whose only trace had been a "lyre all golden" (63) by his side to the Proem of *The Fall of Hyperion*, where dream becomes part of the "sable charm / And dumb enchantment" (I. 10-11) which threatens poetry itself.

57. I borrow Northrop Frye's use of "identity" for the older apocalyptic world to suggest the tension with Keats's more negative use.

58. One of the forerunners of Keats's *Hyperion* poems, Edward Young's *Night Thoughts*, hovers anxiously between the older image of religious *praeparatio* and the seductive twilight zone of *melancholia*. Young's strong sense of *Anfang und Ende* makes all in between into a wilderness of wandering, the valley of the shadow of death, and the twilight vestibule before the final dawn. He prefers evening ("the sweet, the clement, mediatorial hour," Night IX. 272) and the shade to the glaring sun of a Mammon world and looks forward to the advent of everlasting day, but he keeps falling back into a more binary structure. The whole movement of this exodus depends on an affirmative answer to the question he raises in the Preface to Night VI—"Is man immortal, or is he not?"—and though all of the poem is an attempt to affirm the existence of a higher sphere, the anxiety with which the question is posed continually suggests the opposite.

59. See John Jones, *John Keats's Dream of Truth* (London: Chatto & Windus, 1969), pp. 153-54.

60. John Donne, for example, draws on the Pauline distinction between hopeful and purely negative *tristitia* (II Cor. 7:10) to distinguish between the "shadow" of the figure or of the *nondum* of faith and the "shadow" of melancholy or the despair of ever reaching the promised fulfillment. See his "Sermon Preached at St. Paul's Cathedral, London, January 29, 1625" on Ps. 63:7, in E. M. Simpson and G. R. Potter, eds., *The Sermons of John Donne* (Berkeley: Univ. of California Press, 1954), VII, 51-71.

61. See his *Play*, p. 102, and *FQ* III. x. 60.

62. *Blindness and Insight* (New York: Oxford Univ. Press, 1971), p. 152.

63. Wordsworth and Milton are the poles of Keats's speculations on poetic history in the *Letters*. W. J. Bate, in *John Keats* (1963; rpt. New York: Oxford Univ. Press, 1966), p. 307, warns us that we should not approach such an impromptu piece "with formal expectations that are wildly irrelevant" to Keats's intentions on the occasion, but this Epistle, like the confusions of the "Ode on Indolence," would seem nevertheless to be a fruitful focus for the problem of "wandering" in Keats after *Endymion*. See Albert S. Gérard, "Romance and Reality: Continuity and Growth in Keats's View of Art," *Keats-Shelley Journal*, 11 (1962), 19-23, revised and reprinted in his *English Romantic Poetry* (Berkeley: Univ. of California Press, 1968), pp. 217-24; and Stuart M. Sperry, Jr., "Keats's *Epistle to John Hamilton Reynolds*," *ELH*, 36 (1969), 562-74.

64. *Endymion* I. 777-81, as described by Keats in the letter to Taylor, January 30, 1818 (*Letters*, I, 218).

65. *The Prefigurative Imagination of John Keats* (Stanford: Stanford Univ. Press, 1951), p. 138.

66. At the beginning of the poem, this dual stance takes the form of a poetic *style indirect libre* when, for a moment, the poem steps into the mind of the Beadsman ("But no—already had his deathbell rung . . .") before it leaves him outside to his "Rough ashes" (22-27).

67. *Fearful Symmetry* (1947; rpt. Princeton: Princeton Univ. Press, 1969), p. 325.

68. Letter to Haydon, January 23, 1818, in *Letters*, I, 207.

69. "Toward Literary History," in *Beyond Formalism*, p. 371.

70. See J. Lemprière, *A Classical Dictionary* (1816), s.v. "Endymion."

71. Letter to Haydon, January 23, 1818, in *Letters*, I, 207.

72. *Keats: Selected Poetry*, p. xvii.

73. Letter to Reynolds, September 21, 1819, in *Letters*, II, 167.

74. "The Noble Rider and the Sound of Words," in *The Necessary Angel* (New York: Random House, 1951), p. 22.

75. See, in this context, the suggestive remarks of Harold Bloom on the trope of *metalepsis* (the reversal of late for early, or of early for late) in Keats, in *A Map of Misreading*, pp. 152-56, and in the chapter on Keats in his *Poetry and Repression* (New Haven: Yale Univ. Press, 1976).

76. That Keats was not ignorant of these wanderings is indicated by the early, more complete version of "I Stood Tip-Toe" ("The silver lamp—the ravishment—the wonder— / The darkness—loneliness—the fearful thunder," 147-48).

77. "Symbolic Action in a Poem by Keats" (1943), reprinted in his *Perspectives by Incongruity* (Bloomington: Indiana Univ. Press, 1964), pp. 123-41.

78. "On Poetry in General," in *Lectures on the English Poets*, pp. 20-21: "Painting gives the object itself; poetry what it implies. Painting embodies what a thing contains in itself; poetry suggests what exists out of it, in any manner connected with it. . . . Again, as it relates to passion, painting gives the event, poetry the progress of events: but it is during the progress, in the interval of expectation and suspense, while our hopes and fears are strained to the highest pitch of breathless agony, that the pinch of the interest lies. . . . But by the time that the picture is painted, all is over."

79. See the brilliant discussion of this aspect of the poem in Leo Spitzer, "The 'Ode on a Grecian Urn,' or Content vs. Metagrammar," in his *Essays on English and American Literature* (Princeton: Princeton Univ. Press, 1962), p. 72.

80. The audience of "tell" in lines 38-40 ("And, little town, thy streets for evermore / Will silent be; and not a soul to tell / Why thou art desolate can e'er return") is left suggestively open. Tell whom? If it is the town itself, the silence would point to the state of suspended animation on the urn. But if the potential audience of the tale is the poet himself, the suggestion is that no

voice from the past can cross the gap between then and now, the object and the questioning poet.

81. Burke, *Perspectives*, p. 134.

82. See Keats's note on *PL* VII. 420-23, in Forman, ed., *Complete Works*, III, 264.

83. See the interesting reading of the poem in his "Spectral Symbolism and Authorial Self in Keats's *Hyperion*," in *The Fate of Reading*, pp. 57-73.

84. Letter to Reynolds, February 19, 1818, in *Letters*, I, 232.

85. Letter to Woodhouse, October 27, 1818, in *Letters*, I, 387, the letter from which all citations in this paragraph are taken.

86. To George and Georgiana Keats, October 1818, in *Letters*, I, 403-4.

87. On the romance tradition of this fear, see Giamatti, "Poets and Proteus," in *Play*, p. 123.

88. Augustine, in the section on the cursing of the serpent in *De genesi ad litteram* XIX, draws the linguistic analogy in his observation that the serpent is involved in the guilt only in the same sense as we speak of the "lying pen" of the writer.

89. See Forman, III, 265.

90. *Inf.* XXV. 57-58, as it appears in the Henry Cary translation (1814) of the *Divina Commedia*, which Keats read carefully in the summer of 1818. Keats underlined the whole passage of the metamorphosis (54-59), and in particular this image, which is echoed in the burning "leaves" of *The Fall* I. 116. See Robert Gittings, *The Mask of Keats* (London: Heinemann, 1956), p. 39. It is interesting in relation to the theme of trespass that the memory should be of the canto of the "Thieves."

91. I follow John Freccero, "Medusa: The Letter and the Spirit," in *Yearbook of Italian Studies* (1972), p. 10, in associating the Medusa of *Inferno* IX with the Siren of *Purgatorio* XIX, who becomes an attractive siren only when the pilgrim gazes intently on her (10).

92. See Jones, *Keats's Dream of Truth*, p. 193, and Frye, *English Romanticism*, p. 152.

93. See the letter to Bailey, November 22, 1817 (*Letters*, I, 186: "I scarcely remember counting upon any Happiness—I look not for it if it be not in the present hour—nothing startles me beyond the Moment . . ."), and the note on *PL* VII. 420-23, in Forman, III, 264.

94. See Lemprière, *Classical Dictionary*, s.v. "Atlas."

95. See Gittings, *The Mask of Keats*, pp. 5ff.

96. To Reynolds, February 19, 1818, in *Letters*, I, 231.

97. For Keats's use of "bear," see, for example, "Sleep and Poetry," 61-63, and "God of the Meridian," 17-19.

EPILOGUE

1. *Letters on Chivalry and Romance*, p. 4.

2. Walter Pater, "Romanticism" (1876), as it appears in the "Postscript" to his *Appreciations* (London: Macmillan, 1890), p. 255.

3. Ferdinand de Saussure, *Cours de linguistique générale*, 3rd ed. (Paris: Presses universitaires de France, 1965), pp. 166-68; Roman Jakobson, *Essais de linguistique générale*, trans. N. Ruwet (Paris: Editions de Minuit, 1963) and "Closing Statement: Linguistics and Poetics," in *Style in Language*, ed. T. A. Sebeok (Cambridge, Mass.: MIT Press, 1960), pp. 350-77; Hans Vaihinger, *The Philosophy of "As if,"* trans. C. K. Ogden (London: Routledge & Kegan Paul, 1924); Georges Charbonnier, *Entretiens avec Claude Lévi-Strauss* (Paris: Plon, 1961). Further on the "distancing" of language, see Hans Georg Gadamer, *Wahrheit und Methode*, 2nd ed. (Tübingen: Mohr, 1965), pp. 370-71, and Walter Benjamin, *Schriften*, ed. T. W. Adorno et al. (Frankfurt: Suhrkamp Verlag, 1955), ii, 464-65. For a comprehensive survey of concepts of distance from an "origin," see Edward Said's *Beginnings: Intention and Method* (New York: Basic Books, 1975).

4. "La Différance," *Bulletin de la société française de philosophie*, 62, No. 3 (1968), 73-101; reprinted in his *Marges de la philosophie*, pp. 1-29.

5. *Mensonge romantique et vérité romanesque* (Paris: Grasset, 1961).

6. See his *S/Z*, pp. 81ff and pp. 215-16 on "le dévoilement," and *Le plaisir du texte* (Paris: Editions du Seuil, 1973).

7. *Collected Papers* (Cambridge, Mass.: Harvard Univ. Press, 1931), i, 171.

8. The *Tiers Livre* constantly shifts from the literal to the metaphorical sense of terms such as "la guerre" and "debtes." In the discussion of debts, Panurge evades the question of his mismanagement of the revenues of Salmiguondin by shifting to the metaphorical level. In his quest to know whether he will be cuckolded if he marries, he constantly evades what appears to be the obvious and consistent message of the various signs and oracles he consults, and thus extends a quest which, had he immediately agreed to the "obvious" meaning, would have been a very short one. "Diversion" is also one of the most fertile points of encounter between the Montaigne of the "Diversion" essay and the Pascal of the *Pensées* who writes "Rien n'est si insupportable à l'homme que d'être dans un plein repos . . . sans divertissement. . . . Il sent alors son néant" (ii, 131).

9. *Letters on Chivalry and Romance*, p. 4.

10. Jonson's objection, in *Discoveries*, to Spenser's language is discussed in Michael Murrin's *Veil of Allegory*, p. 180.

11. On Bishop Berkeley's *Treatise Concerning the Principles of Human Knowledge* (1710) and climate and primitivistic theories of figurative language, see Wellek, *Rise of English Literary History*, pp. 83-94.

12. See *Les Nuits d'octobre*: x—*Le Rôtisseur* and *Inf.* iv. 151.

13. See his description in *Parnasse contemporain* (1866).

14. Quoted in Owen Barfield, *Romanticism Comes of Age*, rev. ed. (Letchworth: The Rudolf Steiner Press, 1966), p. 156.

15. "Romanticism and Anti-Self-Consciousness," in *Beyond Formalism*, p. 303.

16. Boccaccio in the *Genealogia deorum* interpreted "Demogorgon" as the father of all gods (from a confusion with Plato's *demiourgos*), the terrible "god of the earth" whose name could only be pronounced at great risk. See

Spenser, *FQ* I. i. 37. Coleridge's poem "Ne Plus Ultra" follows "Limbo."

17. "Hölderlin und das Wesen der Dichtung" (1936), in Martin Heidegger, *Erläuterungen zu Hölderlins Dichtung* (Frankfurt am Main: Vittorio Klostermann, 1951), pp. 43-44; "Das ist die dürftige Zeit, weil sie in einem gedoppelten Mangel und Nicht steht: im Nichtmehr der entflohenen Götter und im Nochnicht des Kommenden." For a highly stimulating discussion of the poet's threshold, or preliminary, state, see Angus Fletcher, " 'Positive Negation': Threshold, Sequence, and Personification in Coleridge," in *New Perspectives on Coleridge and Wordsworth*, ed. Geoffrey H. Hartman (New York: Columbia Univ. Press, 1972), pp. 133-64.

18. "Edmond Jabès et la question du livre," in *L'écriture et la différence* (Paris: Editions du Seuil, 1967), pp. 99-116.

19. "Literary History and Literary Modernity," *Blindness and Insight*, pp. 152-61. The tension within representation is contained in such Baudelairean phrases as "la représentation du présent" in "Le peintre de la vie moderne," *Curiosités esthétiques: L'Art romantique et autres Oeuvres critiques de Baudelaire*, ed. Henri Lemaitre (Paris: Garnier, 1962), p. 454.

20. See, respectively, *Confessions* IV. x and the commentary on Ps. 103:2 (Vulgate) in the *Enarrationes in Psalmos*. For recent structuralist uses of the sentence as narrative model, see the essays by Todorov, Greimas, Bremond, and Barthes in *Communications*, 8 (1966).

21. *Sermons and Devotional Writings*, ed. C. Devlin (London: Oxford Univ. Press, 1959), pp. 179-80.

22. *Journals and Papers*, ed. H. House (London: Oxford Univ. Press, 1959), p. 289.

23. *Sermons and Devotional Writings*, pp. 200-201.

24. See, for example, "The Leaden Echo and the Golden Echo," and its "Give beauty back, beauty, beauty, beauty, back to God."

25. Andrew Marvell's ironic resolve, for example, in the *Rehearsal Transpros'd*, to call Samuel Parker "His Morality" rather than "His Grace" stems partly from a sense of the latter's folly in trying to legislate meaning.

26. See Barthes, "L'écriture et le silence" and "L'écriture et la parole," in *Le Degré zéro de l'écriture* (1953; rpt. Paris: Editions du Seuil, 1972), pp. 54-61. The debate begun in Plato's *Cratylus* continues in the opposition of "scientific" and "poetic" language in more recent discussions. Derrida, in "La mythologie blanche," *Marges*, pp. 249-324, notes that the devaluing of polysemous language leads to a suspicion of metaphor, and the debate between the two kinds of language continues in his critique there of Gaston Bachelard, *La Formation de l'esprit scientifique*. Kenneth Burke contrasts the semantic ideal of the logical positivists with the poet's complication of the medium of language in "Semantic and Poetic Meaning," in *The Philosophy of Literary Form: Studies in Symbolic Action* (1941; rpt. New York: Random House, 1957), pp. 121-44. The scandal of metaphoric language for philosophy and science is discussed in Walker Percy, "Metaphor as Mistake," *Sewanee Review*, 66 (1958), 70-99, and the opposition of connotation and denotation analyzed in Gérard Genette, *Figures II* (Paris: Editions du Seuil,

1969), pp. 133ff. For the attempt to reduce the ambiguity of language, see W.V.O. Quine, *Word and Object* (Cambridge, Mass.: MIT Press, 1960), esp. the section on the "Synonymy of Terms."

27. *Oeuvres complètes* (Paris: Gallimard, 1945), p. 284. All references to Mallarmé's work are to this Pléiade edition. Translations mine.

28. "Crise de vers," p. 368.

29. "Enquête sur l'évolution littéraire," p. 869.

30. "Magie," p. 400.

31. "Le Mystère dans les lettres," p. 384.

32. For an analysis of the play of possible referents here, see Paul de Man, *Blindness and Insight*, pp. 176-82.

33. For a suggestive account of the referential patterns of this poem, see François Rastier, "Systématique des isotopies," in A.-J. Greimas et al., *Essais de sémiotique poétique* (Paris: Librairie Larousse, 1972), pp. 80-105. I am indebted to my friend and colleague Peter Nesselroth for bringing this essay to my attention.

34. "Le Mystère dans les lettres," p. 386.

35. "Crayonné au théâtre," p. 296 (*"fictif ou momentané"*).

36. See, for example, "Symphonie littéraire," p. 262, the prose poem "La Déclaration foraine," p. 279, and Yves Bonnefoy on this tension, in "The Poetics of Mallarmé," *Yale French Studies*, No. 54 (1977), pp. 9-21.

37. Paul de Man, *Blindness and Insight*, p. 70.

38. "L'Action restreinte," p. 372.

39. "Hamlet," p. 300.

40. "Son solitaire drame! et qui, parfois . . . semble le spectacle même pourquoi existent la rampe ainsi que l'espace doré quasi moral qu'elle défend, car il n'est point d'autre sujet . . ." ("Hamlet," p. 300).

41. All parenthetical references to *Un Coup de dés* in the text are to page numbers in the Pléiade edition.

42. *S/Z*, p. 120: "La phrase ne peut jamais constituer un *total:* . . . le total, la somme sont pour le langage des terres promises, entrevues *au bout* de l'énumération, mais cette énumération accomplie, aucun trait ne peut la rassembler—ou, si ce trait est produit, il ne fait que *s'ajouter* encore aux autres."

43. The text used in all citations from Valéry is the Pléiade edition of his *Oeuvres*, 2 vols., ed. Jean Hytier (Paris: Gallimard, 1957). "Les Pas" appears in *Charmes*, I, 120. All translations, unless otherwise noted, are from *Collected Works of Paul Valéry*, ed. Jackson Mathews, Bollingen Series xlv (Princeton and Surrey).

44. On the theme of the threshold, or the virtual, in Valéry, see Geoffrey Hartman, *The Unmediated Vision: An Interpretation of Wordsworth, Hopkins, Rilke, and Valéry* (New Haven: Yale Univ. Press, 1954), pp. 111ff, and Céline Sabbagh, "Calypso: a theme of ambiguity, a theme of fascination," *Yale French Studies*, No. 44 (1970), pp. 106-18.

45. "Magie," *Oeuvres*, I, 309.

46. "Au sujet du *Cimetière marin*," I, 1497.

47. "Matin," i, 355.

48. On the conflict between the desire for "un prompt torment" and the retardation of the verse, see Hartman, "Valéry's Fable of the Bee," in *The Fate of Reading*, pp. 223-47.

49. "Au sujet du *Cimetière marin*," i, 1501.

50. "Commentaires de *Charmes*," i, 1510.

51. "Nécessité de la Poésie," i, 1384.

52. Letter xi, p. 106.

53. "Imagination as Value," *The Necessary Angel*, p. 138.

54. "Only we two are one, not you and night, / Nor night and I, but you and I, alone" ("Re-statement of Romance"). All quotations from Stevens' poetry are from *The Palm at the End of the Mind*, ed. Holly Stevens (New York: Alfred A. Knopf, 1967). References in Roman numerals are to sections of poems. Michel Benamou, in *Wallace Stevens and the Symbolist Imagination* (Princeton: Princeton Univ. Press, 1972), pp. 50-52, provides a useful discussion of the difference between the reduction to "nakedness" in Stevens and the search for "purity" in Mallarmé. Stevens himself remained evasive on the subject of his relation to the French poets. See the *Letters of Wallace Stevens*, ed. Holly Stevens (New York: Alfred A. Knopf, 1966), pp. 290, 391, 636, and 795.

55. "Imagination as Value," *The Necessary Angel*, p. 142.

56. Helen Vendler has brilliantly analyzed the hesitations of Stevens' "pensive style" in the first chapter of *On Extended Wings: Wallace Stevens' Longer Poems* (Cambridge, Mass.: Harvard Univ. Press, 1969).

57. "The Noble Rider and the Sound of Words," *The Necessary Angel* p. 31.

58. "Imagination as Value," *The Necessary Angel*, p. 136.

59. Yeats, *The Cutting of an Agate*, pp. 234ff. The alternately positive and negative Stevensian uses of the terms "abstract," "evasion," "imagination," and "romantic" suggest his affinity with the ambivalence of this romance theme. See, for example, his use of "evasion" and "escapism" in *The Necessary Angel*, pp. 30-31, and in *Letters*, p. 402; and of "romantic" in *The Necessary Angel*, pp. 138-39, and in *Opus Posthumous*, ed. Samuel French Morse (New York: Alfred A. Knopf, 1957), pp. 251-52. Penetrating discussions of the centrality of these terms in Stevens are provided in George Bornstein, *Transformations of Romanticism in Yeats, Eliot, and Stevens* (Chicago: Univ. of Chicago Press, 1976), pp. 175-98; Harold Bloom, *Wallace Stevens* (Ithaca: Cornell Univ. Press, 1976), pp. 167-218; and Northrop Frye, "Wallace Stevens and the Variation Form," in *Spiritus Mundi* (Bloomington: Indiana Univ. Press, 1976), pp. 275-94.

60. "The Figure of the Youth as Virile Poet," *The Necessary Angel*, pp. 52-67.

Selected Bibliography

Abrams, M. H. *Natural Supernaturalism: Tradition and Revolution in Romantic Literature*. New York: W. W. Norton, 1971.

Allen, D. C. "Milton's Eve and the Evening Angels." *MLN*, 75 (December 1960), 108-9.

————. "Some Theories of the Growth and Origin of Language in Milton's Age." *Philological Quarterly*, 28, No. 1 (January 1949), 5-16.

Alpers, Paul J. "Narration in *The Faerie Queene*." *ELH*, 44 (1977), 19-39.

————. *The Poetry of "The Faerie Queene."* Princeton: Princeton Univ. Press, 1967.

Anderson, Judith H. *The Growth of a Personal Voice: "Piers Plowman" and "The Faerie Queene."* New Haven: Yale Univ. Press, 1976.

Ariosto, Ludovico. *Opere minori*. Ed. Cesare Segre. Milan: Ricciardi, 1954.

————. *Tutte le opere di Ludovico Ariosto, I: Orlando Furioso*. Ed. Cesare Segre. Milan: Mondadori, 1964.

Arthos, John. *On the Poetry of Spenser and the Form of Romances*. London: George Allen & Unwin, 1956.

Auerbach, Erich. *Mimesis: The Representation of Reality in Western Literature*. Trans. Willard Trask. Princeton: Princeton Univ. Press, 1953.

Baker, Herschel, ed. *Four Essays on Romance*. Cambridge, Mass.: Harvard Univ. Press, 1971.

Barfield, Owen. *Poetic Diction: A Study in Meaning*. 3rd ed. Middletown, Conn.: 1973.

————. *Romanticism Comes of Age*. Rev. ed. Letchworth: The Rudolf Steiner Press, 1966.

Barthes, Roland. *Le Degré zéro de l'écriture*. 1953; rpt. Paris: Editions du Seuil, 1972.

————. *Le Plaisir du texte*. Paris: Editions du Seuil, 1973.

————. *S/Z: Essai*. Paris: Editions du Seuil, 1970.

Bate, W. Jackson. *The Burden of the Past and the English Poet*. New York: Norton, 1970.

Bate, W. Jackson. *John Keats*. 1963; rpt. New York: Oxford Univ. Press, 1966.

Beattie, James. "On Fable and Romance." *Dissertations Moral and Critical*. London, 1783.

Beer, Gillian. *Romance*. London: Methuen, 1970.

Benamou, Michel. *Wallace Stevens and the Symbolist Imagination*. Princeton: Princeton Univ. Press, 1972.

Bennett, Josephine Waters. *The Evolution of "The Faerie Queene."* Chicago: Univ. of Chicago Press, 1942.

Berger, Harry, Jr. *The Allegorical Temper*. 1957; rpt. New Haven: Archon, 1967.

————. "The Discarding of Malbecco: Conspicuous Allusion and Cultural Exhaustion in *The Faerie Queene* III. ix-x." *Studies in Philology*, 66, No. 2 (April 1969), 135-54.

————, ed. *Spenser: A Collection of Critical Essays*. Englewood Cliffs: Prentice-Hall, 1968.

————. "The Spenserian Dynamics." *Studies in English Literature*, 8, No. 1 (Winter 1968), 1-18.

Bloom, Harold. *A Map of Misreading*. New York: Oxford Univ. Press, 1975.

————. *Poetry and Repression: Revisionism from Blake to Stevens*. New Haven: Yale Univ. Press, 1976.

————. *The Ringers in the Tower*. Chicago: Univ. of Chicago Press, 1971.

————. *The Visionary Company*. Rev. ed. Ithaca: Cornell Univ. Press, 1971.

————. *Wallace Stevens: The Poems of Our Climate*. Ithaca: Cornell Univ. Press, 1976.

Boiardo, Matteo Maria. *Orlando Innamorato, Amorum Libri*. Ed. A. Scaglione. 2 vols. Turin: UTET, 1963.

Bornstein, George. *Transformations of Romanticism in Yeats, Eliot, and Stevens*. Chicago: Univ. of Chicago Press, 1976.

Brisman, Leslie. *Milton's Poetry of Choice and its Romantic Heirs*. Ithaca: Cornell Univ. Press, 1973.

Burke, Kenneth. *Perspectives by Incongruity*. Bloomington: Indiana Univ. Press, 1964.

————. *The Philosophy of Literary Form: Studies in Symbolic Action*. 1941; rpt. New York: Random House, 1957.

————. *The Rhetoric of Religion: Studies in Logology*. 1961; rpt. Berkeley: Univ. of California Press, 1970.

Carne-Ross, D. S. "The One and the Many: A Reading of *Orlando Furioso*, Cantos 1 and 8." *Arion*, 5 (Summer 1966), 195-234.

Carscallen, James. "The Goodly Frame of Temperance: The Metaphor of Cosmos in *The Faerie Queene*, Book ii." *University of Toronto Quarterly*, 37, No. 2 (January 1968), 136-55.

Cheney, Donald. *Spenser's Images of Nature: Wild Man and Shepherd in "The Faerie Queene."* New Haven: Yale Univ. Press, 1966.

Cioranescu, A. *L'Arioste en France.* 2 vols. Paris: Les Presses Modernes, 1938-39.

Coleridge, Samuel Taylor. *Biographia Literaria.* Ed. George Watson. London: Dent, 1965.

———. *Coleridge's Miscellaneous Criticism.* Ed. T. M. Raysor. Cambridge, Mass.: Harvard Univ. Press, 1936.

———. *The Complete Poetical Works of Samuel Taylor Coleridge.* Ed. Ernest Hartley Coleridge. 2 vols. 1912; rpt. Oxford: Clarendon Press, 1957.

Colie, Rosalie L. *Paradoxia Epidemica: The Renaissance Tradition of Paradox.* Princeton: Princeton Univ. Press, 1966.

Cope, Jackson. *The Metaphoric Structure of "Paradise Lost."* Baltimore: The Johns Hopkins Press, 1962.

Curtius, Ernst Robert. *European Literature and the Latin Middle Ages.* Trans. Willard Trask. 1953; rpt. New York: Harper & Row, 1963.

Daniélou, Jean. *From Shadows to Reality: Studies in the Biblical Typology of the Fathers.* Trans. Dom Wulstan Hibberd. London: Burns & Oates, 1960.

de Man, Paul. *Blindness and Insight.* New York: Oxford Univ. Press, 1971.

———, ed. *John Keats: Selected Poetry.* New York: Signet, 1966.

Derrida, Jacques. *L'écriture et la différence.* Paris: Editions du Seuil, 1967.

———. *Marges de la philosophie.* Paris: Editions de Minuit, 1972.

Dickstein, Morris. *Keats and His Poetry: A Study in Development.* Chicago: Univ. of Chicago Press, 1971.

Donato, Eugenio. "The Shape of Fiction: Notes Towards a Possible Classification of Narrative Discourses." *MLN*, 86 (1971), 807-22.

Durling, Robert M. *The Figure of the Poet in Renaissance Epic.* Cambridge, Mass.: Harvard Univ. Press, 1965.

Empson, William. *Some Versions of Pastoral.* 1935; rpt. Harmondsworth: Penguin, 1966.

Ferry, Anne Davidson. *Milton's Epic Voice: The Narrator in "Paradise Lost."* Cambridge, Mass.: Harvard Univ. Press, 1963.

Fish, Stanley Eugene. "Interpreting the *Variorum.*" *Critical Inquiry*, 2, No. 3 (Spring 1976), 465-85.

Fish, Stanley Eugene. *Self-Consuming Artefacts: The Experience of Seventeenth-Century Literature*. Berkeley: Univ. of California Press, 1972.

——. *Surprised by Sin: The Reader in "Paradise Lost."* 1967; rpt. Berkeley: Univ. of California Press, 1971.

Fletcher, Angus. *Allegory: The Theory of a Symbolic Mode*. Ithaca: Cornell Univ. Press, 1964.

——. *The Prophetic Moment: An Essay on Spenser*. Chicago: Univ. of Chicago Press, 1971.

Ford, Newell F. *The Prefigurative Imagination of John Keats*. Stanford: Stanford Univ. Press, 1951.

Freccero, John. "Dante and the Neutral Angels." *Romanic Review*, 51, No. 1 (February 1960), 3-14.

——. "Medusa: The Letter and the Spirit." *Yearbook of Italian Studies* (1972), pp. 1-18.

Frenzel, Herbert. *Ariost und die romantische Dichtung*. Cologne: Böhlau-Verlag, 1962.

Frye, Northrop. *Anatomy of Criticism*. 1957; rpt. New York: Atheneum, 1966.

——. *Fables of Identity*. New York: Harcourt, Brace & World, 1963.

——. *Fearful Symmetry*. 1947; rpt. Princeton: Princeton Univ. Press, 1969.

——. *The Return of Eden: Five Essays on Milton's Epics*. Toronto: Univ. of Toronto Press, 1965.

——. *The Secular Scripture: A Study of the Structure of Romance*. Cambridge, Mass.: Harvard Univ. Press, 1976.

——. *Spiritus Mundi: Essays on Literature, Myth, and Society*. Bloomington: Indiana Univ. Press, 1976.

——. *A Study of English Romanticism*. New York: Random House, 1968.

Genette, Gérard. *Figures*. Paris: Editions du Seuil, 1966.

——. *Figures II*. Paris: Editions du Seuil, 1969.

——. *Figures III*. Paris: Editions du Seuil, 1972.

Gérard, Albert S. *English Romantic Poetry*. Berkeley: Univ. of California Press, 1968.

Giamatti, A. Bartlett. *The Earthly Paradise and the Renaissance Epic*. Princeton: Princeton Univ. Press, 1966.

——. "Headlong Horses, Headless Horsemen: An Essay on the Chivalric Epics of Pulci, Boiardo, and Ariosto." *Italian Literature: Roots and Branches*. Ed. G. Rimanelli and K. J. Atchity. New Haven: Yale Univ. Press, 1976. 265-307.

——. *Play of Double Senses: Spenser's "Faerie Queene."* Englewood Cliffs: Prentice-Hall, 1975.

Girard, René. *Mensonge romantique et vérité romanesque.* Paris: Grasset, 1961.

Gittings, Robert. *The Mask of Keats.* London: Heinemann, 1956.

Greene, Thomas M. *The Descent from Heaven: A Study in Epic Continuity.* New Haven: Yale Univ. Press, 1963.

Hamilton, A. C. *The Structure of Allegory in "The Faerie Queene."* Oxford: Clarendon Press, 1961.

Hankins, John Erskine. *Source and Meaning in Spenser's Allegory.* Oxford: Clarendon Press, 1971.

Hartman, Geoffrey H. *Beyond Formalism: Literary Essays 1958-1970.* New Haven: Yale Univ. Press, 1970.

——. *The Fate of Reading and Other Essays.* Chicago: Univ. of Chicago Press, 1975.

——. *The Unmediated Vision: An Interpretation of Wordsworth, Hopkins, Rilke, and Valéry.* New Haven: Yale Univ. Press, 1954.

Hazlitt, William. *Lectures on the English Poets.* 2nd ed. London: Taylor and Hessey, 1819.

Hopkins, Gerard Manley. *Journals and Papers.* Ed. H. House. London: Oxford Univ. Press, 1959.

——. *Sermons and Devotional Writings.* Ed. C. Devlin. London: Oxford Univ. Press, 1959.

Hurd, Bishop Richard. *Letters on Chivalry and Romance.* 2nd ed. London, 1762.

Jameson, Fredric. "Magical Narratives: Romance as Genre." *New Literary History*, 7, No. 1 (Autumn 1975), 135-63.

——. *The Prison-House of Language.* Princeton: Princeton Univ. Press, 1972.

Johnston, Arthur. *Enchanted Ground: The Study of Medieval Romance in the Eighteenth Century.* London: Athlone Press, 1964.

Jones, John. *John Keats's Dream of Truth.* London: Chatto & Windus, 1969.

Keats, John. *The Complete Works of John Keats.* Ed. H. Buxton Forman. 5 vols. Glasgow, 1901.

——. *The Letters of John Keats 1814-1821.* Ed. Hyder Rollins. 2 vols. Cambridge, Mass.: Harvard Univ. Press, 1958.

——. *The Poems of John Keats.* Ed. Miriam Allott. London: Longman Group, 1970.

Ker, W. P. *Epic and Romance: Essays on Medieval Literature.* 2nd ed. London: Macmillan, 1908.

Kermode, Frank. *The Sense of an Ending.* London: Oxford Univ. Press, 1966.

———. *Wallace Stevens.* New York: Grove Press, 1961.

Knight, G. Wilson. *The Burning Oracle.* London: Oxford Univ. Press, 1939.

Lewalski, Barbara K. *Milton's Brief Epic.* Providence: Brown Univ. Press, 1966.

Lewis, C. S. *The Allegory of Love.* 1936; rpt. New York: Oxford Univ. Press, 1958.

Loomis, R. S. *Arthurian Literature in the Middle Ages.* Oxford: Clarendon Press, 1959.

MacCaffrey, Isabel G. *Paradise Lost as "Myth."* Cambridge, Mass.: Harvard Univ. Press, 1967.

———. *Spenser's Allegory: The Anatomy of Imagination.* Princeton: Princeton Univ. Press, 1976.

MacCallum, H. R. "Milton and Figurative Interpretation of the Bible." *University of Toronto Quarterly*, 31, No. 4 (July 1962), 397-415.

———. "Milton and Sacred History: Books xi and xii of *Paradise Lost.*" *Essays in English Literature from the Renaissance to the Victorian Age Presented to A.S.P. Woodhouse.* Ed. Millar MacLure and F. W. Watt. Toronto: Univ. of Toronto Press, 1964.

Madsen, William G. *From Shadowy Types to Truth.* New Haven: Yale Univ. Press, 1968.

Mallarmé, Stéphane. *Oeuvres complètes.* Paris: Gallimard, 1945.

Marinelli, Peter V. "Redemptive Laughter: Comedy in the Italian Romances." *Genre*, 9, No. 4 (Winter 1976-77), 505-26.

Martz, Louis. *The Poetry of Meditation.* Rev. ed. New Haven: Yale Univ. Press, 1962.

Mather, Samuel. *The Figures or Types of the Old Testament.* 2nd ed. London, 1705.

Milton, John. *Complete Prose Works of John Milton.* Ed. Don M. Wolfe et al. New Haven: Yale Univ. Press, 1953-.

———. *John Milton: Complete Poems and Major Prose.* Ed. Merritt Y. Hughes. New York: Odyssey Press, 1957.

———. *The Poems of John Milton.* Ed. Alastair Fowler and John Carey. New York: Longman Group, 1968.

Momigliano, A. *Saggio su l'Orlando Furioso.* 1925; rpt. Bari, 1959.

Mueller, William R. and D. C. Allen, eds. *That Soveraine Light: Essays in Honor of Edmund Spenser 1552-1952.* 1952; rpt. New York: Russell & Russell, 1967.

Murrin, Michael. *The Veil of Allegory*. Chicago: Univ. of Chicago Press, 1969.

Nelson, William, ed. *Form and Convention in the Poetry of Edmund Spenser*. New York: Columbia Univ. Press, 1961.

————. *The Poetry of Edmund Spenser*. New York: Columbia Univ. Press, 1963.

Nohrnberg, James. *The Analogy of "The Faerie Queene."* Princeton: Princeton Univ. Press, 1976.

Panofsky, Erwin. *Hercules am Scheidewege*. Leipzig: Teubner, 1930.

Pater, Walter. *Appreciations*. London: Macmillan, 1890.

————. *The Renaissance*. London: Macmillan, 1873.

Patterson, Charles I. *The Daemonic in the Poetry of Keats*. Urbana: Univ. of Illinois Press, 1970.

Perkins, David. *The Quest for Permanence*. Cambridge, Mass.: Harvard Univ. Press, 1959.

Peter, John. *A Critique of "Paradise Lost."* New York: Columbia Univ. Press, 1960.

Quine, Willard Van Orman. *Word and Object*. Cambridge, Mass.: MIT Press, 1960.

Quint, David. "Astolfo's Voyage to the Moon." *Yale Italian Studies*, 1, No. 4 (Fall 1977), 398–408.

Ramat, Raffaello. *La critica ariostesca dal secolo xvi ad oggi*. Florence: La Nuova Italia, 1954.

Reeve, Clara. *The Progress of Romance*. Colchester, 1785.

Richardson, Jonathan. *Explanatory Notes and Remarks on Milton's "Paradise Lost."* London, 1734.

Richter, David H. *Fable's End: Completeness and Closure in Rhetorical Fiction*. Chicago: Univ. of Chicago Press, 1974.

Ricks, Christopher. *Keats and Embarrassment*. Oxford: Clarendon Press, 1974.

————. *Milton's Grand Style*. Oxford: Clarendon Press, 1963.

Roche, Thomas P., Jr. *The Kindly Flame*. Princeton: Princeton Univ. Press, 1964.

Ryding, William W. *Structure in Medieval Narrative*. The Hague: Mouton, 1971.

Saccone, Eduardo. *Il soggetto del Furioso e altri saggi tra Quattro e Cinquecento*. Naples: Liguori, 1974.

Said, Edward. *Beginnings: Intention and Method*. New York: Basic Books, 1975.

Saintsbury, George. *The Flourishing of Romance*. London: William Blackwood & Sons, 1897.

Scott, Sir Walter. *Essays on Chivalry and Romance*. 1818; rpt. London: Adam and Charles Black, 1892.

Shelley, Percy Bysshe. *Shelley: Poetical Works*. Ed. Thomas Hutchinson. London, 1905. Rev. ed. by G. M. Matthews. London: Oxford Univ. Press, 1970.

Sherwin, Paul S. *Precious Bane: Collins and the Miltonic Legacy*. Austin: Univ. of Texas Press, 1977.

Smith, Barbara H. *Poetic Closure: A Study of How Poems End*. Chicago: Univ. of Chicago Press, 1968.

Spenser, Edmund. *Spenser: Poetical Works*. Ed. J. C. Smith and E. de Selincourt. 1912; rpt. London: Oxford Univ. Press, 1965.

———. *The Works of Edmund Spenser: A Variorum Edition*. Ed. Edwin Greenlaw et al. 11 vols. Baltimore: The Johns Hopkins Press, 1932-57.

Sperry, Stuart M. *Keats the Poet*. Princeton: Princeton Univ. Press, 1973.

Spitzer, Leo. *Classical and Christian Ideas of World Harmony*. Ed. Anna Granville Hatcher. Baltimore: The Johns Hopkins Press, 1963.

———. *Essays on English and American Literature*. Princeton: Princeton Univ. Press, 1962.

———. *Linguistics and Literary History*. Princeton: Princeton Univ. Press, 1948.

Sprigg, Christopher St. John [Christopher Caudwell]. *Romance and Realism*. Ed. Samuel Hynes. Princeton: Princeton Univ. Press, 1970.

Stein, Arnold. *Answerable Style: Essays on "Paradise Lost."* 1953; rpt. Seattle: Univ. of Washington Press, 1967.

Stevens, John. *Medieval Romance*. New York: Norton, 1973.

Stevens, Wallace. *Letters of Wallace Stevens*. Ed. Holly Stevens. New York: Alfred A. Knopf, 1966.

———. *The Necessary Angel*. New York: Random House, 1951.

———. *Opus Posthumous*. Ed. Samuel French Morse. New York: Alfred A. Knopf, 1957.

———. *The Palm at the End of the Mind*. Ed. Holly Stevens. New York: Alfred A. Knopf, 1967.

Stillinger, Jack. *The Hoodwinking of Madeline and Other Essays on Keats's Poems*. Chicago: Univ. of Illinois Press, 1971.

Summers, Joseph H. *The Muse's Method*. London: Chatto & Windus, 1962.

Tasso, Torquato. *Gerusalemme liberata*. Ed. Anna Maria Carini. Milan: Feltrinelli, 1961.

—. *Opere.* Ed. Bortolo Tommaso Sozzi. 2 vols. Turin: UTET, 1955-56.

Thomson, James. *The Castle of Indolence: An Allegorical Poem Written in Imitation of Spenser.* 2nd ed. London, 1748.

Tillyard, E.M.W. *The English Epic and its Background.* London: Chatto & Windus, 1954.

—. *Studies in Milton.* London: Chatto & Windus, 1951.

Tonkin, Humphrey. *Spenser's Courteous Pastoral.* Oxford: Clarendon Press, 1972.

Tuve, Rosemond. *Allegorical Imagery: Some Medieval Books and Their Posterity.* Princeton: Princeton Univ. Press, 1966.

Vaihinger, Hans. *The Philosophy of "As if."* Trans. C. K. Ogden. London: Routledge & Kegan Paul, 1924.

Valéry, Paul. *Oeuvres.* Ed. Jean Hytier. 2 vols. Paris: Gallimard, 1957.

Vendler, Helen H. *On Extended Wings: Wallace Stevens' Longer Poems.* Cambridge, Mass.: Harvard Univ. Press, 1969.

Vinaver, Eugène. *The Rise of Romance.* Oxford: Clarendon Press, 1971.

Waldock, A.J.A. *Paradise Lost and its Critics.* Cambridge: Cambridge Univ. Press, 1947.

Warton, Thomas. *History of English Poetry.* 3 vols. London: 1774-1781.

—. *Observations on "The Faerie Queene" of Spenser.* 2nd ed. 4 vols. London, 1762.

Wasserman, Earl R. *The Finer Tone: Keats' Major Poems.* Baltimore: The Johns Hopkins Press, 1953.

Weigand, Hermann J. *Wolfram's "Parzival."* Ithaca: Cornell Univ. Press, 1969.

Weiskel, Thomas. *The Romantic Sublime.* Baltimore: The Johns Hopkins Press, 1976.

Wellek, René. *The Rise of English Literary History.* Chapel Hill: Univ. of North Carolina Press, 1941.

Wenzel, Siegfried. *The Sin of Sloth: "Acedia" in Medieval Thought and Literature.* Chapel Hill: Univ. of North Carolina Press, 1960.

Williams, Kathleen. *Spenser's World of Glass.* Berkeley: Univ. of California Press, 1966.

Wind, Edgar. *Pagan Mysteries in the Renaissance.* Rev. ed. Harmondsworth: Penguin, 1967.

Wittreich, Joseph Anthony, Jr., ed. *The Romantics on Milton.* Cleveland: Case Western Reserve Univ. Press, 1970.

Woodhouse, A.S.P. "Nature and Grace in *The Faerie Queene.*" *ELH*, 16 (1949), 194–228.

Yeats, William Butler. *The Cutting of an Agate*. New York: Macmillan, 1912.

Zumthor, Paul. *Essai de poétique médiévale*. Paris: Editions du Seuil, 1972.

Index

Works are listed under authors.
Numbers in italics indicate the main discussion

219-22, 227, 237-39, 270-71; in
Mallarmé, 229-30; in Milton, 4, 6,
12, 124-30, 134-38; in Spenser, 58,
61, 64-77, 80-81, 84, 86-88, 91,
94, 98; in Stevens, 237-39; in Valéry, 235-36. *See also* Wandering
Evasion, 81, 104-105, 112, 160-63,
166, 236, 240-42, 272
Evening (twilight): in Keats, 187-91;
197-99; in Milton, 6, 11, 114-25,
128-29, 133, 141-42, 151-52,
157-58, 257-58, 260; in post-
Miltonic poetry, 12, 187, 225,
265, 266; in Spenser, 78
"Evening" or "twilight" vision
(*cognitio vespertina*), 115-17, 120,
128-29, 152, 225
Eve's vision in pool (*PL* IV), 6, 114-
16, 126, 147, 151; after Milton,
187, 188, 194

Ferry, Anne Davidson, 142
Fetishism, 92, 170, 213, 255
Ficino, Marsilio, 57
Figura, 123-28, 247, 266; and figura-
tion, 79-81, 129-38, 222-23; and
Keats, 191-92
Fish, Stanley Eugene, 129-31, 138,
149, 153-54, 261
Fixation, 104, 174, 212-15
Fletcher, Angus, 95, 99, 256
Ford, Newell F., 194
Frye, Northrop, 3, 9, 13, 77, 128,
165, 173, 181, 197

Giamatti, A. Bartlett, 137, 192
Girard, René, 220
Goldsmith, Oliver, 7, 165
Gothic, 14, 130, 161, 164-65, 169,
205, 213
Graduation, 8; in Keats, 8, 172,
194-95; in Milton, 8, 118, 120,
122, 132-35
Gray, Thomas, 12

Greene, Thomas M., 28, 39, 56,
126, 171

Harington, Sir John, 21, 247, 249
Hartman, Geoffrey H., 163, 197-98,
204, 224
Hazlitt, William, 126, 162-63, 187,
198, 202, 204
Heidegger, Martin, 224
Herbert, George, 222-23, 226
Homer, 5, 29, 42, 45, 53, 96. Works:
Iliad, 17, 42-43; *Odyssey*, 43, 50,
75
Hopkins, Gerard Manley, 225-26
Horace, 19
Hurd, Bishop Richard (*Letters on
Chivalry and Romance*), 3, 4, 15,
76, 161, 219, 222, 236

Identity: apocalyptic, 153-54, 189,
266; problem of, in Keats, 204-
205, 208. *See also* Naming
Indolence, 8, 159-61, 168. *See also*
Sloth

Jakobson, Roman, 220
Jameson, Fredric, 4, 7
Janus, 83, 143, 171, 207
Jewel, John, 58
Johnson, Samuel, 144
Jones, John, 213
Jonson, Ben, 222
Joyce, James (*Finnegans Wake*), 97,
131, 221
Justin Martyr, 125

Keats, John, 4-5, 9, 13, 15, 70, *159-
218*; and Dante, 181, 192, 194,
206-208, 212-14, 216-17; and Milton, 8, 157, 167, 175, 184-89, 190,
192-95, 198, 200, 203, 205-206,
209-13, 216-18; Negative Capability in, 9, 14, 171-89, 193-94, 196,
201, 204-206, 208; and Pater, 218,
226; and romance after Milton, 7,

LIBRARY OF CONGRESS CATALOGING IN PUBLICATION DATA

Parker, Patricia A   1946–
  Inescapable romance.

  Bibliography: p.
  Includes index.
  1.   Epic poetry—History and criticism.
2.   Romanticism.   I.   Title.
PN1326.P37   809.1'3   78-70312
ISBN 0-691-06398-2